Mastering AWK Programming

From Basics to Expert Proficiency

Contents

1 Introduction to AWK **11**

1.1 History and Evolution of AWK 11
1.2 What is AWK? 13
1.3 The Purpose of AWK 16
1.4 Installing AWK 17
1.5 AWK vs. Other Text Processing Tools 20
1.6 Basic Structure of an AWK Program 22
1.7 Running Your First AWK Script 25
1.8 Understanding AWK Command Line Syntax 27
1.9 Common Use Cases for AWK 29
1.10 Community and Resources 32

2 AWK Syntax and Fundamentals **35**

2.1 Basic AWK Syntax 35
2.2 The Structure of AWK Programs 38
2.3 AWK Command Line Options 40
2.4 Fields and Records in AWK 42
2.5 Comments in AWK Scripts 45
2.6 Patterns and Actions in AWK 47
2.7 Using Regular Expressions in AWK 50
2.8 AWK Input and Output 52

2.9 Field Separators and Record Separators 55
2.10 Built-in Variables in AWK 58
2.11 Writing and Saving AWK Programs 60

3 Patterns and Actions in AWK **65**
3.1 Introduction to Patterns in AWK 65
3.2 Types of Patterns in AWK 67
3.3 Simple Patterns 69
3.4 Regular Expressions as Patterns 71
3.5 Range Patterns 74
3.6 Compound Patterns 77
3.7 The BEGIN and END Patterns 79
3.8 Action Statements in AWK 81
3.9 Printing with AWK 83
3.10 Skipping and Selecting Records 86
3.11 Combining Patterns and Actions 88

4 Variables and Data Types in AWK **93**
4.1 Introduction to Variables in AWK 93
4.2 Types of Variables in AWK 96
4.3 Predefined Variables 99
4.4 User-defined Variables 102
4.5 Initializing and Assigning Variables 104
4.6 Scope of Variables in AWK 106
4.7 String Variables 108
4.8 Numeric Variables 111
4.9 Arrays in AWK 113
4.10 Built-in Arrays 116
4.11 Best Practices for Using Variables 118

5 Control Structures in AWK **121**

5.1 Introduction to Control Structures 121
5.2 Conditional Statements: if, else if, else 123
5.3 Loops: while and do-while 126
5.4 The for Loop in AWK 128
5.5 Using break and continue 131
5.6 The exit Statement 133
5.7 Pattern Matching with Control Structures 136
5.8 Nested Control Structures 139
5.9 The switch Statement 141
5.10 Error Handling in AWK 144
5.11 Combining Control Structures for Complex Logic 146

6 Built-in Functions in AWK **149**

6.1 Introduction to Built-in Functions 149
6.2 String Functions 152
6.3 Mathematical Functions 155
6.4 Time Functions 157
6.5 Array Functions 160
6.6 I/O Functions 162
6.7 Bitwise Functions 164
6.8 System Functions 166
6.9 Using Functions in AWK Scripts 168
6.10 Combining Functions for Complex Tasks 171
6.11 Extending AWK with User-defined Functions 175

7 Advanced Text Processing with AWK **179**

7.1 Introduction to Advanced Text Processing 179
7.2 Advanced Field Manipulation 182
7.3 Text Substitution and Formatting 185
7.4 Working with Multi-line Records 188

7.5 Splitting and Joining Lines 190
7.6 Dealing with Special Characters 192
7.7 Data Validation and Cleansing 194
7.8 Generating Reports with AWK 197
7.9 Merging and Comparing Files 201
7.10 Error Handling in Text Processing 203
7.11 AWK and Shell Scripting Integration 205

8 Working with Files in AWK **209**
8.1 Introduction to File Handling in AWK 209
8.2 Reading Files with AWK 211
8.3 Writing to Files 213
8.4 Appending Data to Files 216
8.5 Processing Multiple Files 218
8.6 Using AWK with File Redirection 220
8.7 Handling File Errors 223
8.8 Using AWK with Piped Input and Output 225
8.9 Temporary Files and Data Streams 227
8.10 File Permissions and Security 230
8.11 Advanced File Management Techniques 232

9 Debugging and Optimization **237**
9.1 Introduction to Debugging in AWK 237
9.2 Common Errors and Their Solutions 240
9.3 Using Print Statements for Debugging 243
9.4 Debugging with GAWK's Debugger 245
9.5 Profiling AWK Programs 248
9.6 Optimizing AWK Script Performance 251
9.7 Memory Management in AWK 254
9.8 Efficient Data Handling 257

9.9 Avoiding Common Pitfalls 259
9.10 Best Practices for Debugging and Optimization 263

10 Real-world Applications of AWK 267

10.1 Introduction to Real-world Applications 267
10.2 AWK in System Administration 269
10.3 Log File Analysis with AWK 271
10.4 AWK for Data Extraction and Reporting 273
10.5 AWK in Software Development 276
10.6 Text Data Transformation 278
10.7 Processing CSV and TSV Files 280
10.8 AWK in Network Monitoring 283
10.9 Automating Tasks with AWK 285
10.10AWK for Bioinformatics 289
10.11Case Studies of Successful AWK Projects 291

Introduction

AWK is one of the most powerful text processing languages available, and it has been a cornerstone of Unix programming for decades. Designed by Alfred Aho, Peter Weinberger, and Brian Kernighan, AWK is named after its creators and is known for its concise syntax and robust capabilities. This book aims to guide you through mastering AWK, starting from basic concepts and progressing to advanced techniques that are pivotal for text processing, data extraction, and report generation.

AWK excels in handling tasks involving pattern recognition and data manipulation, making it indispensable for anyone working with text files, logs, or any form of structured data. Its versatility and efficiency allow for performing complex transformations with simple, declarative code. Understanding AWK not only equips you with a powerful tool but also enhances your overall skills in data processing and scripting.

To fully appreciate the power of AWK, this book is structured into well-organized chapters, each focusing on essential topics. We will begin by exploring the history and evolution of AWK, setting the foundation for why it remains relevant in modern computing. Subsequently, we delve into the syntax and fundamentals, providing you with the building blocks to write and execute basic AWK scripts.

As you progress, you will learn about patterns and actions, which are core concepts in AWK that allow you to specify conditions and corresponding actions. Variables and data types are crucial for any programming language, and AWK is no different. This book will guide you on how to efficiently use variables to store and manipulate data.

Control structures in AWK, such as loops and conditional statements, will be discussed in depth to enable you to write more complex and logical scripts. Built-in functions, another key feature of AWK, will be covered comprehensively, enabling you to leverage existing functionalities for efficient coding.

We will also explore advanced text processing techniques, demonstrating AWK's capability to handle sophisticated data manipulation tasks that go beyond simple text processing. Working with files is another critical aspect, and this book will provide detailed instructions on reading, writing, and managing files using AWK.

Debugging and optimization are essential for writing robust and efficient scripts. This chapter will equip you with strategies to identify and resolve issues, as well as optimize your AWK programs for better performance. Finally, real-world applications of AWK will be explored through various case studies and practical examples, showing how AWK can be applied to solve real-world problems efficiently.

This book is designed for both beginners and experienced users, with a focus on practical knowledge that can be applied immediately. By the end of this book, you will have a thorough understanding of AWK and be proficient in using it for a wide range of text processing tasks. The aim is to make your experience with AWK both educational and empowering, providing you with the skills to tackle any text processing challenge you may encounter.

Chapter 1

Introduction to AWK

AWK is a versatile and powerful programming language specifically designed for text processing and data extraction. This chapter covers the historical context and evolution of AWK, its purpose and unique features, and how it compares to other text processing tools. Additionally, readers will learn about installing AWK, running their first script, and common use cases, making it an essential starting point for mastering AWK programming.

1.1 History and Evolution of AWK

AWK was created by Alfred Aho, Peter Weinberger, and Brian Kernighan in the 1970s, and its name is derived from their initials. The genesis of AWK occurred within the context of Bell Labs, a renowned institution with a rich history of significant contributions to the field of computer science. AWK was first introduced in 1977 as part of Version 7 Unix. The language was designed to address the need for a tool that could handle simple data extraction and reporting tasks efficiently.

AWK's design was influenced by other programming languages of the time, particularly C and Unix shell scripts. The goal was to create a language that combined the flexibility of pattern scanning and manipulating text, similar to what was possible in regular Unix utilities, with the capabilities of a general-purpose programming language. The initial implementation of AWK became an instant success due to its concise syntax and powerful text processing features.

The first implementation of AWK was very basic and worked primarily with fixed patterns. However, it shortly proved to be powerful enough to handle a variety of text processing tasks, which spurred its adoption in various Unix environments. Various enhancements and refinements have been made to the language since its inception. Perhaps the most significant of these was the introduction of "new" AWK (often referred to as "nawk") in 1985. This version included a more sophisticated implementation of the language, with support for user-defined functions, multiple input streams, and other advanced features.

```
awk '{
    sum += $1
}
END {
    print "Total Sum: " sum
}' datafile.txt
```

During the late 1980s, the language was extended and standardized further, leading to the release of gawk, the GNU implementation of AWK. Gawk introduced additional features such as dynamic regex compilation, advanced array handling, and true multidimensional arrays. This extension aligned with the principles of the GNU project, ensuring that a free and open-source version of AWK was available to the community.

The AWK language continued to evolve within the open-source ecosystem, with input and contributions from numerous programmers around the world. Changes and enhancements to gawk allowed users to perform increasingly complex data processing tasks. This open development model ensured that AWK remained relevant even as other programming languages and tools emerged.

One notable enhancement in gawk is its ability to interface with external C libraries, allowing users to extend AWK's capabilities even further. By using the dlopen() function, it became possible to call C functions directly from AWK scripts. This facility opened the door for AWK scripts to handle more computationally-intensive tasks and interface with a broader range of software and libraries.

```
@load "mylib"
BEGIN {
    mylib_function()
}
```

AWK's influence can also be seen in many contemporary scripting and text processing languages. Languages such as Perl and Python have drawn heavily on AWK's pattern-action paradigm and string manipulation capabilities. Despite the rise of these newer languages, AWK remains a valuable tool for many tasks involving simple data processing, due to its ease of use, compact syntax, and efficiency.

The history and evolution of AWK underscore its central role in the Unix programming environment and its ongoing relevance in the broader field of computer science. Its design principles and robust feature set continue to support a wide variety of application areas, maintaining its status as a cornerstone tool for text processing and data manipulation. Readers looking to master AWK will benefit from understanding this background, appreciating both its origins and its developmental milestones.

1.2 What is AWK?

AWK is a domain-specific language designed for text processing and typically used for data extraction and reporting. The language is named after its three original authors: Alfred Aho, Peter Weinberger, and Brian Kernighan. AWK allows users to write concise programs that define search patterns and actions to be executed when these patterns are encountered in the input text. The language is characterized by its ease of use, powerful pattern matching using regular expressions, and built-in associative arrays.

The basic operation of AWK can be understood as a three-step process:

- **Scan a data file**: AWK reads input data, which is usually text files, line by line.
- **Match lines against patterns**: For each line, AWK evaluates specified patterns.
- **Perform actions on matched lines**: When a pattern is satisfied, corresponding actions are executed.

A crucial feature of AWK is its field-based processing capabilities. It views each line of input as a set of fields, which are by default separated by whitespace. This default behavior can be modified to use different delimiters, making it suitable for processing CSV files and other structured text formats.

For example, consider a simple input file data.txt with the contents:

```
John   Doe    28
Jane   Smith  32
Alice  Brown  25
```

An AWK script to print the first and last names from this file can be written as follows:

```
awk '{ print $1, $2 }' data.txt
```

The expected output will be:

```
John Doe
Jane Smith
Alice Brown
```

In this script, print 1,2 specifies that AWK should print the first and second fields of each line in data.txt. The variable $1 represents the first field, $2 the second field, and so on, up to $NF, where NF is a special variable representing the number of fields in the current record.

AWK's syntax includes the use of patterns, which can be regular expressions, and actions enclosed in braces {}. Patterns can be specified using regular expressions, relational expressions, or special patterns like BEGIN and END. The BEGIN block is used for actions that should be performed before any input lines are read, and the END block is for actions to be performed after all input lines have been processed.

Example:

```
awk 'BEGIN { print "Names and Ages" }
{ print $1, $2, $3 }
END { print "End of File" }' data.txt
```

Output:

```
Names and Ages
John Doe 28
Jane Smith 32
Alice Brown 25
End of File
```

In the above script, the BEGIN block executes before any input is read, initializing the output with the heading, "Names and Ages." The action { print $1, $2, $3 } prints the fields of each line, and the END block appends "End of File" after all lines have been processed.

AWK also provides built-in variables and functions that enhance its text processing capabilities. Some important built-in variables include:

- FS: Field Separator, determines how fields are split in each input line. Default is whitespace.
- OFS: Output Field Separator, determines how fields are sepa-

rated in the output. Default is a single space.

- RS: Record Separator, determines how records (lines) are separated in the input. Default is the newline character.

- ORS: Output Record Separator, determines how records are separated in the output. Default is the newline character.

Customizing these variables allows for flexible manipulation of input and output data formats: Example to process CSV files:

```
awk 'BEGIN { FS = ","; OFS = ":" }
{ print $1, $2, $3 }' data.csv
```

If data.csv contained:

```
John, Doe, 28
Jane, Smith, 32
Alice, Brown, 25
```

The output will be:

```
John:Doe:28
Jane:Smith:32
Alice:Brown:25
```

AWK scripts can become more sophisticated with conditional statements, loops, and user-defined functions. For instance:

```
awk '{
    if ($3 > 30) {
        print $1, $2 ": over 30 years old"
    } else {
        print $1, $2 ": 30 or younger"
    }
}' data.txt
```

The output will be:

```
John Doe: 30 or younger
Jane Smith: over 30 years old
Alice Brown: 30 or younger
```

In this script, an if statement evaluates the condition $3 > 30. Depending on whether the condition is true, it prints the appropriate message.

With these foundational concepts, one can appreciate AWK's capability to handle a broad range of text processing tasks through its succinct and expressive syntax.

1.3 The Purpose of AWK

The purpose of AWK is to provide a scripting language that excels at handling and processing plain text data, particularly structured data such as log files, CSV files, and other delimited text formats. AWK was developed with the goal of simplifying the execution of common text processing tasks that are cumbersome or more complex in other programming languages and shell utilities. By focusing on records and fields, AWK offers an intuitive approach to data extraction, transformation, and reporting.

At its core, AWK operates on a line-by-line basis, treating each line of input as a record. Within each record, fields are identified by separation delimiters, typically whitespace or user-defined characters. This record-and-field paradigm enables AWK to perform sophisticated text manipulations using concise and readable code.

The primary purposes of AWK are:

- **Data Extraction**: AWK allows users to easily extract specific pieces of data from text files based on patterns and conditions. For example, extracting the fifth field from each line of a CSV file can be achieved with minimal code.
- **Text Transformation**: Users can transform text by performing substitutions, rearranging fields, or modifying record formats. AWK provides powerful string manipulation functions to facilitate these transformations.
- **Summarization and Reporting**: AWK can aggregate data and generate summary statistics, such as counts, sums, and averages. Customized reports can be created by formatting the output according to specific requirements.
- **Pattern Scanning and Processing**: By defining pattern-action pairs, AWK programs specify how to process records based on matching patterns. This feature is useful for filtering data, performing conditional processing, and applying actions selectively.

To illustrate the purpose of AWK, consider a scenario where we have a log file named web_logs.txt containing web server access logs. Each line in the log file follows the common log format:

```
192.168.1.1 - - [10/Oct/2023:13:55:36 -0700] "GET /index.html HTTP/1.1" 200 1043
192.168.1.2 - - [10/Oct/2023:13:55:37 -0700] "POST /form HTTP/1.1" 404 167
```

An AWK script can be used to extract and summarize information from these logs. For instance, we may want to count the number of requests for each HTTP status code. The following AWK script accomplishes this task:

```
awk '{status[$9]++} END {for (code in status) print code, status[code]}' web_logs.txt
```

In this script, status[$9]++ increments the count for the status code found in the ninth field of each record. The END block executes after all records have been processed, printing each status code and its corresponding count. The output may look like:

```
200 1
404 1
```

This concise script highlights AWK's capability to perform complex data manipulation tasks with minimal code. By leveraging AWK's inherent strengths, users can efficiently address a wide range of text processing challenges.

Additionally, AWK's purpose extends to:

- **Automating Repetitive Tasks**: AWK scripts can automate repetitive data processing tasks, reducing manual efforts and minimizing errors.
- **Integration with UNIX Tools**: AWK complements other UNIX tools such as grep, sed, and sort, allowing for the construction of powerful data processing pipelines.
- **Portability**: Being available on most UNIX-like systems, AWK scripts can be executed across various environments without modification, ensuring portability and ease of sharing.

AWK's design, focused on simplicity and efficiency, makes it an indispensable tool for users who regularly work with text data. Its pattern-matching capabilities, built-in functions, and straightforward syntax empower users to perform a wide array of data processing tasks, from basic text extraction to complex data transformations and reporting.

1.4 Installing AWK

The installation process for AWK is relatively straightforward and can be accomplished on a variety of operating systems, including Unix-like systems such as Linux and macOS, as well as on Windows. This section provides detailed instructions for installing AWK on these platforms. Since AWK comes pre-installed on many Unix-like systems, the primary focus here will be on ensuring you have the necessary version, as well as installation on Windows systems where AWK is not natively available.

Checking AWK Installation on Unix-like Systems

To determine if AWK is already installed on your system, open a terminal and type the following command:

```
awk --version
```

If AWK is installed, you will see output similar to:

```
GNU Awk 5.1.0, API: 3.2
Copyright (C) 1989, 1991-2020 Free Software Foundation.
```

If AWK is not installed, you will receive a command not found message. In that case, you can install AWK via your package manager.

Installing AWK on Linux

For Debian-based distributions such as Ubuntu, you can install GNU AWK (gawk) using the apt package manager:

```
sudo apt update
sudo apt install gawk
```

For Red Hat-based distributions such as Fedora or CentOS, use dnf or yum for the installation:

```
sudo dnf install gawk
# or
sudo yum install gawk
```

Installing AWK on macOS

On macOS, you can install gawk using the Homebrew package manager. First, ensure that Homebrew is installed by visiting the official Homebrew website. Then, execute the following commands:

```
brew update
brew install gawk
```

After installation, confirm that the installation was successful by re-running the awk –version command.

Installing AWK on Windows

Windows does not come with AWK pre-installed, but you can use several methods to install it. One common approach is to use Cygwin, a large collection of GNU and Open Source tools that provide functionality similar to a Linux distribution on Windows. To install AWK via Cygwin, follow these steps:

- Visit the official Cygwin website and download the setup executable.
- Run the setup executable and follow the installation wizard's instructions.
- During the package selection step, search for and select gawk to include in your installation.
- Complete the installation.

Another approach involves using a Windows Subsystem for Linux (WSL). WSL allows you to run a Linux environment directly on Windows, unmodified, without the overhead of a traditional virtual machine or dual-boot setup. To install AWK using WSL:

- Open a PowerShell or command prompt window as an administrator.
- Install WSL and a Linux distribution, such as Ubuntu, by running:

```
wsl --install -d Ubuntu
```

- Once the installation is complete and you are in the WSL terminal, use the Linux-based steps to install gawk:

```
sudo apt update
sudo apt install gawk
```

Verifying the Installation

Regardless of platform, verifying the installation is critical to ensure that AWK is set up correctly. The following steps illustrate how to verify:

- Open a terminal or command prompt.
- Execute awk –version to check if AWK is recognized and correctly installed.

- Optionally, create and run a simple AWK script for further verification.

A simple test script:

```
echo "Hello, AWK!" | awk '{ print $0 }'
```

Expected output:

```
Hello, AWK!
```

Executing this command verifies that AWK can process input texts and produce the expected output, confirming a successful installation. The detailed steps provided should help ensure AWK is correctly set up, enabling you to proceed with learning and utilizing AWK's capabilities efficiently.

1.5 AWK vs. Other Text Processing Tools

AWK stands out among various text processing tools due to its specific design for pattern scanning and processing. To understand its uniqueness, we must evaluate it against other commonly used text processing utilities such as sed, Perl, and Python. Each tool has its strengths, trade-offs, and particular use cases where it excels.

AWK and sed

sed (stream editor) and AWK both originated in the UNIX ecosystem and serve similar purposes for text processing. However, their designs and capabilities differ significantly.

- **Pattern Matching**: AWK's pattern matching is more versatile, as it allows for conditional blocks akin to if-else constructs found in full-fledged programming languages. This makes it more powerful for complex text processing.

  ```
  awk '/pattern/ { print $1 }'
  ```

  In contrast, sed is primarily designed for basic text manipulation using regular expressions:

  ```
  sed -n '/pattern/p'
  ```

- **Program Structure**: AWK scripts can be more structured with BEGIN and END blocks that execute commands before processing any input lines and after all input lines have been processed, respectively:

```
awk 'BEGIN { print "Start" }
     /pattern/ { print $1 }
     END { print "End" }' filename
```

Conversely, sed operates on a line-by-line basis without such explicit blocks:

```
sed 's/pattern/replacement/' filename
```

AWK and Perl

Perl (Practical Extraction and Report Language) is another flexible tool for text processing, renowned for its regular expression handling and extensive library of modules. Comparing AWK to Perl highlights several distinctions:

- **Simplicity and Readability**: AWK's syntax is simpler and more readable for straightforward tasks, making it more approachable for beginners:

```
awk '{ print $1, $3 }' filename
```

  In Perl, similar tasks often require more verbose code:

```
perl -lane 'print "$F[0] $F[2]"' filename
```

- **Learning Curve**: AWK is generally easier to learn due to its focused feature set, while Perl offers more functionalities at the cost of a steeper learning curve.

AWK and Python

Python is a general-purpose programming language popular for its readability and strong community support. Comparing AWK with Python offers a perspective on their application in text processing:

- **Text Processing Specificity**: AWK is specialized for text processing with built-in features like field and record separation, making it ideal for scripting on the command line:

```
awk -F, '{ print $1 }' filename.csv
```

  While Python can perform similar tasks using libraries like re for regular expressions, the syntax is more elaborate:

```
import csv
with open('filename.csv') as file:
    reader = csv.reader(file)
    for row in reader:
        print(row[0])
```

- **Extensibility and Integration**: Python excels in integrating with various systems and libraries, offering extensive extensibility beyond text processing, including numerical computations, web development, and more.

While AWK thrives in simple and moderately complex text processing tasks due to its domain-specific design, each of the comparative tools—sed, Perl, and Python—brings unique advantages that may be preferred in different contexts. The choice of tool may depend on factors like the complexity of the task, the familiarity of the user with the tool, and specific workflow requirements.

1.6 Basic Structure of an AWK Program

The structure of an AWK program can be understood through its core components: patterns, actions, variables, and functions. An AWK program consists of a series of pattern-action statements, along with optional global variable and function definitions. Each of these parts plays a crucial role in effectively processing and manipulating text data.

Patterns are expressions that specify the conditions under which the associated actions are executed. These conditions can be based on line numbers, regular expressions, or logical combinations thereof. Patterns are optional but typically used to filter input data.

Actions are series of commands enclosed in curly braces {}. These commands are executed when the respective pattern is matched. If no pattern is specified, then by default, the actions apply to all lines of the input. This provides a high level of flexibility and control over data manipulation.

AWK program structure follows the syntax:

```
pattern { action }
```

Let's delve deeper into these components with examples and explanations.

Patterns can be:

- /regular_expression/: Matches lines containing the regular expression.
- BEGIN: Pre-processing action executed before the first input line is read.
- END: Post-processing action executed after the last input line is read.
- NR == 1: Matches only the first line.
- $1 == "value": Matches lines where the first field equals value.
- expression1 && expression2: Logical AND combination.
- expression1 || expression2: Logical OR combination.
- !expression: Logical NOT.

Actions are:

- Sequence of commands.
- Field and record manipulations.
- Print and arithmetic operations.
- Function calls.

A typical AWK command looks like:

```
$ awk 'BEGIN { print "Start" } /pattern/ { action } END { print "End" }' filename
```

The BEGIN block initializes any setup instructions, executes before any line processing begins. The main pattern-action combinations process each line of input data. Finally, the END block runs post-processing instructions.

Consider this simple AWK program example stored in example.awk:

```
// example.awk
BEGIN { print "Processing Start" }
/pattern/ { print $1, $2 }
END { print "Processing End" }
```

When the script is executed:

```
$ awk -f example.awk datafile.txt
```

The output will display the matched lines along with the commands in the BEGIN and END blocks:

```
Processing Start
first_field second_field
...
Processing End
```

Variables in AWK can be predefined or user-defined. Examples of predefined variables include:

- NR: Current record number.
- NF: Number of fields in the current record.
- FS: Input field separator (default is whitespace).
- RS: Input record separator (default is newline).
- OFS: Output field separator.
- ORS: Output record separator.
- $0: Entire input record.
- $n: nth field of the input record.

User-defined variables can be declared and initialized within the BEGIN block or within the action statements as necessary.

Functions in AWK enhance its capability by performing sub-tasks, promoting code modularity and reusability. AWK supports both built-in functions and user-defined functions.

Built-in functions include:

- length(): Returns the length of a string.
- substr(string, start, length): Returns a substring.
- toupper(string): Converts a string to uppercase.
- tolower(string): Converts a string to lowercase.
- match(string, regex): Searches string for regex match.
- split(string, array, delimiter): Splits string into array parts.

A user-defined function example is:

```
function myFunction(parameter1, parameter2) {
  return parameter1 + parameter2
}
```

myFunction can then be called in an action statement:

```
{
  result = myFunction($1, $2)
  print result
}
```

Understanding the basic structure of an AWK program provides a solid foundation for leveraging the language's full capabilities for text processing and data extraction tasks. The subsequent sections will build on these fundamentals, exploring more intricate uses and advanced strategies in AWK programming.

1.7 Running Your First AWK Script

Running your first AWK script involves understanding the basic structure and executing it in a way that parses and processes text input correctly. To illustrate this procedure effectively, we will walk through a simple script to count the number of lines in a file.

Begin by creating a sample text file named sample.txt that contains the following content:

```
This is the first line.
This is the second line.
This is the third line.
```

The objective is to use AWK to count the number of lines in this file. Below is a basic AWK script that accomplishes this task:

```
awk 'BEGIN {count=0} {count++} END {print count}' sample.txt
```

This script involves three important parts:

1. BEGIN block: Executes before processing any lines from the input file. Here, count is initialized to zero. 2. Main block (between { and }): This block processes each line in the input file. For each line, count++ increments the count variable by one. 3. END block: Executes after all lines from the input file have been processed. It prints the final value of count, which represents the total number of lines.

To execute the script, use the following command in a UNIX-like terminal:

```
$ awk 'BEGIN {count=0} {count++} END {print count}' sample.txt
```

The output will be:

```
3
```

This indicates that there are three lines in the sample.txt file.

Next, let's dissect each part more meticulously:

- **BEGIN block**: - Syntax: BEGIN {...commands...} - Purpose: Initialize variables or perform actions before processing any input lines. - In our script: BEGIN {count=0} initializes the count variable.

- **Main block**: - Syntax: {...commands...} - Purpose: Execute commands for each line of input. - In our script: {count++} increments count for each line processed.

- **END block**: - Syntax: END {...commands...} - Purpose: Execute commands after all input lines have been processed. - In our script: END {print count} prints the final value of the count variable.

For a more comprehensive understanding, let's introduce another example. Suppose we want to sum the numbers in the following file named numbers.txt:

```
5
10
15
20
```

The corresponding AWK script to calculate the sum of these numbers is:

```
awk 'BEGIN {sum=0} {sum += $1} END {print "Sum:", sum}' numbers.txt
```

In this example: - sum=0 initializes the sum variable. - sum += $1 adds the value of the first field (the entire line in this case) to the variable sum. - print "Sum:", sum prints a label followed by the total sum.

Execution command in the terminal:

```
$ awk 'BEGIN {sum=0} {sum += $1} END {print "Sum:", sum}' numbers.txt
```

The output will be:

```
Sum: 50
```

By understanding these examples, it is possible to write and execute basic AWK scripts that perform initial text processing tasks. The above scripts introduced fundamental constructs such as BEGIN, main processing blocks, and END, which form the underpinning of many AWK programs.

It is also valuable to use script files for larger and more complex AWK programs. Save the AWK script in a file, for example script.awk, then run it using:

```
$ awk -f script.awk inputfile.txt
```

This approach ensures easier editing, reusability, and better management of scripts.

1.8 Understanding AWK Command Line Syntax

In mastering AWK programming, understanding its command line syntax is crucial. The AWK command line syntax can be expressed as:

```
awk [ options ] 'program' file ...
```

Here, options are various command-line options that modify the behavior of the AWK interpreter, 'program' is the AWK script or individual commands to be executed, and file specifies the input files.

Options:

AWK provides several options that influence its operation. The most commonly used options include:

- -f program_file: Read the AWK program from the file specified instead of the command line. This is useful for larger scripts.
- -F fs: Specify the input field separator, fs.
- -v var=value: Assign a value to a variable before execution begins.
- -b: Use the binary mode for fread or fread parsing.
- -W compat or -W traditional: Use compatibility mode or traditional AWK mode respectively.

Program:

The 'program' segment includes the AWK instructions to be executed. It is commonly encapsulated in single quotes to prevent confusion with the shell. The basic structure of an AWK program is a series of pattern-action statements. Each statement has the form:

```
pattern { action }
```

Patterns determine when the action is performed and can consist of regular expressions, relational expressions, or special expressions such as BEGIN and END. Actions are a sequence of AWK commands and expressions.

Patterns: AWK patterns can match against records or lines in the input. Some common patterns include:

- /regexp/: Matches lines containing the regular expression.
- expr: Matches lines where the expression evaluates to true.
- BEGIN: Executes action(s) before processing any input lines.
- END: Executes action(s) after processing all input lines.

Actions: Actions are enclosed in braces { } and define what processing to perform. Common actions encompass expressions, control statements, and built-in functions. Examples include:

- print statement: Outputs text.

  ```
  { print $0 }
  ```

- if statement: Conditional execution.

  ```
  { if ($1 > 100) print $1 }
  ```

- for loop: Repeated execution.

  ```
  { for (i=1; i<=NF; i++) print $i }
  ```

- Built-in functions like length, tolower, toupper, etc.

  ```
  { print tolower($0) }
  ```

Files:

The file argument specifies the input files for processing. If no file is provided, AWK reads from standard input. Multiple files can be processed in sequence:

```
awk 'program' file1 file2 ...
```

Examples:

1. Using AWK to print lines containing the string "error" in a file named log.txt:

```
awk '/error/ { print $0 }' log.txt
```

Output:

[Matching lines from log.txt containing 'error']

2. Specifying the field separator as a comma, printing the first and second fields from data.csv:

```
awk -F ',' '{ print $1, $2 }' data.csv
```

Output:

[First and second fields from data.csv]

3. Assigning variables via the command line:

```
awk -v threshold=100 '{ if ($1 > threshold) print $1 }' numbers.txt
```

Output:

[Values greater than 100 from numbers.txt]

Understanding these basic components of the AWK command line syntax will enable users to leverage AWK's full potential for text processing tasks.

1.9 Common Use Cases for AWK

AWK is an indispensable tool for those engaged in text processing and data extraction due to its versatility and the relatively simple commands required to execute complex tasks. Here, we will explore some common use cases for AWK, offering practical examples to ensure clarity and ease of understanding.

1. Pattern Matching and Data Extraction

One of the primary strengths of AWK is its ability to search for patterns in text and extract corresponding data. AWK scripts allow for the use of regular expressions to define these patterns, making it easy to filter columns and lines based on specific criteria.

Consider an example where we want to extract the names and scores of students who have scored above 75 in a list stored in students.txt:

```
awk '$3 > 75 { print $1, $2 }' students.txt
```

Here, the script processes each line in students.txt. The condition $\$3 > 75$ checks if the third field, presumably the score, is greater than 75. If true, it prints the first two fields, presumably the student's first and last names.

```
Alice Johnson
Bob Smith
Carol White
```

2. Field Manipulation and Reformatting

AWK makes it easy to manipulate text by specifying fields and rearranging them as needed. This can be particularly useful in preprocessing data for further analysis.

Suppose we have a file data.csv with fields separated by commas, and we want to switch the first and second fields. Here is an example:

```
awk 'BEGIN { FS = ","; OFS = "," } { print $2, $1, $3 }' data.csv
```

In this script, FS (Field Separator) and OFS (Output Field Separator) are both set to commas. The command then prints the second field, followed by the first and third fields.

```
2008, Smith, 4000
2009, White, 5000
2010, Johnson, 6000
```

3. Summarizing Data

AWK can perform aggregation and summarization of data within files. This is useful for generating concise reports from large datasets.

For example, if we need the total sales amount from a sales report stored in sales.txt, where the amount is in the second field, the following script will sum these values:

```
awk '{ sum += $2 } END { print "Total Sales: ", sum }' sales.txt
```

The script adds the values of the second field for each line to the sum variable. After processing all lines, it outputs the total sales amount.

```
Total Sales: 15000
```

4. Text Transformation and Substitution

AWK supports robust text transformation functionalities, such as searching and replacing within fields. These tasks typically involve the gsub (global substitute) function.

For instance, assume we have a file report.txt, and we need to replace all instances of “error” with “warning”:

```
awk '{ gsub(/error/, "warning"); print }' report.txt
```

The gsub function searches for the pattern "error" and replaces it with "warning" in each line before printing the modified line.

```
Warning: Memory usage is high
Warning: Disk space is low
```

5. Validating Data Integrity

Another common use of AWK is validating data to ensure it meets certain criteria. AWK scripts can check for conditions and highlight or report anomalies.

For example, we can validate entries in data.txt to report lines where the value in the second field is negative:

```
awk '$2 < 0 { print "Invalid entry on line " NR ": " $0 }' data.txt
```

This command checks each line and prints a message if the second field is negative. NR is the AWK built-in variable representing the current record number (line number), and $0 is the entire line.

```
Invalid entry on line 3: Widget, -120, Chicago
```

6. Conditional Processing

AWK’s conditional processing capabilities allow executing different actions based on pattern matches or other conditions, making it ideal for handling complex data.

Imagine we have a log file server.log and want to separate error and info messages into different files. We can use:

```
awk '/error/ { print > "errors.log" } /info/ { print > "info.log" }' server.log
```

This script directs lines containing "error" to errors.log and those containing "info" to info.log.

```
errors.log:
2023-10-01 10:00:00 ERROR: Disk failure

info.log:
2023-10-01 12:00:00 INFO: System rebooted successfully
```

AWK’s versatility extends beyond these examples, offering a robust set of features for a multitude of text processing tasks. Mastering these common use cases opens the door to efficiently managing and transforming textual data in various practical scenarios.

1.10 Community and Resources

The utility and versatility of AWK have garnered a robust and dynamic community of users, developers, and educators who continually contribute to its growth and the dissemination of knowledge. Understanding and leveraging these community-driven resources can significantly enhance your proficiency in AWK programming. This section provides an in-depth overview of the various resources and community hubs that are essential for anyone looking to master AWK.

Online Forums and Discussion Groups

The AWK community thrives in numerous online forums and discussion groups, where you can ask questions, share insights, and troubleshoot issues. Some notable platforms include:

- Stack Overflow: The awk tag on Stack Overflow is a valuable resource for finding solutions to specific problems, reading expert answers, and participating in discussions.
- Reddit: Subreddits such as r/commandline and r/programming frequently feature discussions on AWK programming techniques and best practices.
- Unix&Linux Stack Exchange: This site is particularly useful for Unix-based AWK queries, given AWK's deep integration with Unix-like systems.

Mailing Lists and Newsgroups

Traditional mailing lists and newsgroups remain active avenues for in-depth discussions and announcements related to AWK. Prominent lists include:

- comp.lang.awk: A Usenet newsgroup dedicated to discussions about AWK.
- bug-gnu-utils@gnu.org: This mailing list addresses both bugs and general discussions about the GNU versions of various utilities, including gawk.

Documentation and Tutorials

High-quality documentation and tutorials are indispensable for mastering AWK. Key resources include:

- GNU AWK User's Guide: Available online, this guide offers comprehensive coverage of gawk, the GNU implementation of AWK.
- The AWK Programming Language by Alfred V. Aho, Brian W. Kernighan, and Peter J. Weinberger: This seminal book is often considered the definitive resource for learning AWK.
- fuctions.awk: Online repositories such as awk1-libraries provide reusable function collections that can augment your AWK scripts.

Community-Contributed Scripts and Libraries

One of the best ways to learn AWK is by studying and utilizing community-contributed scripts and libraries. Websites like GitHub host numerous AWK repositories. For example:

- GitHub's #awk topic: Searching #awk on GitHub reveals a variety of AWK scripts and projects shared by users worldwide.
- Awesome-AWK: A curated list of AWK scripts, libraries, and resources available on GitHub, often listed as awesome-awk.

Conferences and Meetups

Engagement with peers through conferences and meetups can provide valuable insights and networking opportunities. International conferences such as:

- FOSDEM: The Free and Open Source Developers' European Meeting often includes talks relevant to AWK and other text processing tools.
- Linux Foundation Events: Events organized by the Linux Foundation frequently feature sessions on AWK and related technologies.

Local meetups organized via platforms such as Meetup.com can also be useful for connecting with local AWK developers and enthusiasts.

Educational Platforms

Several educational platforms and resources offer structured AWK courses, including:

- Coursera and edX: While AWK-specific courses may be limited, these platforms often include modules on AWK within larger courses on Unix or data processing.
- YouTube: Channels dedicated to command-line programming and Unix tools frequently cover AWK, providing video tutorials ranging from beginner to advanced levels.

Social Media and Blogs

Social media platforms and blogs are excellent for staying up-to-date with the latest developments in AWK. Notable mentions include:

- Twitter: Follow tags like #awk and users who frequently tweet about text processing and AWK.
- Technical Blogs: Blogs by industry experts often contain deep dives into specific AWK use cases and advanced techniques. Examples include regular updates on the GNU Project blog.

Embracing these diverse resources and engaging with the AWK community will not only accelerate your learning process but also keep you informed about the latest advancements and best practices in AWK programming.

Chapter 2

AWK Syntax and Fundamentals

This chapter provides a comprehensive overview of the basic syntax and fundamental elements of AWK programming. Topics include the structure of AWK programs, command line options, fields and records, comments, patterns and actions, and the use of regular expressions. Readers will also learn about input and output operations, field and record separators, built-in variables, and best practices for writing and saving AWK scripts. This foundational knowledge is essential for anyone aiming to proficiently utilize AWK for text processing tasks.

2.1 Basic AWK Syntax

AWK is a powerful text processing language that allows users to easily manipulate data files, perform pattern matching, and generate reports. Understanding the basic syntax of AWK is essential for writing efficient and readable AWK programs. This section will cover the fundamental components of AWK syntax, including patterns, actions, and the general structure of AWK commands.

An AWK program consists of a sequence of pattern-action statements:

```
pattern { action }
```

The pattern specifies the conditions under which the action is performed. If no pattern is specified, the action is applied to every line of the input. Likewise, if no action is specified, the default action is to print the entire line. Both pattern and action are optional, but at least one must be present.

```
BEGIN { action }
END { action }
```

AWK also supports the use of BEGIN and END patterns, which allow actions to be executed before processing any input lines (BEGIN) or after all input has been processed (END). These are special patterns that do not match any input lines, but provide a way to execute setup or cleanup code.

Example:

```
awk 'BEGIN {print "Start"} {print $0} END {print "End"}' file.txt
```

This AWK command will print "Start" before processing any lines, print each line of file.txt, and then print "End" after all lines have been processed.

AWK Patterns:

Patterns can be composed of regular expressions, relational expressions, or logical combinations of other patterns. Below are some common pattern forms:

- **Regular expressions:** Matches lines containing the regular expression.

```
/pattern/
```

- Relational expressions: Matches lines wherein the specified condition is true.

```
$1 > 100
```

- **Boolean combinations:** Combines patterns using logical operators (&&, ||, !).

```
$1 > 100 && /pattern/
```

AWK Actions:

An action is a sequence of statements enclosed in curly braces {} that are executed for each line that matches the pattern. Some commonly used statements include:

- print: Outputs text to standard output.

```
print $0
```

- printf: Outputs formatted text.

```
printf "%s %s\n", $1, $2
```

- assignment: Assigns a value to a variable.

```
sum += $1
```

- control statements: Includes conditionals and loops.

```
if (condition) { ... } else { ... }
for (i = 1; i <= N; i++) { ... }
```

Example:

```
awk '/error/ { print $0 }' logfile.txt
```

This command prints any line from logfile.txt that contains the word "error".

Field Variables:

In AWK, input lines are automatically divided into fields, which can be accessed using the field variables $1, $2, ..., $NF, where NF is a built-in variable representing the number of fields in a line. $0 represents the entire input line.

```
{$1 = toupper($1); print $0 }
```

This action converts the first field of each line to uppercase, then prints the modified line.

Built-in Functions:

AWK provides numerous built-in functions for mathematical operations, string manipulation, and more. Some commonly used functions include:

- length(): Returns the length of a string.

```
length($1)
```

- toupper(): Converts a string to uppercase.

```
toupper($1)
```

- substr(): Extracts a substring from a string.

```
substr($1, 2, 5)
```

By adhering to these fundamental concepts and mastering the basic syntax of AWK, users can unlock the full potential of AWK for efficient text processing and data manipulation tasks.

2.2 The Structure of AWK Programs

An AWK program is composed of a sequence of pattern-action statements. The structure of an AWK program typically follows the syntax:

pattern { action }

In this syntax, *pattern* specifies the conditions under which the *action* is executed. Each pattern-action pair is executed for each line of input that matches the pattern. The default action is to print the current record if no action is specified.

The essential components of an AWK program include the BEGIN and END patterns, which might appear as follows:

```
BEGIN {
    # Initialization code
}
{
    # Main processing code
}
END {
    # Cleanup code
}
```

Explanation of Components:

- BEGIN Block: The BEGIN block is executed before any input lines are read. It is typically used for initialization tasks such as setting variables, printing headers, or opening files.

- Default Block: The block without any specific pattern is executed for every input line. This is where the main processing logic goes.

- END Block: The END block is executed after all input lines have been processed. It is used for cleanup activities, such as printing summaries, closing files, or freeing resources.

Example:

The following AWK program demonstrates the use of BEGIN, default, and END blocks:

```
BEGIN {
    print "Processing begins."
    line_count = 0
}
{
    line_count++
    print $0 # Print each line
}
END {
    print "Processing ends."
    print "Total lines processed:", line_count
}
```

If this script is saved in a file named process.awk and executed using the command awk -f process.awk input.txt, the output for an input file input.txt containing three lines line1, line2, and line3 would be:

```
Processing begins.
line1
line2
line3
Processing ends.
Total lines processed: 3
```

Pattern Matching:

Patterns in AWK can be regular expressions, relational expressions, or special patterns such as BEGIN and END. For instance, to print lines that contain the word "error":

```
awk '/error/ { print $0 }' logfile.txt
```

In this example, the pattern is the regular expression /error/, and the action { print $0 } prints the lines that match the pattern.

Multiple Patterns and Actions:

Each pattern-action pair should be enclosed in curly braces. An AWK program can have multiple such pairs:

```
BEGIN {
    print "Start"
```

```
}
$1 ~ /^[a-zA-Z]/ {
    print "Line starts with a letter:", $0
}

$1 ~ /^[0-9]/ {
    print "Line starts with a number:", $0
}

END {
    print "End"
}
```

In the above script, the pattern $1 ~ /^[a-zA-Z]/ determines if the first field of the input line starts with a letter, whereas the pattern $1 ~ /^[0-9]/ checks if the first field starts with a number. The corresponding actions print the matched lines with appropriate messages.

Actions:

Actions are sequences of statements enclosed in curly braces. They can consist of built-in functions, variable assignments, control statements, and other expressions. For example:

```
{
    sum += $2
    count++
}

END {
    avg = sum / count
    print "Average value:", avg
}
```

In this example, the default action computes the sum of the values in the second field and counts the number of records. The END block calculates and prints the average.

By understanding and leveraging the structure of AWK programs, users can effectively perform a wide range of text processing tasks with precision and efficiency.

2.3 AWK Command Line Options

AWK command line options play a crucial role in controlling the behavior of AWK programs when they are executed. Understanding these options allows users to fine-tune their scripts, handle various input types, and manage outputs appropriately. This section will delve into the primary command line options available in AWK and explain their usage.

- -F fs: This option sets the input field separator, FS, to the value specified by fs. This can be particularly useful for processing data files with a consistent but unconventional delimiter.

```
awk -F, '{print $1, $2}' data.csv
```

- -v var=val: It assigns a value to a variable var before the script starts executing. This can be used to pass parameters into the AWK script from the command line.

```
awk -v min_age=18 '$3 >= min_age {print $1, $2}' data.txt
```

- -f progfile: This option allows the user to specify an AWK program file, progfile, containing the AWK script. This is useful for executing larger AWK programs stored in separate files.

```
awk -f myscript.awk inputfile.txt
```

- –: This option signifies the end of command line options. This allows the user to safely pass file names or other strings that might start with a hyphen to the AWK program.

```
awk -- '{print $1}' -file.txt
```

- -W compat or –compat: Enables compatibility mode. When this mode is activated, gawk behaves more similarly to regular AWK, which can help when migrating scripts from other AWK implementations.

```
gawk --compat -f oldscript.awk inputfile.txt
```

- -W trace or –trace: This debugging option shows each statement of the AWK program that is executed. This can be very useful for troubleshooting complex scripts.

```
gawk --trace -f debugscrip.awk inputfile.txt
```

- -W lint or –lint: Provides warnings about constructs that are dubious or non-portable to other AWK implementations. This is useful for writing more robust and portable AWK scripts.

```
gawk --lint -f portablescript.awk inputfile.txt
```

- -W lint=fatal or –lint=fatal: Extends the –lint functionality by treating warnings as errors. This can enforce strict code quality during the development process.

```
gawk --lint=fatal -f strictscript.awk inputfile.txt
```

- –re-interval: Enables interval expressions in regular expressions, which are disabled by default in some versions of gawk for compatibility reasons. Interval expressions allow specifying a range of occurrences for a pattern.

```
gawk --re-interval '/a{2,5}/ {print $0}' textfile.txt
```

- -W exec or –exec progfile: An option similar to -f, but treats the specified file as an executable script and immediately processes the following input files. This allows embedding AWK scripts directly in executable files.

```
awk --exec myscript.awk inputfile.txt
```

- –traditional: Forces gawk to behave like traditional awk, disabling gawk-specific extensions. This can help in maintaining backward compatibility with older AWK scripts.

```
gawk --traditional -f script.awk inputfile.txt
```

To comprehend the implications of these options effectively, one should consider the operational context in which the AWK script will be executed. Parameters such as field delimiters, compatibility requirements, and debugging needs significantly influence the choice and combination of options used. Consistent practice with these command line options will enable users to harness the full power of AWK scripting for various text processing tasks.

2.4 Fields and Records in AWK

In AWK, data input is processed in the form of records and fields. Understanding these concepts is fundamental to using AWK effectively for text processing tasks. Each line in the input stream is treated as a record. Records are subsequently divided into smaller units known as fields.

Records: By default, AWK considers each line of input to be a record. The sequence of records can be processed one line at a time. The built-in variable NR (Number of Records) keeps track of the current record count. For example:

```
awk '{ print NR, $0 }' input.txt
```

When executed, this command prints the record number followed by the content of each record:

```
1 This is the first line of the file.
2 This is the second line of the file.
3 This is the third line.
```

Fields: Within each record, fields are typically separated by whitespace (spaces or tabs). The built-in variable NF (Number of Fields) denotes the number of fields in the current record. Fields are accessed using the dollar sign $ followed by the field number.

```
awk '{ print $1, $2 }' input.txt
```

The above command prints the first and second fields of each record:

```
This is
This is
This is
```

Field Separator: The default field separator is whitespace, but it can be changed using the FS variable. For example, if the fields in a file are separated by commas, you can set FS to a comma:

```
awk 'BEGIN { FS = "," } { print $1, $2 }' input.csv
```

This script sets the field separator to a comma and prints the first and second fields of each record from the input file input.csv.

Modifying Field Separator at the Command Line: The -F option allows a user to set the field separator directly from the command line:

```
awk -F"," '{ print $1, $2 }' input.csv
```

Output Field Separator: The OFS variable controls the output field separator, which is also whitespace by default. To change the output field separator to a comma:

```
awk 'BEGIN { OFS = "," } { print $1, $2 }' input.txt
```

Records Separator: Similar to fields, the record separator can be changed using the RS variable. For example, consider separating records based on blank lines instead of newlines:

```
awk 'BEGIN { RS = "" } { print NR, $0 }' input.txt
```

In this scenario, each blank-line-separated block becomes a single record, and NR will reflect the number of such records.

Modifying Record Separator at the Command Line: The -v option allows setting the record separator from the command line:

```
awk -v RS="" '{ print NR, $0 }' input.txt
```

Multicharacter Field Separators: Multicharacter separators can be used by assigning a regular expression to FS. For example, to separate fields by either a comma or a semicolon:

```
awk 'BEGIN { FS = "[,;]" } { print $1, $2 }' input.txt
```

Changing Field Values: Fields are not just read-only. You can modify the value of a field within a record:

```
awk '{ $1 = "Modified"; print $0 }' input.txt
```

This script replaces the first field of each record with the word "Modified".

Combining Fields and Records: Let's consider a practical example. Here is a script that computes the average of numbers in the second field of a file:

```
awk '{ sum += $2 } END { if (NR > 0) print "Average:", sum / NR }' data.txt
```

This script accumulates the sum of the second field in sum, and after processing all records, it calculates and prints the average.

Consistent Field Access Across Records: When working on a file with inconsistent field counts across records, NF and mentioned fields will reflect only existing fields per record:

```
awk '{ print $1, $2, "Fields:", NF }' incomplete.txt
```

Knowing how to handle fields and records in AWK is crucial for effective text and data processing. Mastery of these elements enables you to manipulate and analyze structured data efficiently.

2.5 Comments in AWK Scripts

Comments are essential in any programming language, serving as guidelines and explanations within the code. They provide a means for programmers to document their code, making it more readable and maintainable. In AWK, comments follow specific syntactical rules that facilitate this process effectively.

To include a comment in an AWK script, one must use the hash character ('#'). Any text that follows this character on the same line is treated as a comment and is ignored by the AWK interpreter during execution. It is critical to ensure that comments are written clearly and are strategically placed to enhance the understanding of the code.

The following example demonstrates how to include comments in an AWK script:

```
# This AWK script prints the first column of the input file

awk '{ print $1 }' inputfile.txt

# End of script
```

In this example, the comment # This AWK script prints the first column of the input file provides a descriptive explanation of the script's purpose. Similarly, the # End of script comment indicates the conclusion of the script.

It is considered a best practice to use comments liberally, particularly in complex scripts, to elucidate the logic and purpose of various segments of code. This not only aids others who might read the code but also serves as a reminder to the original author when revisiting the script after some time.

Inline Comments: AWK also allows for inline comments, where comments can be placed at the end of a line of code. This technique is useful for providing quick notes about specific parts of the line, as shown in the following example:

```
awk '{ print $1 }' inputfile.txt # Print the first column
```

In this case, the comment # Print the first column immediately follows the AWK command, offering a brief explanation without interfering with the code's readability.

Multi-line Comments: Although AWK does not support multi-line comments natively, a common workaround is to place a comment character at the beginning of each line. This method ensures that multiple lines of text are treated as comments. The example below illustrates this approach:

```
# This script performs the following tasks:
# 1. Reads the input file
# 2. Prints the first column
# 3. Ignores the rest of the columns

awk '{ print $1 }' inputfile.txt
```

Here, each line of the descriptive block is preceded by a #, marking it as a comment. This method is widely accepted and used to provide detailed explanations or instructions within the code.

Comments also play a crucial role during debugging. They can be used to temporarily disable lines of code by converting them into comments. This technique helps identify issues without deleting the actual code. Consider the following example:

```
awk '{
  print $1
  # print $2 # This line is disabled for debugging purposes
}' inputfile.txt
```

In the example, the line print $2 is commented out, temporarily preventing its execution. This allows developers to isolate and test specific parts of the code while preserving the original logic.

Another important aspect is the documentation of script parameters and usage. Commenting at the beginning of scripts to explain input parameters, expected output format, and usage instructions is very beneficial. Here is an illustration of this practice:

```
# This script takes an input file and prints the first column
# Usage: awk -f script.awk inputfile.txt

awk '{ print $1 }'
```

By documenting usage instructions and parameters, the script becomes more user-friendly, reducing the likelihood of misuse and errors.

Readers should note that excessive commenting of self-explanatory code can lead to clutter and reduced readability. Comments should add value by offering insights and clarifications that are not immediately apparent from the code itself. Balancing the amount and detail of comments is essential to maintain clean, readable, and interpretable scripts.

In AWK programming, comments are a powerful tool for documentation, explanation, and debugging. Proper use of comments enhances the code's maintainability and provides a clearer understanding for both the original author and others who may work with the code in the future.

2.6 Patterns and Actions in AWK

In AWK programming, a key feature is its ability to process text based on specified patterns and perform actions when these patterns are matched. This combination of patterns and actions makes AWK powerful and versatile for text-processing tasks.

Patterns in AWK determine which input records are selected for processing. Input records that match a pattern will trigger a corresponding action. An action is a sequence of commands enclosed in curly braces {} that specifies what to do with the selected records.

Patterns can take several forms, including regular expressions, relational expressions, and logical combinations of these. By mastering the use of patterns and actions, one can automate complex text manipulations efficiently.

Example of AWK Program with Patterns and Actions

Consider the following AWK script:

```
awk '{ if ($1 > 100) print $0 }'
```

In this example, the pattern is a conditional statement $\$1 > 100$, which checks if the first field of each record is greater than 100. The action is the $\mathrm{print}\ \$0$ statement, which prints the entire record if the condition is true.

Types of Patterns in AWK

- **Regular Expressions:** A regular expression pattern matches any input record that contains the specified regular expression. For instance:

  ```
  /pattern/ {
      action
  }
  ```

  If $\mathrm{pattern}$ is found in an input record, the specified action is executed.

- **Relational Expressions:** A relational expression pattern performs a comparison. If the condition evaluates to true, the action is executed. Example:

```
$3 == "abc" {
    print $0
}
```

In this example, the action is executed if the third field of the input record is equal to "abc".

- **Pattern Ranges:** A pattern range is specified by two patterns separated by a comma. The action is executed for all records between the start and the end pattern inclusively. Example:

```
/start_pattern/, /end_pattern/ {
    action
}
```

- **Logical Operators:** Patterns can be combined using logical operators such as && (AND), || (OR), and ! (NOT). Example:

```
($1 > 50) && ($2 < 100) {
    print $0
}
```

  This pattern-action block prints records where the first field is greater than 50 and the second field is less than 100.

- **Pattern Blocks:** AWK supports multiple pattern-action blocks within the same script. Each pattern-action block is independent and executed sequentially. Example:

```
pattern1 {
    action1
}
pattern2 {
    action2
}
```

Omitting Patterns

When the pattern is omitted, the action applies to all input records by default. Example:

```
awk '{ print $0 }'
```

This script prints every input record because no specific pattern limits its scope.

Using BEGIN and END Patterns

AWK provides two special patterns: BEGIN and END. These patterns allow actions to be performed before processing any input records and after all input records have been processed, respectively.

BEGIN is often used to initialize variables or perform actions that need to occur once:

```
awk 'BEGIN { print "Start processing..." }'
```

Similarly, END is useful for summarizing or finalizing results:

```
awk 'END { print "Processing complete." }'
```

Combining BEGIN and END with Regular Patterns

An AWK script can contain BEGIN, END, and regular pattern-action blocks. An example illustrating this combination:

```
awk 'BEGIN { print "Start" }
    /pattern/ { print $0 }
    END { print "End" }'
```

In this script, "Start" is printed before any input is processed, records containing "pattern" are printed during processing, and "End" is printed after all input records are processed.

Practical Example: Filtering Logs

Consider a log file named system.log with varying levels of message severity. Here is an AWK script to filter and print warnings and errors:

```
awk '/WARNING/ || /ERROR/ { print $0 }' system.log
```

This script prints all records containing either "WARNING" or "ERROR".

Advanced Pattern Examples

Combining complex patterns and actions can be very powerful. Example:

```
awk 'BEGIN { print "Log Analysis" }
/ERROR/ { errorCount++ }
/WARNING/ { warningCount++ }
END {
    print "Total Errors:", errorCount
    print "Total Warnings:", warningCount
}' system.log
```

In this advanced example, the script initializes two counters for errors and warnings. It increments the respective counters upon encountering "ERROR" or "WARNING" in the input records. At the end, it prints the total counts of errors and warnings.

Understanding and correctly using patterns and actions in AWK can significantly enhance the capability to handle diverse text processing tasks effectively. With practice, combining patterns with appropriate actions allows one to extract, manipulate, and analyze data efficiently.

2.7 Using Regular Expressions in AWK

Regular expressions (regex) are essential tools in AWK for pattern matching and text processing. They allow for sophisticated string manipulations by specifying patterns that define a search space. AWK employs regex to match records and fields within its input data, enabling a variety of operations from simple searches to complex parsing and transformations.

To use regex in AWK, follow the syntax:

```
pattern { action }
```

The pattern can be any regex enclosed in forward slashes /. When a line or record matches the pattern, the associated action block is executed.

Basic Regular Expressions

- abc: Matches the exact string abc.
- a.c: The period . matches any single character except a newline.
- a*: Matches zero or more occurrences of a.
- a+: Matches one or more occurrences of a (extended regex).
- a?: Matches zero or one occurrence of a (extended regex).
- a{n,m}: Matches at least n and at most m occurrences of a.

For example, consider the following AWK program:

```
awk '/^a/ { print $0 }' input.txt
```

The regex â matches lines that start with the character a. The program prints each line of input.txt that begins with a.

Character Classes

- [abc]: Matches any one of the characters a, b, or c.

- [âbc]: Matches any character except a, b, or c.
- [a-z]: Matches any lowercase letter.
- [A-Z]: Matches any uppercase letter.
- [0-9]: Matches any digit.

Use character classes to match groups of characters. For instance:

```
awk '/[0-9]/ { print $0 }' input.txt
```

This script prints lines containing at least one digit.

Anchors and Boundaries Anchors are special characters used to specify the position within a line.

- ^: Matches the beginning of a line.
- $: Matches the end of a line.
- \b: Matches a word boundary (extended regex).
- \B: Matches a non-word boundary (extended regex).

For example:

```
awk '/^hello/ { print $0 }' input.txt
```

Prints lines that start with hello.

Grouping and Alternation Grouping and alternation enhance regex flexibility.

- Parentheses () group parts of patterns.
- The pipe | represents alternation.

For instance:

```
awk '/(foo|bar)/ { print $0 }' input.txt
```

This script prints lines containing either foo or bar.

Special Characters in AWK In AWK scripts, special characters like /, $, and & need escaping to match them literally. For example, the following matches a line containing a dollar sign:

```
awk '/\$/ { print $0 }' input.txt
```

Advanced Usage with Backreferences Backreferences are used for capturing groups and referencing them later in the pattern. They are especially useful for tasks like identifying repeated sequences.

Consider an example where we want to match two consecutive words that are the same:

```
awk '/\b([a-zA-Z]+) \1\b/ { print $0 }' input.txt
```

Here, \b asserts word boundaries, and ([a-zA-Z]+) captures a word in \1, which is then referenced to match the subsequent same word.

Using Regular Expressions with Built-in AWK Functions Built-in AWK functions like gsub(), sub(), and match() facilitate regex operations directly within actions.

- gsub(regex, replacement, target): Replaces all occurrences of regex in target with replacement.
- sub(regex, replacement, target): Replaces the first occurrence of regex in target with replacement.
- match(string, regex): Searches string for regex and returns the starting position if found.

Example usage of gsub():

```
awk '{ gsub(/[0-9]+/, "NUM", $0); print $0 }' input.txt
```

This script replaces all numeral sequences in each line of input.txt with the string "NUM".

Educating readers about the proper usage of regular expressions in AWK significantly enhances their ability to perform complex text manipulations effectively. By understanding the syntax and application of regex, it is possible to leverage AWK's full potential for text processing tasks.

2.8 AWK Input and Output

In AWK programming, handling input and output is a fundamental process that dictates how data is read, processed, and displayed. Understanding the mechanisms of input and output operations is crucial for effective text processing and manipulation. This section delves deeply into the various methods and options available for managing input and output in AWK.

Reading Input

AWK processes input data through files, standard input, or command-line arguments. By default, AWK reads input one line at a time from the specified input files or standard input if no files are provided. Each line is treated as a record, and AWK divides these records into fields using spaces or tabs as the default field separator.

The following basic example demonstrates reading input from a file:

```
awk '{ print $0 }' inputfile.txt
```

Here, the contents of inputfile.txt are read line by line, and $0 represents the entire line. Thus, this script simply prints out each line of the file.

Redirecting Input

It is possible to redirect input from files or standard input using shell redirection. Consider the following scenario where input is passed via standard input:

```
echo "test data" | awk '{ print $1 }'
```

In this example, echo produces the string "test data," and the pipe (|) passes this string as input to the AWK script. The script prints the first field, $1, of the input, which is "test".

Using getline for Input Control

The getline function in AWK provides advanced control over reading input. It can be used to read the next line from the current input file or from a different file specified explicitly. It also allows reading from command output.

Example of basic getline usage:

```
awk '{
    while ((getline line < "inputfile.txt") > 0) {
        print line
    }
    close("inputfile.txt")
}'
```

This script opens inputfile.txt, reads each line into the variable line, and prints it. The close function is used to close the file after reading.

Output Operations

AWK supports various methods for directing and formatting output. The print and printf functions are primary tools for generating output.

Using print

The print function sends its arguments to standard output with a default space separator and automatically appends a newline character.

Example of using print:

```
awk '{ print $1, $2 }' inputfile.txt
```

This prints the first and second fields of each line in inputfile.txt, separated by spaces.

Using printf

For more controlled and formatted output, printf in AWK functions similarly to the C language printf. It allows specifying format strings and customizing the output.

Example using printf:

```
awk '{
    printf "Name: %s, Age: %d\n", $1, $2
}' inputfile.txt
```

Assuming inputfile.txt contains names and ages, this script prints each record in a formatted manner, specifying that the first field is a string (%s) and the second field is a decimal number (%d).

Redirecting Output to Files

Output redirection in AWK can be conducted using the > and » operators within the print and printf functions. The > operator redirects output to a file, creating the file if it does not exist or overwriting it if it does. The » operator appends output to the end of the file.

Example of output redirection:

```
awk '{ print $1 > "outputfile.txt" }' inputfile.txt
```

This script writes the first field of each record from inputfile.txt to outputfile.txt, overwriting the file if it exists.

Using the append operator:

```
awk '{ print $1 >> "outputfile.txt" }' inputfile.txt
```

This appends the first field of each record to outputfile.txt.

Piping Output to Commands

AWK can send its output directly to other commands using the pipe symbol (|) within the print and printf functions.

Example of piping output:

```
awk '{ print $1 | "sort" }' inputfile.txt
```

This script extracts the first field from each record of inputfile.txt and pipes it to the sort command for sorting.

Closing Files and Pipes

To ensure efficient resource management, AWK provides the close function to explicitly close files or pipes opened during the execution of the script.

Example of closing a file:

```
awk '{
    print $1 > "outputfile.txt"
    close("outputfile.txt")
}' inputfile.txt
```

In this script, the file outputfile.txt is closed explicitly after writing each record's first field. This is particularly useful in long-running scripts or those that open multiple files and pipes.

Effective use of input and output operations in AWK is achieved through a thorough understanding of these features, enabling robust and flexible text processing workflows.

2.9 Field Separators and Record Separators

In AWK, data is parsed into records and fields based on defined separators. This allows for powerful data manipulation by specifying how lines of input are divided. Understanding and effectively utilizing field separators and record separators is crucial for mastering AWK programming.

The default behavior in AWK treats each line of input as a record, and each word within a line as a field. By default, the field separator is any whitespace (spaces or tabs), and the record separator is the newline character. However, AWK provides flexibility to define custom separators as needed.

The field separator is specified using the FS variable or the -F option in the command line, while the record separator is specified using the RS variable. Let us delve deeper into these concepts with detailed examples.

Using the FS Variable

The FS variable is used to define the input field separator. Consider the following AWK code:

```
awk 'BEGIN { FS = "," } { print $1, $2 }' inputfile.csv
```

This code snippet sets the field separator to a comma. It processes each line of inputfile.csv, printing the first and second fields. Suppose inputfile.csv contains the following data:

```
apple,banana,cherry
1,2,3
hello,world,!
```

The output will be:

```
apple banana
1 2
hello world
```

Using the -F Option

Alternatively, the command line option -F can be used to set the field separator:

```
awk -F "," '{ print $1, $2 }' inputfile.csv
```

This achieves the same result as setting FS within the BEGIN block. The flexibility in specifying field separators allows AWK scripts to handle various data formats effortlessly.

Using Regular Expressions in Field Separators

AWK allows the use of regular expressions to define more complex field separators. For example, to set the field separator as either a comma or a semicolon:

```
awk 'BEGIN { FS = "[,;]" } { print $1, $3 }' inputfile
```

Given an inputfile with the following content:

```
apple;banana,cherry
1,2;3
hello;world;!
```

The output will be:

```
apple cherry
1 3
hello !
```

Manipulating Record Separators

The record separator is defined by the RS variable. By default, RS is set to the newline character, indicating that each line is a separate record. However, it can be customized to define records based on other delimiters. For instance, to set the record separator as a semicolon:

```
awk 'BEGIN { RS = ";" } { print $1 }' inputfile
```

Consider an inputfile with the following data:

```
Record1;Record2;Record3
Record4;Record5
```

The output will be:

```
Record1
Record2
Record3
Record4
Record5
```

Combining FS and RS

AWK's flexibility shines when both FS and RS are used in tandem. For example, if records are separated by a double newline and fields by a comma, the script can be designed as follows:

```
awk 'BEGIN { FS = ","; RS = "\n\n" } { print $1, $2 }' inputfile
```

Suppose inputfile contains:

```
field1a,field1b,field1c

field2a,field2b,field2c

field3a,field3b
```

The output will be:

```
field1a field1b
field2a field2b
field3a field3b
```

Multiline Records

For more complex data structures, multiline records can be processed by setting RS to an appropriate regular expression that captures the delimiter. For instance:

```
awk 'BEGIN { RS = "\n\n+" } { print $0 }' inputfile
```

Given an inputfile:

```
record line 1
record line 2

record line 3
record line 4
```

The output will maintain the entire multiline records as units:

```
record line 1
record line 2

record line 3
record line 4
```

This reveals the power of AWK in handling complex data structures with simple configurations of FS and RS. Proper use of these variables can greatly enhance the efficiency and clarity of AWK scripts. Understanding their nuances facilitates precise data parsing and manipulation, leading to more effective text processing solutions. As with any powerful tool, practice and experimentation with different datasets and separators strengthen proficiency in using AWK for diverse text-processing tasks.

2.10 Built-in Variables in AWK

AWK provides a set of built-in variables that are automatically initialized and can be used to control program behavior or to extract specific information about data being processed. Understanding and utilizing these built-in variables effectively is crucial for writing efficient and powerful AWK scripts. Here, we will explore some of the most commonly used built-in variables in AWK, their purposes, and examples of how they are applied.

FS (Field Separator): This variable defines the field separator character used to split input records into fields. By default, FS is set to a space character. You can change it to any other character or regular expression to suit your data format.

```
awk 'BEGIN { FS="," } { print $1, $2 }' data.csv
```

In this example, FS is set to a comma, which means AWK will split each line of data.csv into fields based on commas.

OFS (Output Field Separator): This variable defines the output field separator, i.e., the character used to separate fields when printing them. By default, OFS is a space character.

```
awk 'BEGIN { FS=","; OFS="|" } { print $1, $2 }' data.csv
```

Here, OFS is set to a pipe character, so the fields $1 and $2 will be printed separated by a pipe.

RS (Record Separator): This variable specifies the character or regular expression used to separate records. By default, RS is set to a newline character, meaning each line in the input is treated as a record.

```
awk 'BEGIN { RS=""; FS="\n" } { print $1 }' data.txt
```

In this example, RS is set to an empty string, causing each paragraph (block of text separated by one or more blank lines) to be considered a single record. FS is set to a newline to split the fields.

ORS (Output Record Separator): This variable determines the character or string used to separate output records. By default, ORS is a newline character.

```
awk 'BEGIN { ORS="%" } { print $1 }' data.txt
```

Here, each record will be printed followed by a percent sign instead of a newline.

NF (Number of Fields): This variable contains the number of fields in the current record. It is read-only and is dynamically updated as AWK processes each record.

```
awk '{ print "Number of fields:", NF }' data.txt
```

This command will print the number of fields in each record of data.txt.

NR (Number of Records): This variable holds the current record number, starting from 1. It is read-only and increments as AWK processes each record.

```
awk '{ print "Record number", NR }' data.txt
```

In this script, NR is used to display the record number for each line in data.txt.

FNR (File Number of Records): Similar to NR, but FNR is reset to 1 at the beginning of each input file when processing multiple files.

```
awk '{ print FILENAME, ":", FNR }' file1.txt file2.txt
```

This command prints the file name and the record number within each file for all records in file1.txt and file2.txt.

FILENAME: This variable contains the name of the current input file being processed.

```
awk '{ print FILENAME, ":", $0 }' file1.txt file2.txt
```

The script above prints each record from file1.txt and file2.txt along with the respective file name.

ARGC and ARGV: These variables are analogous to the arguments passed to a C program. ARGC is the number of command line arguments, including the name of the AWK program. ARGV is an array that contains the actual arguments.

```
awk 'BEGIN { for (i = 0; i < ARGC; i++) print ARGV[i] }' filename
```

This script prints all the command line arguments received by the AWK program.

Other useful built-in variables include CONVFMT for converting numbers to strings, FIELDWIDTHS for specifying field widths for fixed-width input, IGNORECASE for case-insensitive matching, and OFMT for output format specification.

Understanding these built-in variables and their applications enables more precise and flexible data processing in AWK. Including these variables in your scripts as needed can greatly enhance your text processing capabilities.

2.11 Writing and Saving AWK Programs

When an AWK script is lengthy or often reused, it is practical to write it in a file and execute that file. This section covers the essential aspects of writing and saving AWK programs, including practical conventions for naming, structuring, and running AWK scripts.

To create an AWK script, begin by writing the program code into a text file. It is common to save AWK scripts with a .awk extension for clarity. Below is an example of an AWK script stored in a file named example.awk:

```
# This AWK script calculates the sum of the second field

BEGIN {
    sum = 0;
}

{
    sum += $2;
}

END {
    print "Sum:", sum;
}
```

Running an AWK Script File

To run the AWK script from a file, use the following command syntax:

```
$ awk -f scriptfile inputfile
```

Here, -f option informs AWK that the program code is in the file scriptfile. Below is an example of how to run the previously written example.awk script on an input file named data.txt.

```
$ awk -f example.awk data.txt
```

Setting Executable Permissions

For convenience, an AWK script can be made executable by setting the appropriate permissions. Add the following shebang line to the top of the AWK script, which tells the system to execute the script using the AWK interpreter:

```
#!/usr/bin/awk -f
```

Ensure the path to the AWK interpreter is correct for the system being used. After adding the shebang line, set the executable permission with the chmod command:

```
$ chmod +x example.awk
```

This allows executing the script directly without specifying the awk command explicitly:

```
$ ./example.awk data.txt
```

Useful Conventions for Writing AWK Scripts

Adopting a consistent style and following conventions make AWK scripts easier to understand and maintain. Below are recommended best practices:

- Start scripts with comments explaining their purpose and usage.
- Use meaningful variable names and avoid single-character variables where clarity is critical.
- Group related code segments using functions or clarifying comments.
- Indent code within BEGIN, END, and pattern-action blocks for readability.

Here is an improved version of the previous example script with these conventions applied:

```
#!/usr/bin/awk -f
# example.awk - Calculate the sum of the second field
# Usage: ./example.awk data.txt

BEGIN {
    # Initialize sum variable
    sum = 0;
}

{
    # Add the second field to sum
    sum += $2;
}

END {
    # Print the final sum
    print "Sum:", sum;
}
```

Debugging AWK Scripts

Errors in AWK scripts are typically identified through careful review and manual testing, as AWK's debugging capabilities are limited compared to other languages. However, several common strategies can facilitate debugging:

- **Print intermediate results**: Insert print statements to display values of variables at various stages.
- **Check syntax**: Verify the script for syntax errors using awk -f scriptfile without specifying the input file.
- **Simplify conditions**: Break down complex conditions and expressions into simpler ones that can be individually verified.

For example, adding print statements to the script can help track how the sum is accumulated:

```
#!/usr/bin/awk -f
# example.awk - Debugging version
# Usage: ./example.awk data.txt

BEGIN {
    sum = 0;
}

{
    print "Current line:", $0;
    print "Second field:", $2;
    sum += $2;
    print "Current sum:", sum;
}

END {
```

```
    print "Final Sum:", sum;
}
```

Supplying input data would provide verbose output, revealing the script's internal state during execution.

Conclusion

Writing and saving AWK programs as script files provide numerous benefits, including reusability, clarity, and ease of execution. Following naming conventions, organizing code effectively, and employing simple debugging techniques facilitate efficient development and maintenance of AWK scripts.

Chapter 3

Patterns and Actions in AWK

This chapter delves into the core concepts of patterns and actions in AWK, detailing various types of patterns such as simple patterns, regular expressions, range patterns, and compound patterns. It explains the use of the BEGIN and END patterns and illustrates how to leverage action statements for processing data. Readers will also learn about printing, record selection, and how to effectively combine patterns and actions to perform complex text processing tasks. This knowledge is crucial for harnessing the full power of AWK.

3.1 Introduction to Patterns in AWK

Patterns in AWK are the core components that dictate the applicability of actions on input data. A pattern is a rule or a condition that determines whether or not a particular action is executed on a record (a line of input). Understanding how patterns work in AWK is crucial as it allows users to filter and manipulate data efficiently. Patterns are evaluated sequentially as the input is processed, and they can be simple or highly complex depending on the matching criteria required.

In AWK, a pattern can be:

- A regular expression that matches certain text in the input.

- A fixed string that explicitly states the desired text to match.
- A relation or logical expression involving AWK internal variables or fields.
- A range of lines determined by a start and end pattern.
- A pattern combining multiple criteria using logical operators.

When a pattern matches a given record, the associated action is executed. If no pattern is specified, the action applies to every record by default.

```
awk '{ print $0 }' filename
```

In the above command, there is no explicit pattern, so the action print $0 is executed for every record in the input file. Here, $0 represents the entire record.

Patterns often involve the use of regular expressions:

```
awk '/pattern/ { print $1 }' filename
```

In this example, the pattern pattern specifies a regular expression. The action print $1 is executed only for those records containing the specified pattern. Here, $1 refers to the first field of the record.

AWK also supports relational expressions as patterns:

```
awk '$3 > 100 { print $1, $3 }' filename
```

This pattern checks if the third field ($3) of a record is greater than 100. If the condition is satisfied, the action print $1, $3 is executed, printing the first and third fields of the matching record.

Logical operators such as && (logical AND), || (logical OR), and ! (logical NOT) allow the combination of multiple conditions to form compound patterns:

```
awk '$3 > 100 && $1 ~ /^[A-Za-z]+$/ { print $0 }' filename
```

In this script, the pattern consists of two conditions combined using the logical AND operator. The first condition checks if the third field exceeds 100, and the second condition, using a regular expression, verifies if the first field ($1) contains only alphabetic characters. The action print $0 is executed when both conditions are met.

Another essential concept in AWK patterns is the use of the BEGIN and END patterns. The BEGIN pattern allows specifying actions to be executed before any input records are read:

```
awk 'BEGIN { print "Starting processing..." } { print $0 }' filename
```

Here, the message "Starting processing..." is printed before any input is processed. The subsequent action print $0 executes for each record in the input.

Similarly, the END pattern facilitates actions to execute after all input records are processed:

```
awk '{ print $0 } END { print "Processing finished." }' filename
```

In this example, the action print "Processing finished." executes after all input records are read and processed.

Range patterns enable defining a range of lines where actions are applicable. A range pattern consists of two patterns separated by a comma:

```
awk '/start/,/end/ { print $0 }' filename
```

Here, the pattern matches every record between lines containing start and end, inclusive. The action print $0 is executed for each line within this range.

Comprehending these fundamental types of patterns equips users with the ability to construct complex filters and transformations, enabling precise text processing with AWK. This flexibility in defining the criteria for applying actions empowers users to handle a wide variety of data extraction and manipulation tasks efficiently and effectively.

3.2 Types of Patterns in AWK

In AWK, patterns are utilized to specify which lines of input data are processed by action statements. A pattern can be any of several constructs: a simple pattern, a regular expression, a range pattern, or a compound pattern. Each of these pattern types can be employed to filter input records effectively and apply specific actions to those that match. Understanding these patterns is essential for unleashing the full potential of AWK for text and data processing.

Simple Patterns: Simple patterns in AWK are typical conditions that evaluate to true or false. These conditions can involve relational operators, arithmetic comparisons, or string comparisons. Simple patterns are evaluated for each input record, and if the condition holds true, the corresponding action is executed.

For example, consider the following AWK program:

```
awk '$3 > 100 { print $1, $3 }' data.txt
```

In this instance, the pattern $\$3 > 100$ is a simple pattern that checks if the third field of each record is greater than 100. If this condition is met, the action print $1, $3 is executed, printing the first and third fields of the matching records.

Regular Expressions as Patterns: AWK also allows the use of regular expressions as patterns to match input lines against specific text patterns. Regular expressions offer a powerful way to search for patterns within text and are central to many AWK operations.

For example:

```
awk '/^Error/ { print $0 }' log.txt
```

Here, the regular expression pattern /Êrror/ matches lines that start with the string "Error." The action print $0 prints the entire record (line) that matches this pattern.

Range Patterns: Range patterns in AWK are specified by two patterns separated by a comma and match all lines from a record that satisfies the first pattern to a record that satisfies the second pattern.

For example:

```
awk '/start/,/end/ { print $0 }' document.txt
```

The above AWK command matches and prints all lines between and including the lines that match the patterns /start/ and /end/.

Compound Patterns: Compound patterns are constructed using logical operators to combine two or more patterns. These logical operators are && (logical AND), || (logical OR), and ! (logical NOT).

Consider the following example:

```
awk '$1 == "John" && $3 > 100 { print $0 }' people.txt
```

In this case, the compound pattern $1 == "John" && $3 > 100 combines two simple patterns using the logical AND operator. This pattern matches lines where the first field is "John" and the third field is greater than 100.

Understanding and effectively using these types of patterns is crucial for performing sophisticated data processing tasks in AWK. Each pattern type offers unique capabilities that, when combined with the power of AWK's action statements, provide a versatile toolkit for managing and transforming text data.

3.3 Simple Patterns

In AWK, a simple pattern is a basic conditional expression that determines whether a specific action should be executed on a line or record. These patterns can be based on conditions such as the content of the fields, comparisons, or simply the presence of a specified value. Understanding simple patterns is a fundamental aspect of mastering AWK's text processing capabilities, as it forms the basis for more complex pattern matching and data manipulation.

AWK operates by scanning each line of input and evaluating the specified patterns. If a pattern matches, the corresponding action is executed. If no action is specified, the default action is to print the matching line. Below, we explore several common types of simple patterns in AWK and demonstrate how they are used with examples.

Literal Matching

A simple pattern can be a literal value that matches exactly against any field in the record. This type of pattern comes in handy when you need to filter lines containing a specific value. For instance, considering a file data.txt containing the following text:

```
Alice 25 Developer
Bob   30 Designer
Charlie 28 Manager
Alice 32 Architect
```

To match and print all lines containing the name Alice, the following command would suffice:

```
awk '/Alice/ { print }' data.txt
```

The pattern /Alice/ searches for the literal string "Alice" in any field of the record and executes the default print action.

Field Comparison

Another common scenario is to perform a comparison on a specific field.

Suppose our goal is to find all records where the second field (age) is greater than 28:

```
awk '$2 > 28 { print }' data.txt
```

In this example, $\$2 > 28$ is the pattern that checks whether the second field is greater than 28. If this condition is satisfied, the line is printed.

Pattern Matching with Variables

Simple patterns can also involve AWK variables, either built-in or user-defined. Built-in variables such as NR (Number of Records) and NF (Number of Fields) play a crucial role in defining patterns. Below is an example that prints every third line of the input file:

```
awk 'NR % 3 == 0 { print }' data.txt
```

Here, $NR \% 3 == 0$ is the pattern that matches on every third line by checking the modulus of the record number.

Range Patterns with Simple Conditions

Simple patterns can be combined to form range patterns. These patterns match all lines between a starting and ending condition. For example, to process lines between the first occurrence of Alice and the first occurrence of Charlie, the following command is applicable:

```
awk '/Alice/, /Charlie/ { print }' data.txt
```

In this case, the range pattern /Alice/, /Charlie/ ensures that all lines from the one containing "Alice" to the one containing "Charlie" (inclusive) are processed.

Compound Patterns with Logical Operators

Simple patterns can be combined using logical operators such as && (AND), || (OR), and ! (NOT). For instance, to print lines where the second field is greater than 28 and less than 32:

```
awk '$2 > 28 && $2 < 32 { print }' data.txt
```

Here, $\$2 > 28 \&\& \$2 < 32$ represents the compound pattern that ensures both conditions are satisfied simultaneously.

When filtering lines that do not contain a specific value, the NOT operator can be utilized. To exclude records containing the word Alice:

```
awk '!/Alice/ { print }' data.txt
```

In this example, the pattern $!/\mathrm{Alice}/$ evaluates to true for lines not containing the string "Alice."

Understanding and employing simple patterns fundamentally enhance your ability to process text files efficiently using AWK. As we proceed, these foundational concepts will serve as building blocks for mastering more intricate patterns and actions in AWK, enabling you to tackle complex data processing tasks with ease.

3.4 Regular Expressions as Patterns

Regular expressions are a powerful tool used to describe patterns in text. In AWK, regular expressions are a central feature that allows for sophisticated pattern matching. When used as patterns in AWK, regular expressions enable the selection of input records that match the specified criteria. This section delves into the syntax and usage of regular expressions within the context of AWK, providing detailed examples to illustrate their application.

In AWK, regular expressions are defined within slashes $/$ $/$. For example, $/\mathrm{pattern}/$ is a regular expression that matches any input record containing the substring "pattern." The regular expression pattern-matching capability in AWK supports various metacharacters that enable complex matching rules. The most common metacharacters include ., $*$, $+$, $?$, [], $\{\}$, $()$, $|$, $\hat{}$, and $\$$.

- . - Matches any single character except a newline.
- $*$ - Matches zero or more occurrences of the preceding element.
- $+$ - Matches one or more occurrences of the preceding element.
- $?$ - Matches zero or one occurrence of the preceding element.
- [] - A bracket expression that matches any one of the enclosed characters.
- $\{\}$ - Defines a quantifier for the number of occurrences.
- $()$ - Groups expressions.
- $|$ - Alternation operator, offering a choice between patterns.
- $\hat{}$ - Matches the beginning of a line.

- $ - Matches the end of a line.

To illustrate the use of regular expressions in AWK, consider a dataset where each line contains information about employees in a company, such as name, position, and department:

```
John Doe, Manager, Sales
Jane Smith, Engineer, Development
Jim Brown, CTO, Administration
Jack Black, Engineer, Development
```

Suppose we want to select all lines that contain the word Engineer. Using a regular expression pattern, we can achieve this easily:

```
awk '/Engineer/' employee_data.txt
```

The output of this command will be:

```
Jane Smith, Engineer, Development
Jack Black, Engineer, Development
```

Beyond matching literal text, regular expressions in AWK can employ metacharacters for more flexible matching. For instance, to match all lines where the position is either Manager or Engineer, we can use the alternation operator |:

```
awk '/Manager|Engineer/' employee_data.txt
```

This command outputs:

```
John Doe, Manager, Sales
Jane Smith, Engineer, Development
Jack Black, Engineer, Development
```

To match lines that start with Jack, we use the caret ^ metacharacter:

```
awk '/^Jack/' employee_data.txt
```

The output will be:

```
Jack Black, Engineer, Development
```

Similarly, to match lines that end with Development, we use the dollar sign $:

```
awk '/Development$/' employee_data.txt
```

This yields:

```
Jane Smith, Engineer, Development
Jack Black, Engineer, Development
```

Bracket expressions allow for matching any one of the enclosed characters. For instance, to match any line with a name starting with 'J', followed by any character, and then 'n', we use:

```
awk '/J.n/' employee_data.txt
```

Resulting in:

```
John Doe, Manager, Sales
Jane Smith, Engineer, Development
```

With regular expressions, it is also possible to define character ranges inside brackets. To match names starting with a capital letter from 'A' to 'J', followed by any two characters, we use:

```
awk '/^[A-J].. /' employee_data.txt
```

The output is:

```
Jane Smith, Engineer, Development
Jim Brown, CTO, Administration
Jack Black, Engineer, Development
```

Quantifiers extend the versatility of regular expressions. For example, to match occurrences where the first name is followed by a title with at least three characters, we use curly braces:

```
awk '/^J.{2,},/' employee_data.txt
```

The output will be:

```
John Doe, Manager, Sales
Jack Black, Engineer, Development
```

Grouping expressions with parentheses allows for complex pattern definitions. For instance, to match any line where the department is either Sales or Administration, we use:

```
awk '/, (Sales|Administration)$/' employee_data.txt
```

Leading to the following output:

```
John Doe, Manager, Sales
Jim Brown, CTO, Administration
```

Combining anchors, metacharacters, and grouping can create more sophisticated patterns. If we want to match lines with a name that starts with 'J', positioned as either Manager or Engineer and belonging to any department, we use:

```
awk '/^J.*(Manager|Engineer),/' employee_data.txt
```

This yields:

```
John Doe, Manager, Sales
Jane Smith, Engineer, Development
Jack Black, Engineer, Development
```

Regular expressions in AWK are not limited to matching fixed patterns. They can be dynamically constructed and used within programs. This flexibility allows for a broad range of text processing tasks, from simple searches to complex data extraction.

3.5 Range Patterns

Range patterns in AWK facilitate the selection of blocks of text between two specified patterns. These patterns are instrumental when the goal is to process or extract sections of data that are bounded by known start and end markers.

A range pattern takes the form:

```
pattern1, pattern2
```

Here, pattern1 marks the beginning of the range, and pattern2 marks the end. AWK will match all the lines from the line containing pattern1 up to and including the line containing pattern2.

Consider the following sample file sample.txt:

```
Header Information
Data Block Start
Item 1
Item 2
Item 3
Data Block End
Footer Information
```

To extract and print the lines between Data Block Start and Data Block End, the AWK command would be:

```
awk '/Data Block Start/,/Data Block End/' sample.txt
```

The output will be:

```
Data Block Start
Item 1
Item 2
Item 3
Data Block End
```

In this example, the range pattern /Data Block Start/,/Data Block End/ instructs AWK to begin the match at the line containing Data Block Start and continue matching until the line containing Data Block End.

The range pattern match is inclusive; both the starting and ending patterns are included in the matched output. This inclusiveness can be essential for scenarios where the delimiters are necessary for context.

Range patterns can also be employed in more complex scenarios by integrating them with action statements:

```
awk '/Data Block Start/,/Data Block End/ { print toupper($0) }' sample.txt
```

This command converts all the characters in the range to uppercase:

```
DATA BLOCK START
ITEM 1
ITEM 2
ITEM 3
DATA BLOCK END
```

The range pattern is combined with an action statement that utilizes the toupper() function to transform the matched lines' content.

Range patterns can be constructed using any valid AWK pattern, including regular expressions and compound patterns:

```
awk '/^Start/,/End$/' sample.txt
```

In this case, the regular expression ^Start matches any line starting with 'Start', and End$ matches any line ending with 'End'.

AWK evaluates the line in two steps: first to check if it matches pattern1, thereby starting the range; and second to check if it matches pattern2, thereby concluding the range. If the entire file is being processed, AWK will stop checking for the range once it has identified the end pattern.

The versatility of range patterns is heightened by the ability to impart logic within the actions. For example, keeping a count of lines within a specified range:

```
awk '/Data Block Start/,/Data Block End/ { count++ } END { print count }' sample.
    txt
```

This script counts the number of lines between (and including) Data Block Start and Data Block End. The END block then prints the count:

Understanding range patterns extends beyond just matching known lines. It can be used to specify conditions dynamically. Suppose the input file size is substantial and you need to process blocks of text dynamically based on different patterns. The range pattern within AWK becomes a powerful tool, allowing scalable and flexible text processing.

Algorithm 1: Range Pattern Matching in AWK

Input: File: sample.txt, StartPattern: pattern1, EndPattern: pattern2

Output: Matching Lines

```
begin
    foreach line in sample.txt do
        if line.matches(StartPattern) then
            inRange ← true
        if inRange then
            print line;
            if line.matches(EndPattern) then
                inRange ← false;
```

This pseudo-code uses AWK-like logic within an algorithmic framework to highlight the process of matching lines within a range pattern.

Range patterns serve as an invaluable mechanism in AWK for the targeted extraction and processing of text within defined boundaries, reducing the complexity of pattern specification in individual records and enabling concise and effective data manipulation.

3.6 Compound Patterns

AWK allows the creation of compound patterns by combining simple patterns. This enables more sophisticated and versatile matching criteria for processing data. Compound patterns can be formed using the logical operators && (logical AND), || (logical OR), and ! (logical NOT). These operators allow for complex conditional statements that facilitate the selection of records for which multiple patterns should be true, where at least one of several patterns should be true, or where a pattern should not be true.

Consider the following example where we have a dataset consisting of student names and their test scores in various subjects. This dataset is stored in a file named students.txt. Each line in the file contains the student's name, followed by their scores in three subjects: Mathematics, Physics, and Chemistry.

```
John Doe, 85, 78, 90
Jane Smith, 82, 88, 91
Alice Brown, 80, 70, 85
Bob White, 72, 56, 77
```

To process this data with compound patterns, we use the following AWK script:

```
awk -F, '{ if ($2 >= 80 && $3 >= 80) print $0 }' students.txt
```

In this script, the pattern condition $2 >= 80 && $3 >= 80 evaluates to true only if the scores in both Mathematics ($2) and Physics ($3) are 80 or higher. The action print $0 prints the entire record.

The output of this script, when executed, would be:

```
Jane Smith, 82, 88, 91
```

This demonstrates the use of the logical AND operator to create a compound pattern. Let's consider a more complex scenario where we want to print the records of students who either have scored 80 or above in Mathematics or 70 or below in Physics. The corresponding AWK script would be:

```
awk -F, '{ if ($2 >= 80 || $3 <= 70) print $0 }' students.txt
```

Here, the pattern $2 >= 80 || $3 <= 70 uses the logical OR operator. This condition is true if either the Mathematics score ($2) is 80 or higher, or the Physics score ($3) is 70 or lower. The action remains the same, printing the entire matching record.

The output for the above script with our dataset would be:

```
John Doe, 85, 78, 90
Jane Smith, 82, 88, 91
Alice Brown, 80, 70, 85
Bob White, 72, 56, 77
```

Lastly, consider using the logical NOT operator in combination with the AND and OR operators. Suppose we want to filter out students who scored below 75 in Chemistry. The script could be written as:

```
awk -F, '{ if (!($4 < 75)) print $0 }' students.txt
```

Here, $!\$4 < 75$ is the compound pattern that negates the condition of Chemistry score being less than 75. Therefore, it matches records where the Chemistry score is 75 or higher.

The output when this script is executed will be:

```
John Doe, 85, 78, 90
Jane Smith, 82, 88, 91
Alice Brown, 80, 70, 85
```

For scenarios where multiple conditions and logical operators are to be combined, it is essential to use parentheses to ensure the intended precedence of operations. Consider a situation where we want to print records for students who scored 80 or above in Mathematics and scored either 88 or above in Physics or 85 or above in Chemistry. The AWK script for this would be:

```
awk -F, '{ if ($2 >= 80 && ($3 >= 88 || $4 >= 85)) print $0 }' students.txt
```

In this script, the expression inside the parentheses $\$3 >= 88 || \$4 >= 85$ is evaluated first due to the precedence rules of logical operators. The AND operator then combines this result with the Mathematics score condition.

The resulting output is:

```
Jane Smith, 82, 88, 91
```

Using compound patterns provides AWK with powerful capabilities to perform sophisticated text processing tasks. By leveraging the logical operators and crafting thoughtful conditions, you can effectively filter and manage data to meet complex criteria. This nuanced control is instrumental in achieving mastery over text processing with AWK.

3.7 The BEGIN and END Patterns

The BEGIN and END patterns in AWK are special patterns that enable programmers to execute code before any input lines are read and after all input lines have been processed, respectively. Unlike other patterns in AWK that are matched against input records, BEGIN and END patterns are not associated with specific input records but with the process's lifecycle.

The BEGIN pattern allows initialization and setup tasks to be performed before the main input processing begins. Statements in the action block associated with BEGIN run only once, regardless of the number of input lines. This can be particularly useful for setting variables, initializing data structures, or printing headers.

```
BEGIN {
  FS = ","
  print "Name", "Age", "Occupation"
}
```

In this example, the BEGIN pattern is used to set the field separator FS to a comma and print a header. These actions will occur only once, at the start of the script execution.

The END pattern is similarly unique but is used for tasks that should be executed after all input lines have been processed. This is useful for tasks such as summarizing results, closing files, or printing footers.

```
END {
    print "Processing complete."
}
```

Here, the END pattern prints a message after all input lines have been processed, indicating the completion of processing.

Combining BEGIN and END is a common practice in AWK scripting for tasks that require pre-processing and post-processing actions. The following example illustrates a complete AWK script that uses both patterns:

```
BEGIN {
    FS = ","
    print "Name", "Age", "Occupation"
}
{
    print $1, $2, $3
}
END {
    print "Total records processed: " NR
}
```

In this script, the BEGIN block initializes the field separator and prints the header. The main action block processes each line of the input, printing the first three fields. The END block prints the total number of records processed, using the built-in NR variable that holds the number of records read so far.

The BEGIN and END patterns provide a structured workflow within AWK scripts. They enable the clean organization of initialization and finalization tasks, ensuring that the core logic remains focused on processing individual records.

When using the BEGIN and END patterns, be mindful of their sequence. AWK ensures that the BEGIN block executes first, followed by actions specified for each record, and concludes with the END block. This orderly execution can be relied upon for tasks that need a specific routine to be followed.

For more complex applications, AWK scripts can include multiple BEGIN and END blocks to organize different initialization and cleanup tasks. When multiple BEGIN or END patterns are present, they execute in the order they are encountered in the script.

```
BEGIN {
    print "Start of Script"
}
BEGIN {
    FS = ","
}
{
    print $1, $2, $3
}
END {
    print "End of record processing"
}
END {
    print "Script complete."
}
```

Here, two BEGIN blocks initialize different settings and print a message at the start of the script. Similarly, two END blocks handle the final messages after record processing completes.

Utilizing the BEGIN and END patterns skillfully can result in more organized and maintainable AWK scripts. Their utility spans from simple tasks, such as printing headers and footers, to more complex preprocessing and postprocessing operations that form an integral part of data processing pipelines. The ability to execute code at the start and end of reading input files adds a powerful dimension to AWK's pattern-action paradigm.

3.8 Action Statements in AWK

In AWK, action statements are executed when the pattern associated with them matches an input record. They dictate what operations are performed on the matched records and how the output is generated. Understanding how to employ these action statements effectively is crucial for performing even the most complex data processing tasks.

An action statement is enclosed in curly braces {} and can encompass a combination of print statements, variable assignments, arithmetic operations, functions, and control flow statements. The general format for an action statement in AWK is as follows:

```
pattern { action1; action2; ...; actionN }
```

Each action can span multiple lines and may consist of one or more commands. Below, we discuss the various components and capabilities of AWK action statements.

Printing with print and printf: The print statement is the most commonly used action in AWK to display data. It outputs the specified text or variables to the standard output, typically the terminal. Variables and text can be concatenated using a comma.

```
# Assuming a sample input file 'data.txt' containing:
# 1 John 25
# 2 Jane 30
# 3 Doe 22

awk '{ print $1, $2, $3 }' data.txt
```

```
1 John 25
2 Jane 30
3 Doe 22
```

The printf function in AWK, inspired by the C programming language, allows formatted output. It takes a format string followed by a list of objects to be printed. The format string can specify width, precision, and type of the output.

```
awk '{ printf("%-5s %-10s %3d\n", $1, $2, $3) }' data.txt
```

```
1     John        25
2     Jane        30
3     Doe         22
```

Variable Assignments and Arithmetic: AWK allows assignment of values to variables within an action statement. These variables can be used to perform calculations, store intermediate results, or control program flow.

```
awk '{ sum = $3 + 5; print $1, sum }' data.txt
```

```
1 30
2 35
3 27
```

Built-in and User-defined Functions: AWK provides a variety of built-in functions such as string manipulation functions (substr(), index(), length()), mathematical functions (sin(), cos(), sqrt()), and others. Here is the use of the length() function to find the length of the second field:

```
awk '{ print $2, length($2) }' data.txt
```

```
John 4
Jane 4
Doe 3
```

Additionally, users can define their own functions within AWK scripts. A user-defined function in AWK is declared using the function keyword, as shown below:

```
awk '
function add_five(x) {
    return x + 5
}

{ print $1, add_five($3) }' data.txt
```

```
1 30
2 35
3 27
```

Control Flow Statements: Just like many programming languages, AWK supports control flow statements such as if, for, while, and do...while. These allow for more complex and conditional actions based on the input data.

An example using the if statement:

```
awk '{
    if ($3 > 25) {
        print $2 " is older than 25."
    } else {
        print $2 " is 25 or younger."
    }
}' data.txt
```

```
John is 25 or younger.
Jane is older than 25.
Doe is 25 or younger.
```

For loop example:

```
awk '{
    sum = 0
    for (i = 1; i <= NF; i++) {
        sum += $i
    }
    print "Sum:", sum
}' integers.txt
```

```
# Assuming integers.txt contains:
# 1 2 3
# 4 5 6
# 7 8 9

Sum: 6
Sum: 15
Sum: 24
```

While loop example:

```
awk '{
    i = 1
    while (i <= NF) {
        printf "%s ", $i
        i++
    }
    print ""
}' words.txt
```

```
# Assuming words.txt contains:
# Hello World
# Welcome to AWK

Hello World
Welcome to AWK
```

By combining patterns and action statements, AWK enables powerful text and data processing capabilities. Whether the task is as simple as printing data or as complex as performing conditional calculations and iterative processing, mastering action statements is essential for fully leveraging the power of AWK.

3.9 Printing with AWK

The `print` statement is one of the fundamental features of AWK for producing output. It provides a versatile and flexible mechanism to print messages and data. There are two main variations of the print statement: the print statement and the printf statement. The print statement is simpler and more convenient for most tasks, while printf offers more control over the output format.

print can be used to output fixed strings, the contents of variables, field values, or computed expressions. By default, the print statement separates each item to be printed with a single space and terminates the output with a newline character.

```
awk '{ print $1, $3 }' input.txt
```

This command reads input.txt line by line, printing the first and third fields of each line, separated by a space. If input.txt contains:

```
apple orange banana
one two three
red blue green
```

The output of the AWK command will be:

```
apple banana
one three
red green
```

The print statement can also include fixed strings. These strings should be enclosed in double quotes, and they will be printed as they are.

```
awk '{ print "Field 1:", $1, "Field 3:", $3 }' input.txt
```

This command will produce the following output:

```
Field 1: apple Field 3: banana
Field 1: one Field 3: three
Field 1: red Field 3: green
```

To avoid the default space separator and newline termination, one can use the printf statement which provides format control analogous to the C language's printf function. The printf statement requires a format string as its first argument, followed by the data to be formatted.

```
awk '{ printf "%-10s %-10s\n", $1, $3 }' input.txt
```

This command formats the first and third fields as left-justified strings within columns of width 10 characters each. The format string %-10s %-10s\n specifies two left-justified string fields each 10 characters wide, followed by a newline character \n.

```
apple    banana
one      three
red      green
```

AWK's print and printf can work with variables and expressions. For instance, an expression's result can be printed with other values.

```
awk '{ sum = $2 + $3; print "Sum:", sum }' input.txt
```

Given an input.txt with numerical values:

```
5 10 15
2 4 6
8 16 32
```

The AWK command produces:

```
Sum: 25
Sum: 10
Sum: 48
```

Field variables, named variables, and expressions within print statements can be separated by commas or concatenated directly. When separated by commas, AWK manages output separation using the value of the OFS (output field separator) variable, which defaults to a space.

```
awk '{ OFS = ","; print $1, $2 }' input.txt
```

Assuming input.txt contains:

```
first second third
one two three
alpha beta gamma
```

The resulting output will be:

```
first,second
one,two
alpha,beta
```

Concatenation can be done without commas:

```
awk '{ print $1 $2 }' input.txt
```

will produce:

```
firstsecond
onetwo
alphabeta
```

Using the ORS (output record separator) variable, which defaults to a newline, one can change the line termination behavior.

```
awk '{ ORS="; "; print $1, $2 }' input.txt
```

Given the same input.txt, this command yields:

```
first second; one two; alpha beta;
```

Print statements are essential for debugging AWK programs by displaying intermediate variable values and expressions' outcomes. This can help verify the correctness of the data processing logic and ensure expected results.

3.10 Skipping and Selecting Records

In AWK programming, the ability to skip and select records is integral for efficient data processing. This functionality allows the programmer to control which records are processed and which are ignored, ensuring that operations are performed on only relevant data. This section explores techniques for skipping and selecting records, using various AWK patterns and conditions.

We start with the concept of record selection using patterns. AWK processes records from the input file sequentially. By default, a record is a line of text. Each record can be selected based on patterns such as regular expressions, comparison operators, or predefined conditions.

To illustrate, let us consider an example where we wish to select records that contain the word error. The following AWK command will achieve this:

```
awk '/error/' input_file.txt
```

This command specifies a pattern /error/, which matches any record containing the string error. If a record matches this pattern, AWK prints it to the standard output.

A more complex scenario may involve selecting records based on the value in a specific field. Suppose we have a file called data.txt where the second field represents a numeric value, and we want to select records where this value is greater than 100:

```
awk '$2 > 100' data.txt
```

Here, $\$2 > 100$ serves as the pattern. AWK evaluates this condition for each record, and only prints those records where the second field is greater than 100. The variable $\$2$ refers to the second field of the current record.

AWK also provides versatility in skipping records using the next statement. The next statement causes AWK to stop processing the current record and move to the next one. Consider an example where we want to skip records containing the word ignore:

```
awk '/ignore/ { next } { print }' input_file.txt
```

In this command, the pattern /ignore/ matches records containing the word ignore. When such a record is encountered, the action next is executed, causing AWK to skip to the next record without performing any further actions on the current one. The pattern-action pair { print } ensures that all other records are printed.

We can also combine multiple patterns and actions to create complex record selection criteria. For instance, to select records where the second field is greater than 100 but not equal to 150, we use the following command:

```
awk '$2 > 100 && $2 != 150' data.txt
```

This command uses the logical AND operator && to combine conditions, resulting in the selection of records where both conditions are satisfied.

For skipping and selecting records, AWK supports a variety of built-in functions that can be used within patterns. An example involves selecting records based on string length using the length function. To select records with more than 80 characters:

```
awk 'length($0) > 80' input_file.txt
```

The function length($0) returns the length of the entire record. The condition length($0) > 80 is used to match records having more than 80 characters.

Another useful AWK feature is the ability to process only a specific range of records. This is achieved using range patterns, denoted by two patterns separated by a comma, pattern1, pattern2. Records are selected starting from the one that matches pattern1 up to and including the one that matches pattern2. For example, to select records from the beginning of the file up to the record containing end:

```
awk 'NR==1, /end/' input_file.txt
```

The NR==1 condition matches the first record, and the /end/ pattern matches the record containing the word end. Together, they define a range pattern.

Finally, we can filter records based on user-defined functions to encapsulate complex logic. Consider an example function that checks whether a field contains only numeric characters:

```
function is_numeric(s) {
  return s ~ /^[0-9]+$/
}

awk 'is_numeric($1)' data.txt
```

This user-defined function is_numeric uses a regular expression to check if the input string s contains only digits. The AWK command then uses this function within its pattern to select records where the first field contains only numeric characters.

By leveraging these techniques, one can efficiently control record processing in AWK, ensuring that only pertinent data is analyzed and manipulated.

3.11 Combining Patterns and Actions

In AWK, the power of pattern-directed scanning and processing comes to its full potential when patterns and actions are combined in a cohesive manner. AWK scripts perform filtering and data transformation through this combination, improving both efficiency and expressiveness in processing text files. This section explores how to leverage the interplay of patterns and actions for more sophisticated text processing tasks.

Patterns define the conditions under which specific actions are executed. When a pattern is matched against a record, the associated action is performed. This mechanism allows for precise control over which data is processed and how it is manipulated.

An AWK program consists of a sequence of pattern { action } rules and performs the following steps:

- Reads an input record.
- Tests the input record against each pattern.
- Executes the action for the patterns that match.

Consider the following example, which uses both a pattern and an action to process text data:

```
awk '$3 > 100 { print $1, $2, $3 }' data.txt
```

This command prints the first, second, and third fields of the records in data.txt where the third field is greater than 100. Here, $3 > 100 is the pattern, and print $1, $2, $3 is the action.

More complex combinations of patterns and actions can be achieved by using compound patterns, logical operators, and block structures. Compound patterns are formed using logical operators like && (AND), || (OR), and ! (NOT).

Compound Patterns and Actions:

```
awk '($3 > 50 && $3 <= 150) || $1 ~ /John/ { print $0 }' data.txt
```

In this example, the command prints the entire record if the third field is between 50 and 150 (inclusive) or if the first field matches the regular expression /John/.

Usage of BEGIN and END Patterns: The BEGIN and END patterns allow for actions to be performed before and after processing all the input records, respectively. These patterns do not require an associated pattern-matching condition as they are implicitly executed.

```
awk 'BEGIN { print "Start of processing" }
     { if ($2 ~ /^A/) print $1, $2 }
     END { print "End of processing" }' data.txt
```

In this script:

- The BEGIN block prints "Start of processing" before any data is processed.
- The main block prints the first and second fields for records where the second field starts with the letter 'A'.

- The END block prints "End of processing" after all records have been processed.

Selective Printing and Record Modifications: AWK allows for selective printing and modifications of records by combining various actions with conditional patterns. This example modifies a specific field based on a condition and prints the modified record:

```
awk '{ if ($3 > 100) $3 = $3 * 2; print $1, $2, $3 }' data.txt
```

The action script in this case:

- Checks if the third field is greater than 100.
- If true, doubles the value of the third field.
- Prints the first, second, and modified third fields.

Nested Actions with Multiple Conditions: Complex logical operations can be performed using nested actions with multiple conditions. This allows for multi-level filtering and processing of records.

```
awk '{ if ($2 == "A") {
        if ($3 > 100)
            $3 = $3 * 2;
        else
            $3 = $3 / 2;
    }
    print $1, $2, $3 }' data.txt
```

In this script:

- The primary condition checks if the second field equals "A".
- A nested condition further checks if the third field is greater than 100.
- Based on the third field's value, it either doubles or halves the third field.
- Finally, it prints the first, second, and modified third fields.

Using Functions within Actions: AWK supports user-defined functions, which can be called within actions to modularize and reuse code. This feature is crucial for maintaining cleaner, more readable scripts.

```
function process_record(field) {
    return (field > 100) ? field * 2 : field / 2;
}

awk '{ $3 = process_record($3); print $1, $2, $3 }' data.txt
```

Here, the script defines a function process_record that determines how the third field is processed, and then calls this function within the action block.

Combining patterns and actions in AWK allows for precise and powerful text processing capabilities, making it a versatile tool for automating data extraction and transformation tasks. Through logical patterns, conditional actions, and the integration of functions, AWK scripts can efficiently address complex requirements.

Chapter 4

Variables and Data Types in AWK

This chapter covers the use of variables and data types in AWK, including predefined and user-defined variables. It discusses how to initialize and assign variables, their scope, and the differences between string and numeric variables. The chapter also introduces arrays and built-in arrays, providing best practices for efficient use. Understanding these concepts is essential for effective data manipulation in AWK scripts.

4.1 Introduction to Variables in AWK

Variables in AWK serve as symbolic names for storing data values that can be manipulated within a program. They play an essential role in computational logic by allowing for the dynamic handling of data, facilitating the execution of various operational commands and functions. Understanding the concept and usage of variables is fundamental to effectively writing and interpreting AWK scripts.

In AWK, variables do not need to be explicitly declared before usage, providing flexibility and ease of use for the programmer. This feature distinguishes AWK from many other programming languages that require variable declarations prior to utilization. When a variable in AWK is first encountered, it is automatically created and initialized to a default value.

The default initialization behavior assigns numeric variables a value of zero (0) and string variables a null string (""). This automatic handling ensures the variable's immediate readiness for subsequent operations without manual pre-initialization.

Consider the following simple AWK script:

```
BEGIN {
    x = 10; # numeric variable initialization
    y = "Hello"; # string variable initialization
    z; # implicitly initialized to zero (numeric)
    print x, y, z;
}
```

Executing this script generates the output:

```
10 Hello 0
```

In the examples above, x and y are explicitly initialized, while z is implicitly initialized. Since z is not assigned any value, it defaults to zero, as displayed in the output.

Variables in AWK can be broadly classified into predefined variables and user-defined variables. Predefined variables are intrinsic to the AWK programming environment, with specific functionalities tied to the system and input-processing behaviors. They provide essential control and informative mechanisms that facilitate script writing and execution.

On the other hand, user-defined variables are declared and utilized by the programmer to manage and manipulate data within the script's logical and operational context. These variables offer flexibility and customizability, allowing programmers to define meaningful names and assign specific values that represent the data or control elements of the program.

The dynamic nature of AWK variables also extends to their data types. A single variable in AWK can hold either a string or a numeric value, depending on the context of its usage and assignment. This dynamism allows a variable to switch data types based on operations performed within the script.

Consider the following example illustrating the dynamic behavior of variable data types:

```
BEGIN {
    a = 5; # numeric assignment
    print a; # outputs: 5

    a = a " apples"; # string concatenation
```

```
    print a; # outputs: 5 apples

    a = a + 2; # numeric operation causing conversion
    print a; # outputs: 7
}
```

The output for the above script execution is:

```
5
5 apples
7
```

Initially, the variable a is assigned a numeric value of 5. When concatenated with the string " apples", a becomes a string. Subsequently, performing a numeric addition operation forces a back into a numeric context by extracting the numeric prefix, resulting in the value 7.

String values in AWK are primarily sequences of characters enclosed in double quotes. AWK provides various string functions to manipulate and handle string data efficiently, which will be elaborated in subsequent sections.

Given AWK's propensity for handling data from input streams, variables prove indispensable for capturing and processing data fields. The special variables $1, $2, ..., $NF are used to reference individual fields in the current input record. The variable $0 holds the entire record.

Consider the following AWK script used for data field processing:

```
{
    first = $1;
    second = $2;
    print "First field:", first, "Second field:", second;
}
```

For an input file containing:

```
Alice 23
Bob 30
Charlie 27
```

The AWK script execution yields:

```
First field: Alice Second field: 23
First field: Bob Second field: 30
First field: Charlie Second field: 27
```

In this script, the variable first captures the value of the first field, while second captures the second field, demonstrating the linkage and processing of input data fields through the assignment of values to variables.

Understanding the foundational aspects of AWK variables sets the stage for exploring more complex constructs and functionalities, such as arrays and built-in variables, to be discussed in the subsequent sections. Mastery of variables in AWK enables proficient data manipulation and introduces flexibility and control necessary for effective scripting and data processing.

4.2 Types of Variables in AWK

AWK, as a data-driven scripting language, supports various types of variables to facilitate different types of data manipulation. Understanding these types is fundamental to leveraging the full power of AWK in your scripts. In AWK, variables do not need explicit declaration and can be assigned dynamically. The core types of variables in AWK are string variables, numeric variables, and arrays. Each type serves its specific purpose and provides unique functionality.

String Variables

String variables in AWK hold sequences of characters and are used extensively in text processing. AWK handles strings in a flexible way, allowing them to be assigned, concatenated, and manipulated using built-in functions. For example:

```
BEGIN {
    str1 = "Hello"
    str2 = "World"
    result = str1 " " str2
    print result
}
```

```
Hello World
```

Here, str1 and str2 are string variables. The assignment of result demonstrates string concatenation, which combines str1 and str2 with a space in between.

Numeric Variables

Numeric variables in AWK store numerical values, which can be integers or floating-point numbers. AWK treats numbers with high flexibility, automatically converting between strings and numbers when needed. Arithmetic operations are performed using standard operators:

```
BEGIN {
```

```
    num1 = 10
    num2 = 5.5
    sum = num1 + num2
    print sum
}
```

```
15.5
```

In this example, num1 and num2 are numeric variables. The operation num1 + num2 results in sum, demonstrating AWK's capability to handle floating-point arithmetic.

Arrays

Arrays in AWK are associative, meaning that their indices can be either numbers or strings. This distinguishes AWK arrays from arrays in many other programming languages where indices are typically numeric. Handling data in this manner provides significant flexibility. Here is an example illustrating array manipulation:

```
BEGIN {
    fruits["apple"] = 3
    fruits["orange"] = 5
    fruits["banana"] = 2

    for (fruit in fruits) {
        print fruit, fruits[fruit]
    }
}
```

```
apple 3
orange 5
banana 2
```

In this script, fruits is an associative array where each fruit name ("apple", "orange", "banana") is used as a key to store corresponding values. The for loop iterates over all keys in the array, allowing access to each key-value pair.

Dynamic Typing in AWK

One of the key aspects of AWK is its dynamic typing. Unlike statically typed languages where variable types must be explicitly defined, AWK determines the type of a variable at runtime based on its value. This means that a variable can hold a string in one context and a number in another, depending on how it is used. Consider the following:

```
BEGIN {
```

```
    var = "10"
    print var + 0
    var = var " apples"
    print var
}
```

```
10
10 apples
```

In the above script, var initially holds a string "10". When used in an arithmetic context (var + 0), it is treated as a number. Later, var is concatenated with another string, demonstrating its dynamic type conversion capability.

Built-in Variables

AWK also provides a set of built-in variables that carry specific information about the data being processed or the execution environment. Some of the commonly used built-in variables include:

- FS: Field separator for input (default is whitespace).
- OFS: Output field separator (default is whitespace).
- RS: Record separator for input (default is newline).
- ORS: Output record separator (default is newline).
- NR: Number of records processed so far.
- NF: Number of fields in the current record.

For example, the variable NR can be used to track the number of lines (records) processed:

```
{
    print "Processing record number:", NR
}
```

```
Processing record number: 1
Processing record number: 2
Processing record number: 3
...
```

These built-in variables provide essential information that can be used to control and manipulate the processing logic within AWK scripts.

Understanding the various types of variables and their flexible handling is crucial for writing efficient and effective AWK programs, capable of handling both numerical computations and textual data manipulations with ease.

4.3 Predefined Variables

AWK provides several predefined variables, which contain information about the input data, the environment, and the state of the program being executed. These variables are automatically initialized and offer significant advantages by simplifying the process of capturing essential data without explicitly defining them. Below is a detailed exploration of some key predefined variables in AWK:

FS: The Field Separator Variable

The $FS variable determines the delimiter used to divide input lines into fields. By default, FS is set to white space, which means any sequence of spaces and tabs. You can change FS to another character or a regular expression depending on how the input data is structured. For example:

```
BEGIN {
    FS = ","
}

In this example, \texttt{FS} is set to a comma, so fields in each input line will be split
    where a comma is found.

\texttt{NF}: The Number of Fields Variable

The \texttt{\$NF} variable holds the number of fields in the current record. This is
    particularly useful for iterating over fields in a record or checking the format
    consistency of the data.

\begin{lstlisting}
{
    print "Number of fields:", NF
}
```

If you run this program on a line with two comma-separated fields, the output will be:

```
Number of fields: 2
```

NR: The Number of Records Variable

The $NR variable represents the number of input records processed so far. This can be used for tasks such as processing records in a particular range or debugging purposes.

```
{
    print "Processing record number:", NR
}
```

Given a file with three lines, the output of this program will be:

```
Processing record number: 1
Processing record number: 2
Processing record number: 3
```

FNR: The File Number of Records Variable

The $FNR variable provides the number of input records read from the current file. Unlike NR, FNR is reset to 1 when a new file is started. This is particularly useful when processing multiple files and you need to retain a count specific to each file.

```
{
    print "Processing record number in current file:", FNR
}
```

With two files containing three lines each, the output will be:

```
Processing record number in current file: 1
Processing record number in current file: 2
Processing record number in current file: 3
Processing record number in current file: 1
Processing record number in current file: 2
Processing record number in current file: 3
```

OFS: The Output Field Separator Variable

The $OFS variable defines the output field separator, which is used when AWK prints the fields of a record. By default, OFS is a single space. Changing OFS helps in formatting output data as per requirement.

```
BEGIN {
    OFS = "|"
}
{
    print $1, $2, $3
}
```

For an input line like "a b c", the output will be:

```
a|b|c
```

ORS: The Output Record Separator Variable

The $ORS variable defines the output record separator, which is appended to the end of an output record. By default, ORS is a newline character.

```
BEGIN {
    ORS = "---"
```

```
}
{
    print $0
}
```

For an input file with two lines, the output will be:

```
line1---
line2---
```

RS: The Input Record Separator Variable

The $RS variable sets the input record separator, which determines how records are split. By default, RS is a newline character. Setting RS to another character or a regular expression customizes input processing.

```
BEGIN {
    RS = ""
}
{
    print $0
}
```

In this case, RS is set to the empty string, causing AWK to read records separated by blank lines.

ARGC and ARGV: Argument Count and Argument Vector Variables

$ARGC stores the number of command-line arguments, and $ARGV is an array containing the actual arguments. These variables are helpful for scripts requiring complex command-line argument processing.

```
BEGIN {
    for (i = 0; i < ARGC; i++) {
        print ARGV[i]
    }
}
```

Executing this script with awk -f script.awk file1 file2, the output will enumerate the program name and file arguments:

```
awk
script.awk
file1
file2
```

Each predefined variable in AWK supports powerful data handling and script control, enhancing code readability and reducing the need for extensive user-defined variables.

4.4 User-defined Variables

In AWK, user-defined variables are fundamental for creating flexible and dynamic scripts. They allow programmers to store and manipulate data efficiently, providing the means to perform complex data processing tasks. User-defined variables in AWK do not require explicit declaration before use. Their first appearance in the script, whether through assignment or usage in an expression, serves as their declaration.

To initialize a user-defined variable, simply assign a value to it. AWK variables are dynamically typed, which means their type is inferred from the context of their initial assignment. If a variable is assigned a numeric value, it is treated as a numeric variable. Conversely, assigning a string value results in the variable being treated as a string.

Consider the following example where we define two variables, num and text:

```
BEGIN {
    num = 42
    text = "Hello, AWK!"
    print num
    print text
}
```

This example initializes num with the numeric value 42 and text with the string "Hello, AWK!". The print statements then output the values of these variables:

```
42
Hello, AWK!
```

Variables can be freely reassigned to either strings or numbers within the same script. The following illustrates variable reassignment:

```
BEGIN {
    var = 100 # Initial assignment as numeric
    print var # Output: 100
    var = "AWK" # Reassigned as string
    print var # Output: AWK
}
```

This dynamic typing feature is both powerful and flexible but demands careful attention to variable usage, especially when performing operations that depend on variable types.

Operations on User-defined Variables

AWK supports a variety of operations on user-defined variables, including arithmetic operations, string concatenation, and assignment operators. Here is an example showcasing arithmetic operations on numeric variables:

```
BEGIN {
    a = 10
    b = 20
    sum = a + b
    difference = a - b
    product = a * b
    quotient = b / a
    remainder = b % a

    print "Sum:", sum
    print "Difference:", difference
    print "Product:", product
    print "Quotient:", quotient
    print "Remainder:", remainder
}
```

This script outputs the following:

```
Sum: 30
Difference: -10
Product: 200
Quotient: 2
Remainder: 0
```

String concatenation is performed automatically by juxtaposing variables or expressions:

```
BEGIN {
    str1 = "Hello, "
    str2 = "world!"
    message = str1 str2 # Concatenation
    print message # Output: Hello, world!
}
```

Scope of User-defined Variables

In AWK, the scope of a variable determines where it can be accessed within a script. Variables defined in the BEGIN block, or before any patterns and actions, are available throughout the entire AWK script. Here is an example illustrating variable scope:

```
BEGIN {
    globalVar = "Accessible everywhere"
}

{
    blockVar = $1 # Variable local to the current block
    print globalVar, blockVar
}
```

In this example, globalVar can be accessed within any pattern-action block, while blockVar is only accessible within the block where it is defined.

Best Practices for User-defined Variables

When using user-defined variables in AWK: - Use meaningful variable names to enhance script readability. - Avoid using predefined variable names for user-defined variables to prevent conflicts. - Initialize variables explicitly to avoid unintended behavior from uninitialized variables. - Be mindful of variable scope to ensure that variables are accessible where needed and avoid unintentional overwriting of variables with the same name.

The intentional use of user-defined variables enriches AWK scripts, allowing for more sophisticated data manipulation and processing. With careful attention to variable initialization, scope, and type, effective and efficient AWK programming can be achieved.

4.5 Initializing and Assigning Variables

In AWK programming, initializing and assigning variables is a fundamental aspect that dictates the overall flow of data manipulation. Variable initialization refers to the initial allocation of a value to a variable, while assignment involves updating the variable's value during script execution.

The syntax for initializing and assigning variables in AWK is straightforward. Variables in AWK can be initialized with numeric or string values, and this can happen either within a script or on the command line.

When dealing with variables in AWK, it's essential to understand the dual nature of variables which can store either string or numeric data. AWK dynamically determines the type of a variable based on the context in which it's used.

Consider the following example script demonstrating variable initialization and assignment within an AWK script:

```
BEGIN {
    x = 10 # Numeric initialization
    y = "hello" # String initialization
    z = x + 5 # Assignment using a numeric expression
    a = y " world" # Assignment using a string expression
    print x, y, z, a
}
```

```
10 hello 15 hello world
```

In this example, the variable x is initialized with a numeric value 10, and y is initialized with the string "hello". The variable z is assigned the result of the numeric expression x + 5, and a is assigned the concatenated result of the string expression y " world". The print statement outputs the values of these variables, demonstrating how they have been initialized and assigned.

Variables can also be initialized directly from the command line when invoking an AWK script. This can be particularly useful for passing parameters into AWK programs. For example:

```
awk 'BEGIN { print x }' x=20
```

```
20
```

In this case, the variable x is initialized to 20 before the script is executed.

It is also possible to reassign values to variables within the execution of an AWK program. This enables dynamic manipulation of data throughout the lifecycle of the script. Consider the example:

```
{
   count = count + 1 # Incrementing the counter
   sum = sum + $1 # Summing the first field of each input line
}
END {
   print "Count:", count
   print "Sum:", sum
}
```

```
Count: <number_of_lines>
Sum: <total_sum_of_first_fields>
```

Here, the variables count and sum are reassigned in each iteration of the main processing block. The count variable keeps a record of the number of lines processed, while the sum variable accumulates the value of the first field of each line.

It is crucial to note that AWK considers uninitialized variables as zero if used in a numeric context and as an empty string if used in a string context. For example:

```
BEGIN {
    print "Uninitialized numeric:", u_var + 0
    print "Uninitialized string:", u_var "test"
}
```

```
Uninitialized numeric: 0
Uninitialized string: test
```

In this script, u_var is an uninitialized variable. When added to zero in a numeric context, it defaults to 0. When concatenated with a string, it defaults to an empty string.

Explicit initialization of variables at the beginning of a script can prevent unintended behavior caused by uninitialized variables. Moreover, documenting the intent of each variable by initializing them improves script readability and maintainability.

Properly initializing and assigning variables lays the groundwork for the effective utilization of variables in AWK scripts, enabling robust data processing and manipulation. This essential skill allows a programmer to control the flow of data and maintain clear and maintainable code.

4.6 Scope of Variables in AWK

Understanding the scope of variables in AWK is fundamental for writing efficient and error-free scripts. Variable scope determines the accessibility and lifetime of a variable within different parts of an AWK program. In AWK, the scope of a variable is influenced by the blocks in which it is defined and used. The two principal scopes are global and local.

Global variables in AWK are accessible from any part of the script, including BEGIN and END blocks, pattern-action statements, and functions. These variables are implicitly declared by simply using them anywhere in the code. Global variables persist throughout the execution of the AWK program unless explicitly modified or redefined.

Local variables, on the other hand, have their scope limited to the function in which they are declared. They are declared using the *var* keyword within the function body. Their values are not accessible outside this function, ensuring that any operations on them do not affect variables of the same name in other parts of the script.

Consider the following script to illustrate these concepts:

```
BEGIN {
    global_var = "I'm a global variable"
}

{
    print global_var
    function_example()
}

function function_example() {
    var local_var = "I'm a local variable"
    print local_var
}
```

When executed, this script produces the following output:

```
I'm a global variable
I'm a local variable
```

In this example, global_var is defined in the BEGIN block and is accessible in the main action block and within the function_example. However, local_var is only accessible within function_example and cannot be referenced outside of this function.

It is important to distinguish between defining and initializing variables. Defining a variable means declaring its existence, which implicitly sets its scope (global or local). Initializing a variable means assigning it an initial value. Uninitialized variables in AWK have a default value of zero for numeric context or an empty string for string context.

To clarify, the following script demonstrates variable reinitialization and shadowing:

```
BEGIN {
    x = 10
    print x
}

{
    print x
    example_function()
    print x
}

function example_function() {
    var x = 5
    print x
}
```

The output of this script is:

```
10
10
5
10
```

Here, the global variable x is reset to 10 in the BEGIN block, printed in the main action block, and remains 10 after example_function executes. Within example_function, a new local variable x is declared and initialized to 5, thereby shadowing the global variable x within the function's scope. This shadowing ensures that the global x remains unchanged when control returns to the main block.

To avoid unintentional conflicts or unintended variable shadowing, it is advisable to use descriptive and unique variable names, especially in larger scripts where the same names might be inadvertently reused in different scopes.

The concept of variable scope is also closely tied to the scope resolution within nested functions. When dealing with nested functions, the innermost function's local variables take precedence over the outer function's local variables of the same name. This nested scope visibility can be useful for controlling variable lifetimes and accessibility within complex AWK scripts:

```
function outer_function() {
    var x = 3
    print "outer x:", x
    inner_function()
}

function inner_function() {
    var x = 4
    print "inner x:", x
}
```

Executing the following code snippet with calls to outer_function:

```
BEGIN {
    outer_function()
}
```

Produces the output:

```
outer x: 3
inner x: 4
```

In this case, the inner function defines and initializes its own local variable x, which shadows x in the outer function. Understanding these nuanced details of the variable scope ensures precise and predictable behavior in AWK scripts, avoiding debugging complications tied to variable conflicts and unexpected overwrites. Here is the corrected LaTeX text of this section, following the guidelines provided and ensuring proper formatting and escaping of special characters:

4.7 String Variables

AWK is particularly adept at handling text processing, making string variables a critical component in many AWK scripts. String variables in AWK can store sequences of characters, which can include letters, numbers, spaces, and special characters. Unlike some other languages, AWK does not distinguish between single and double quotes for defining strings, and automatic type conversion between strings and numbers is a notable feature. This section delves into the manipulation, comparison, and assignment of string variables, alongside an exploration of built-in string functions.

String variables in AWK are straightforward to use. A string can be assigned to a variable using the assignment operator =. Here is an example:

```
name = "John Doe"
company = 'Acme Corporation'
```

Both examples above are functionally equivalent, showcasing AWK's flexibility regarding quotation marks.

String Concatenation

A common operation on strings is concatenation, in which two or more strings are combined into one. In AWK, concatenation can be achieved using the concatenation operator, represented by simply placing two variables next to each other with a space in between.

```
greet = "Hello, "
person = "John"
greeting = greet person
print greeting
```

The output of this script is:

```
Hello, John
```

AWK merges the strings greet and person without requiring an explicit operator, making the syntax clean and concise.

String Comparison

String comparison in AWK follows the same principles as numeric comparison, using relational operators such as ==, !=, <, >, <=, and >=. These comparisons are based on lexicographical ordering, which compares strings based on the ASCII values of their characters.

```
word1 = "apple"
word2 = "banana"
if (word1 < word2) {
    print word1 " comes before " word2
}
```

The output of this code snippet will be:

```
apple comes before banana
```

This comparison uses the ASCII values of the characters, where 'a' has a lower value than 'b', making "apple" come before "banana".

Supported String Functions

AWK provides a set of powerful built-in functions for string manipulation. These functions include length(), substr(), index(), match(), split(), gsub(), and sub(). Each serves a specific purpose in string processing:

- length(string): Returns the length of string.
- substr(string, start, length): Extracts a substring starting from position start and having length characters.
- index(string, search): Returns the position of the first occurrence of search in string, or 0 if not found.
- match(string, regex): Matches regex within string and returns the starting position.
- split(string, array, separator): Splits string into array based on separator.
- gsub(regex, replacement, string): Globally substitutes all occurrences of regex with replacement in string.
- sub(regex, replacement, string): Substitutes the first occurrence of regex with replacement in string.

Examples of String Functions

Using these functions facilitates complex string manipulations efficiently. Below are examples demonstrating their usage:

```
text = "The quick brown fox jumps over the lazy dog"

# length function
print length(text) # Output: 43

# substr function
print substr(text, 5, 5) # Output: quick

# index function
print index(text, "fox") # Output: 17

# match function
position = match(text, /[a-z]+ dog/)
print position # Output: 36

# split function
split(text, words, " ")
for (i in words) {
    print words[i]
}

# gsub function
gsub("o", "0", text)
print text # Output: The quick br0wn f0x jumps 0ver the lazy d0g
```

```
# sub function
sub("lazy", "sleepy", text)
print text # Output: The quick brown fox jumps over the sleepy dog
```

The examples above illustrate the practical applications of the string functions. The length function determines the length of text, substr extracts the word "quick", and index locates the starting position of "fox". The match function identifies the starting position of the substring matching the regular expression /[a-z]+ dog/. The split function breaks the text into individual words which are then printed iteratively. The gsub function replaces all occurrences of 'o' with '0', and sub replaces the first occurrence of "lazy" with "sleepy".

AWK's handling of string variables, coupled with its built-in functions, enables robust manipulation of text data, ensuring scripts are both concise and powerful. Understanding and utilizing these features effectively increases the efficiency and clarity of data processing tasks.

4.8 Numeric Variables

In AWK, numeric variables play a crucial role in handling numerical data, performing arithmetic operations, and controlling flow logic. Numeric variables can store integer and floating-point numbers, enabling a variety of mathematical operations. Understanding how to define, manipulate, and use these variables is fundamental for efficient scripting in AWK.

Defining Numeric Variables

Numeric variables in AWK are defined dynamically; there is no need for explicit declaration. An uninitialized variable holds the value zero by default. You can assign a numeric value to a variable using the assignment operator =. For instance:

```
x = 10
y = 3.14
```

In this code, x is assigned an integer value of 10, and y is assigned a floating-point value of 3.14.

Arithmetic Operations

AWK supports basic arithmetic operations: addition (+), subtraction (-), multiplication (*), division (/), and modulus (%). These operations can be performed on numeric variables to manipulate numerical data. Below is an example:

```
a = 5
b = 2

sum = a + b # Addition
diff = a - b # Subtraction
prod = a * b # Multiplication
quot = a / b # Division
mod = a % b # Modulus (remainder)
```

The above code snippet demonstrates how to perform arithmetic operations on variables a and b, resulting in the computation of their sum, difference, product, quotient, and modulus.

Operator Precedence

In AWK, operator precedence follows standard arithmetic rules, where multiplication, division, and modulus have higher precedence than addition and subtraction. Parentheses can alter the order of operations to ensure specific evaluations. For example:

```
result = 10 + 5 * 2 # result is 20 (5*2 is evaluated first)
result = (10 + 5) * 2 # result is 30 (10+5 is evaluated first)
```

Understanding operator precedence helps in designing accurate and efficient AWK scripts.

Increment and Decrement Operators

AWK also supports the increment (++) and decrement (–) operators, which are shorthand for adding or subtracting one from a variable. They can be used as prefix or postfix operators:

```
counter = 5

counter++ # Post-increment: evaluates to 5, then adds 1
++counter # Pre-increment: adds 1, then evaluates to 6

counter-- # Post-decrement: evaluates to 6, then subtracts 1
--counter # Pre-decrement: subtracts 1, then evaluates to 4
```

The placement of ++ or – (before or after the variable) determines whether the increment/ decrement takes place before or after the variable's current value is used in an expression.

Built-in Mathematical Functions

AWK provides built-in mathematical functions to handle more complex numerical computations. Some of the most commonly used functions include:

- sqrt(x): Returns the square root of x.
- exp(x): Returns the exponential of x.
- log(x): Returns the natural logarithm of x.
- sin(x), cos(x), and tan(x): Return the sine, cosine, and tangent of x (where x is in radians).
- int(x): Returns the integer part of x.
- rand(): Returns a random number between 0 and 1. Seeds can be set using srand().

Example usage of these functions:

```
value = 9

sqrt_val = sqrt(value) # 3.0
log_val = log(value) # 2.197224
int_val = int(3.14) # 3

# Set a seed for random number generation
srand(10)
rand_val = rand() # random number between 0 and 1
```

Type Conversion

In AWK, explicit and implicit type conversions between strings and numeric values occur as necessary. When a string is used in a numeric context, AWK automatically attempts to convert it to a number, using the initial part of the string that interprets as a valid number. Conversely, when a number is used in a string context, it is converted to its string representation.

```
str = "123"
num = str + 0 # Converts string "123" to number 123

num = 456
str = num "" # Converts number 456 to string "456"
```

Conversion is gracefully handled, ensuring that numeric values are accurately processed in their respective contexts.

4.9 Arrays in AWK

Arrays in AWK offer a powerful mechanism to handle collections of data efficiently. Unlike many programming languages that only support numerically indexed arrays, AWK allows arrays to be indexed by both numbers and strings. This flexibility makes it possible to use arrays as associative arrays, which can be beneficial for a range of tasks, such as counting frequencies of elements or storing tabular data.

In AWK, arrays are dynamically sized, meaning you don't need to declare their size in advance. An array in AWK can be created and used simply by assigning a value to a specific index.

An array can be declared and initialized as follows:

```
arr["key"] = "value"
arr[1] = 10
```

In the above code, arr["key"] assigns the value "value" to the array entry indexed by the string "key", and arr[1] assigns the value 10 to the array entry indexed by the number 1.

Accessing Array Elements

Accessing elements in an array is straightforward. You use the index inside square brackets to retrieve the stored value. Here's an example:

```
print arr["key"]
print arr[1]
```

This will output:

```
value
10
```

Iterating Over Arrays

To traverse all elements in an array, AWK provides the for loop with the in keyword. This allows you to iterate through each index in the array, retrieving both index and corresponding value.

```
for (i in arr) {
    print i, arr[i]
}
```

This loop will output each index and its associated value.

Checking for Existence of an Index

To check if a particular index exists in an array, the following syntax can be used:

```
if ("key" in arr) {
    print "key exists in array"
}
```

This conditional statement checks if the index "key" exists in array arr.

Deleting Array Elements

AWK offers the delete statement to remove specific elements from an array, including all its entries:

```
delete arr["key"]
delete arr[1]
```

To delete all the elements of an array, you can iterate over the array and delete each element:

```
for (i in arr) {
    delete arr[i]
}
```

Multidimensional Arrays

AWK supports multidimensional arrays, achieved by using a composite key constructed as a concatenation of indices. The indices are separated by the value of the built-in variable SUBSEP.

Here is an example:

```
arr[1, 2] = 5
arr["a", "b"] = "value"
```

Elements of a multidimensional array are accessed in the same manner:

```
print arr[1, 2] # Outputs: 5
print arr["a", "b"] # Outputs: value
```

Moreover, you can iterate over a multidimensional array:

```
for (i in arr) {
    split(i, idx, SUBSEP)
    print "Indices:", idx[1], idx[2], "Value:", arr[i]
}
```

The split function is used here to extract the individual indices from the composite key.

Built-in Arrays

AWK provides some built-in arrays that facilitate specific tasks. One of the most commonly used built-in arrays is ARGV, which holds the command line arguments that are passed to an AWK program. Another built-in array, ENVIRON, holds the environment variables.

ARGV example:

```
BEGIN {
    for (i in ARGV) {
```

```
        print "ARGV[", i, "] =", ARGV[i]
    }
}
```

This script will print all the command line arguments passed to the AWK script.

ENVIRON example:

```
BEGIN {
    for (var in ENVIRON) {
        print var, ENVIRON[var]
    }
}
```

This will output all the environment variables and their values.

Understanding the use and manipulation of arrays in AWK is crucial for efficient data processing and management. Arrays are versatile, handling data of varied types, indexing schemes, and sizes, streamlining complex operations within simple AWK scripts.

4.10 Built-in Arrays

AWK provides several built-in arrays that enhance its data processing capabilities and streamline scripting by offering pre-defined functionalities. These arrays are automatically maintained by AWK and do not require explicit initialization. Understanding the built-in arrays is crucial for effective data manipulation and accessing metadata during the execution of AWK programs.

ARGC and ARGV

The array ARGV and the variable ARGC are used to manage command-line arguments in AWK. ARGV is an array that holds each argument passed to the AWK script, while ARGC stores the count of those arguments.

```
awk 'BEGIN {
  for (i = 0; i < ARGC; i++)
    print "ARGV[" i "] is " ARGV[i]
}' file1 file2
```

This example processes each command-line argument passed to the AWK script and prints its index and value. If executed with:

```
$ awk -f script.awk file1 file2
```

The output will be:

```
ARGV[0] is awk
ARGV[1] is file1
ARGV[2] is file2
```

The first element, ARGV[0], is always the command used to invoke AWK, and the subsequent elements contain the program parameters.

ENVIRON

ENVIRON is an associative array that provides access to the environment variables of the system where AWK is running. Each element of ENVIRON corresponds to an environment variable, with the array indices representing the variable names and the array values storing their respective values.

```
awk 'BEGIN {
  print "PATH is", ENVIRON["PATH"]
}'
```

When executed, this script retrieves and prints the value of the PATH environment variable:

```
PATH is /usr/local/bin:/usr/bin:/bin
```

FILENAME

The FILENAME variable, although not an array, is closely related to built-in arrays and indispensable when dealing with multiple files in AWK. It contains the name of the current input file being processed. In contexts involving command-line arguments or data streams, FILENAME is invaluable for segregating and processing data based on source files.

```
awk '{ print FILENAME, $0 }' file1 file2
```

This command prefixes each line of output with the name of the file it originated from:

```
file1 line from file1
file1 another line from file1
file2 line from file2
file2 another line from file2
```

PROCINFO

The PROCINFO array holds details about the execution environment and process-related information. This array includes elements such as the file read and write buffers, system time, version, and more.

```
awk 'BEGIN {
  print "AWK version is", PROCINFO["version"]
```

```
}'
```

Running this script yields the version of AWK:

```
AWK version is 20200507
```

Another useful element of PROCINFO is "sorted_in", which indicates the sort order of array elements when iterating with a for...in loop if sorting is specified.

SYMTAB

The SYMTAB array represents AWK's symbol table, providing a programmatic access point to global variables and functions. SYMTAB is less commonly used but is powerful for introspective purposes or advanced programmatic manipulation.

```
awk 'BEGIN {
  SYMTAB["x"] = 5
  print "The value of x is", x
}'
```

In this example, an entry is added to SYMTAB, and accessing this variable through x outputs:

```
The value of x is 5
```

Direct interaction with SYMTAB should be handled cautiously to avoid unintended side effects or conflicts within the script.

These built-in arrays and special variables collectively potentiate AWK with powerful tools for intricate data manipulations and metadata access. By leveraging these constructs, one can write more efficient, concise, and potent AWK programs.

4.11 Best Practices for Using Variables

Effective use of variables in AWK can significantly enhance the readability, maintainability, and efficiency of your scripts. The following best practices will ensure that you utilize variables in ways that adhere to these principles.

Choose Meaningful Variable Names: Selecting clear and descriptive variable names is crucial. Use names that convey the purpose and content of the variable. For instance, instead of naming a variable x, use total_count or average_value. Consistent and logical naming conventions facilitate understanding and collaboration.

Avoid Using AWK Reserved Variable Names: Some variable names in AWK are reserved for built-in variables, such as NR, NF, and FS. To prevent any conflict or unexpected behavior, it is prudent to avoid using these names for user-defined variables.

Initialize Variables Explicitly: Although AWK initializes variables to default values (e.g., numeric variables to 0 and string variables to an empty string), it is recommended to initialize variables explicitly. This practice enhances clarity regarding the variable's initial state and makes the code more predictable.

```
BEGIN {
    total_count = 0;
    sum_value = 0.0;
    concatenated_string = "";
}
```

Use Variables Locally When Possible: In AWK, variables can either be global or local. Local variables, which are defined within functions, prevent unintentional interference with other parts of the code. To declare a local variable within a function, list it after the function's parameter list.

```
function calculate_sum(arr, n, i, sum) {
    sum = 0;
    for (i = 1; i <= n; i++) {
        sum += arr[i];
    }
    return sum;
}
```

Handle Variable Scope Appropriately: Understanding the scope of variables is essential. Global variables are accessible throughout the program, while local variables are confined to the functions in which they are declared. Always consider the scope to avoid inadvertent modifications to global variables.

```
BEGIN {
    global_sum = 10;
}

function add_value(value) {
    local_sum = global_sum + value;
    return local_sum;
}

{
    print add_value($1);
}
```

Consistently Format Numerical and String Variables: AWK allows for flexible treatment of numeric and string variables. However, it is best practice to explicitly format variables to the appropriate type, especially when performing arithmetic operations or string manipulations. This prevents unexpected type coercion and ensures predictable results.

```
{
    numeric_value = $1 + 0; # Ensuring numeric type
    string_value = $2 ""; # Ensuring string type
    print numeric_value, string_value;
}
```

Use Built-in Variables Judiciously: AWK provides several useful built-in variables, such as FS (field separator) and OFS (output field separator). When employed judiciously, these built-in variables can greatly simplify your code and improve its readability.

```
BEGIN {
    FS = ",";
    OFS = "\t";
}
{
    print $1, $2, $3;
}
```

Comment Your Code: Commenting is an invaluable practice that helps others (and yourself) understand the purpose and functionality of variables within your script. Include comments that explain the rationale behind variable initialization, significant computations, or any non-obvious logic within the code.

```
{
    # Initialize count of records processed
    record_count = 0;

    # Sum of values in the first column
    sum_column1 = 0;

    # Iterate over all records
    while ((getline line) > 0) {
        record_count++;
        fields = split(line, arr, ",");
        sum_column1 += arr[1];
    }
    print "Total Records: ", record_count;
    print "Sum of First Column: ", sum_column1;
}
```

Adhering to these best practices ensures that your AWK scripts are efficient, maintainable, and easy to understand. Proper variable usage not only prevents errors but also enhances the readability and reliability of your code.

Chapter 5

Control Structures in AWK

This chapter explores the control structures available in AWK, including conditional statements (if, else if, else), various types of loops (while, do-while, for), and the use of break and continue commands. It also covers the exit statement, pattern matching within control structures, nested control structures, the switch statement, and error handling mechanisms. These control structures are vital for implementing complex logic in AWK scripts.

5.1 Introduction to Control Structures

Control structures are fundamental constructs in programming that dictate the flow of execution within a script or program. In AWK, control structures enable conditional execution of statements, looping over data, and handling exceptions, allowing the development of complex data processing workflows. Understanding and mastering control structures is essential for writing efficient and meaningful AWK programs.

The primary control structures in AWK are conditional statements, loops, and the switch statement. Each of these has a specific syntax and purpose.

Conditional Statements: In AWK, the if, else if, and else statements are used to perform conditional logic. These statements allow you to execute blocks of code only if certain conditions are met. The general form of an if statement in AWK is as follows:

```
if (condition) {
    # Code block to execute if condition is true
} else if (another_condition) {
    # Code block to execute if another_condition is true
} else {
    # Code block to execute if none of the above conditions are true
}
```

Loops: AWK provides several looping constructs to iterate over data. The basic loops in AWK are the while, do-while, and for loops. These loops are used to execute a block of code multiple times, either based on a condition or over a specified range. The syntax for each loop type is:

```
# while loop
while (condition) {
    # Code block to execute while condition is true
}

# do-while loop
do {
    # Code block to execute
} while (condition);

# for loop
for (initialization; condition; increment) {
    # Code block to execute while condition is true
}
```

The switch Statement: The switch statement is used to simplify the handling of multiple conditional branches. It functions by evaluating a single expression and matching it against various cases. The layout of a switch statement in AWK appears as follows:

```
switch (expression) {
    case value1:
        # Code block to execute if expression == value1
        break;
    case value2:
        # Code block to execute if expression == value2
        break;
    default:
        # Code block to execute if none of the cases match
}
```

Break and Continue: The break and continue statements provide additional control over loops. The break statement immediately exits the loop it is in, while the continue statement skips the current iteration and proceeds with the next iteration of the loop.

```
# Example using break
```

```
for (i = 1; i <= 10; i++) {
    if (i == 5) {
        break; # Exit loop when i equals 5
    }
    print i;
}

# Example using continue
for (i = 1; i <= 10; i++) {
    if (i % 2 == 0) {
        continue; # Skip even numbers and continue with next iteration
    }
    print i;
}
```

The exit Statement: The exit statement is used to terminate the execution of an AWK script before reaching the end of the input data. It can be used to return a status code.

```
if (some_condition) {
    exit; # Exits the AWK script immediately
}
```

By mastering these control structures, AWK programmers can create scripts that perform intricate tasks efficiently. The following sections will delve deeper into each control structure, providing examples and best practices for their use.

5.2 Conditional Statements: if, else if, else

Conditional statements are a fundamental part of programming languages and are used to perform different actions based on different conditions. In AWK, the most commonly used conditional statements are if, else if, and else. These statements control the flow of execution depending on whether a condition evaluates to true or false.

The syntax for an if statement in AWK is straightforward:

```
if (condition) {
    // statements to execute if the condition is true
}
```

Here, condition is an expression that AWK evaluates. If condition is true (i.e., it evaluates to a non-zero value), the block of code within the curly braces is executed.

To handle multiple conditions, the else if and else clauses are used in conjunction with if. This can create a chain of conditional checks that are evaluated in sequence:

```
if (condition1) {
    // statements to execute if condition1 is true
} else if (condition2) {
    // statements to execute if condition2 is true
} else {
    // statements to execute if none of the above conditions are true
}
```

The else if clause allows specifying additional conditions if the initial if condition is false. If all conditions are false, the code within the else block (if provided) is executed. Each condition in the chain is evaluated only if all preceding conditions are false.

Practical Examples

To solidify the understanding of if, else if, and else statements, consider the following practical examples. These examples involve classic scenarios one might encounter when processing data with AWK.

```
# Sample AWK script to categorize numbers as positive, negative, or zero
{
    if ($1 > 0) {
        print $1 " is positive"
    } else if ($1 < 0) {
        print $1 " is negative"
    } else {
        print $1 " is zero"
    }
}
```

When this script is executed over a file with numbers, it categorizes each number as positive, negative, or zero. For instance, given an input file numbers.txt with the following content:

```
10
-5
0
7
-3
```

Running the script will produce the following output:

```
10 is positive
-5 is negative
0 is zero
7 is positive
-3 is negative
```

Combining Pattern Matching with Conditional Statements

Pattern matching can be combined with conditional statements to enhance data processing. Patterns can control when certain blocks of code are executed, while if statements add further decision-making capabilities.

For example, consider processing a text file where you wish to print a message based on the presence of a specific keyword:

```
# Sample AWK script to print messages based on keyword matches
/ERROR/ {
    if ($2 == "CRITICAL") {
        print "Critical error found: " $0
    } else if ($2 == "WARNING") {
        print "Warning error found: " $0
    } else {
        print "Non-critical error found: " $0
    }
}
```

This script illustrates how AWK can be used to selectively process lines containing the word ERROR, with further refinement based on the second field in each matching line. Given an input file log.txt:

```
ERROR CRITICAL Disk failure
ERROR WARNING CPU usage high
ERROR INFO Service restarted
```

Executing the AWK script will result in the following output:

```
Critical error found: ERROR CRITICAL Disk failure
Warning error found: ERROR WARNING CPU usage high
Non-critical error found: ERROR INFO Service restarted
```

Handling Multiple Conditions Efficiently

Using the if, else if, and else statements, one can manage complex decision-making processes in AWK with ease. Consider the following more advanced example which involves grading marks.

```
# Sample AWK script to assign grades based on marks
{
    if ($1 >= 90) {
        print $1 ": Grade A"
    } else if ($1 >= 80) {
        print $1 ": Grade B"
    } else if ($1 >= 70) {
        print $1 ": Grade C"
    } else if ($1 >= 60) {
        print $1 ": Grade D"
    } else {
        print $1 ": Grade F"
```

```
    }
}
```

For an input file marks.txt:

```
95
82
68
54
77
85
```

The script will yield the following output:

```
95 : Grade A
82 : Grade B
68 : Grade D
54 : Grade F
77 : Grade C
85 : Grade B
```

This detailed examination of if, else if, and else demonstrates their critical role in regulating program flow. Combining them with pattern matching and other conditions allows for precise and flexible data handling operations in AWK scripts.

5.3 Loops: while and do-while

In AWK, loop structures are essential for executing code repeatedly based on specific conditions. The while and do-while loops provide mechanisms to iterate over code blocks, enabling the processing of data in an efficient manner. Understanding these loops helps in creating more dynamic AWK scripts capable of handling various data manipulation tasks.

The while loop in AWK checks its condition before executing the loop body. If the condition evaluates to true, the loop body is executed. This process continues as long as the condition remains true. The general syntax for the while loop is as follows:

```
while (condition) {
    # code block to be executed
}
```

Here is an example demonstrating the while loop:

```
BEGIN {
    count = 1
    while (count <= 5) {
        print "Count is: " count
        count++
```

```
    }
}
```

The above script initializes a variable count to 1. The loop continues as long as count is less than or equal to 5. Within each iteration, the script prints the current value of count and then increments it.

```
Count is: 1
Count is: 2
Count is: 3
Count is: 4
Count is: 5
```

Now let's look at the do-while loop. Unlike the while loop, the do-while loop checks its condition after executing the loop body. Consequently, the loop body executes at least once regardless of the condition. The syntax for the do-while loop is as follows:

```
do {
    # code block to be executed
} while (condition)
```

Consider this example of a do-while loop:

```
BEGIN {
    count = 1
    do {
        print "Count is: " count
        count++
    } while (count <= 5)
}
```

This script behaves similarly to the previous example, with the key difference being that the loop body is guaranteed to execute at least once since the condition is evaluated after the body.

```
Count is: 1
Count is: 2
Count is: 3
Count is: 4
Count is: 5
```

The choice between while and do-while loops depends on the specific needs of the algorithm being implemented. If the loop body should execute zero or more times, the while loop is appropriate. If the loop body should execute at least once, the do-while loop is a better option.

To illustrate a practical use case, consider processing a file where each line contains numerical values. The goal is to calculate the sum of numbers until a specific threshold is reached. Below is an AWK script using the while loop for this task:

```
BEGIN {
    threshold = 100
```

```
    sum = 0
    while (getline < "data.txt" > 0) {
        sum += $1
        if (sum >= threshold) {
            break
        }
    }
    print "Sum reached: " sum
}
```

In this script, the while loop reads each line from data.txt and adds the first field $1 to sum. Once sum reaches or exceeds the threshold, the loop terminates.

```
Sum reached: 102
```

Similarly, a do-while loop can be employed to ensure that at least one line is processed before the condition is checked:

```
BEGIN {
    threshold = 100
    sum = 0
    do {
        if (getline < "data.txt" <= 0) {
            break
        }
        sum += $1
    } while (sum < threshold)
    print "Sum reached: " sum
}
```

In this scenario, the script guarantees that the first line is read and processed before evaluating the condition.

```
Sum reached: 105
```

These examples underscore the flexibility and utility of while and do-while loops in AWK programming. Being able to choose the right loop structure based on the requirements allows for more precise and effective data handling.

5.4 The for Loop in AWK

The for loop in AWK provides a powerful mechanism to iterate over ranges of values or elements in an array. It offers flexibility and control, allowing complex logic implementations efficiently. In this section, we will explore the syntax, usage scenarios, and nuances of the for loop in AWK, along with illustrative examples.

Basic For Loop Syntax

A basic for loop in AWK has three main components: initialization, condition, and increment. The general syntax is as follows:

```
for (initialization; condition; increment)
{
    // Body of the loop
}
```

- initialization: Sets up the loop control variable. - condition: A boolean expression that is evaluated before each iteration. If true, the loop body is executed; if false, the loop terminates. - increment: Updates the loop control variable after each iteration.

Example: Iterating Over a Range

Consider a scenario where we want to print numbers from 1 to 5. The corresponding for loop in AWK looks like this:

```
BEGIN {
    for (i = 1; i <= 5; i++)
        print i
}
```

```
1
2
3
4
5
```

The initialization sets i to 1, the condition checks if $i <= 5$, and the increment increases i by 1 after each iteration. The loop prints the value of i in each iteration until i exceeds 5.

Nested For Loops

AWK supports nested for loops, which are loops within loops. These are particularly useful in scenarios like matrix operations or when dealing with multi-dimensional arrays.

```
BEGIN {
    for (i = 1; i <= 3; i++) {
        for (j = 1; j <= 3; j++) {
            print "i = " i ", j = " j;
        }
    }
}
```

```
i = 1, j = 1
i = 1, j = 2
i = 1, j = 3
i = 2, j = 1
i = 2, j = 2
i = 2, j = 3
i = 3, j = 1
i = 3, j = 2
i = 3, j = 3
```

Here, the outer loop iterates i from 1 to 3, and for each iteration of the outer loop, the inner loop iterates j from 1 to 3, producing a series of combinations.

For-In Loops: Iterating Over Arrays

AWK provides another form of the for loop specifically designed for iterating over elements in an array. The syntax uses the in keyword:

```
for (index in array)
{
    // Body of the loop
}
```

Example: Iterating Over Array Elements

Consider an array of student grades:

```
BEGIN {
    grades["Alice"] = 85;
    grades["Bob"] = 92;
    grades["Charlie"] = 88;

    for (student in grades)
        print student, grades[student];
}
```

```
Alice 85
Bob 92
Charlie 88
```

In this example, the loop iterates over each student in the grades array and prints out the student's name and corresponding grade.

Handling Unordered Arrays

It is important to note that the iteration order when using for-in loops over arrays is not specified. AWK does not guarantee any particular order in which the elements are accessed. This behavior underscores the importance of not relying on any specific order when using for-in loops.

Using Unlabeled in a For Loop

In certain situations, the condition part of a for loop could be omitted. This creates an infinite loop, which can be controlled using break or exit statements to terminate the loop under specific conditions.

```
BEGIN {
    sum = 0;
    for (i = 1; ; i++) {
        sum += i;
        if (sum > 50)
            break;
    }
    print "Sum:", sum, "Iterations:", i;
}
```

```
Sum: 55 Iterations: 11
```

In this example, the condition part is left blank, making the loop potentially infinite. However, the if (sum > 50) break; statement ensures it terminates when sum exceeds 50. This demonstrates an advanced use case where the loop control flows based on logical conditions rather than just a numerical condition.

Proper utilization of the for loop in AWK can significantly enhance script performance and readability, especially when dealing with complex data processing tasks. Understanding the mechanics and flexibility of for loops is essential for mastering AWK programming.

5.5 Using break and continue

In AWK, the break and continue statements are crucial for controlling the flow within loops. Understanding the behavior and correct usage of these statements enables the development of more sophisticated and efficient scripts. This section details how these statements function and provides practical examples of their application within while, do-while, and for loops.

The break statement is employed to exit a loop prematurely, irrespective of the loop's condition. When break is invoked, the control of the program is transferred to the statement immediately following the loop. This is particularly useful for scenarios where certain conditions, when met, require the cessation of further iterations.

Consider the following example, which uses the break statement within a while loop:

```
BEGIN {
    i = 1
    while (i <= 10) {
        if (i == 5) {
            break
```

```
        }
        print i
        i++
    }
}
```

In this script, the output will be:

```
1
2
3
4
```

When i equals 5, the if condition evaluates to true, and the break statement terminates the loop. Therefore, the values 5 through 10 are not printed.

The continue statement, on the other hand, skips the remaining statements in the current iteration and proceeds with the next iteration of the loop. This statement is useful for situations where specific conditions necessitate bypassing the rest of the loop's body.

Examine the following example using the continue statement:

```
BEGIN {
    for (i = 1; i <= 10; i++) {
        if (i % 2 == 0) {
            continue
        }
        print i
    }
}
```

The output of this script will be:

```
1
3
5
7
9
```

Here, continue is invoked when i is an even number (i.e., when i % 2 == 0), causing the print statement to be bypassed for those iterations.

Both break and continue can be used within nested loops, affecting only the innermost loop where they are called. Consider the following example:

```
BEGIN {
    for (i = 1; i <= 3; i++) {
        for (j = 1; j <= 3; j++) {
            if (j == 2) {
                continue
            }
            print "i =", i, "j =", j
        }
    }
```

```
}
```

This nested loop will produce the following output:

```
i = 1 j = 1
i = 1 j = 3
i = 2 j = 1
i = 2 j = 3
i = 3 j = 1
i = 3 j = 3
```

In this case, when j equals 2, the continue statement causes the loop to skip directly to the next iteration of the inner for loop, leaving the values $j = 2$ unprinted.

Similarly, here is an example with the break statement:

```
BEGIN {
    for (i = 1; i <= 3; i++) {
        for (j = 1; j <= 3; j++) {
            if (j == 2) {
                break
            }
            print "i =", i, "j =", j
        }
    }
}
```

The output will be:

```
i = 1 j = 1
i = 2 j = 1
i = 3 j = 1
```

In this script, when j equals 2, the break statement terminates the inner loop, and the next iteration of the outer loop begins.

These usage patterns of break and continue in AWK demonstrate their effectiveness in managing loop execution. By allowing sensitive control over the program flow, they are powerful tools in a programmer's arsenal for fine-tuning program behavior for various conditions and scenarios. This refined control is essential in writing precise, efficient, and readable scripts.

5.6 The exit Statement

The exit statement in AWK provides a mechanism to terminate the execution of an AWK program prematurely. This can be particularly useful in scenarios where further processing is unnecessary or conditional requirements mandate an early termination. The basic syntax and usage of the exit statement are straightforward, but its proper application requires understanding its interaction with both control structures and the overall program flow.

The exit statement can be called with or without an optional numeric argument. The general form is as follows:

```
exit [expression]
```

Here, expression is optional and, if provided, sets the exit status of the AWK program. By default, if no expression is given, AWK exits with a status of zero (indicating successful execution).

Consider the following example where the exit statement is used without an expression:

```
BEGIN {
    print "Starting the processing..."
    if (some_condition) {
        print "Condition met, exiting program."
        exit
    }
    print "This will not be printed if exit is executed."
}
```

If some_condition evaluates to true, the program prints the message "Condition met, exiting program." and then terminates. Consequently, the last print statement will not execute.

When the exit statement is provided with an expression, this expression can relay an exit status back to the operating system. This is particularly helpful for scripts whose success or failure needs to be interpreted by other scripts or system processes.

```
BEGIN {
    if (error_occurred) {
        print "An error occurred, exiting with status 1."
        exit 1
    }
}
```

In this case, if error_occurred is true, the AWK script exits with a status of 1, traditionally used to signal an error condition to the calling environment.

An interesting aspect of the exit statement is its interaction with the END block. Even if exit is called in the main body of the script, AWK will still execute the END block, unless the exit statement itself is located within this block.

```
BEGIN {
    print "Processing records..."
}
```

```
{
    if (\$1 == "stop") {
        print "Stop record encountered, exiting."
        exit
    }
}

END {
    print "This message will still be printed."
}
```

Here, if the first field of any record is "stop", the script prints "Stop record encountered, exiting." and terminates the main processing loop. However, the "This message will still be printed." line within the END block will execute, demonstrating that the END block is always respected.

Another example demonstrates using exit to conditionally terminate processing based on specific input data:

```
{
    if (\$1 == "error") {
        print "Error detected in line: " \$0
        exit 1
    }
    # Normal processing code
}
```

If the script detects a record whose first field is "error", it prints the error message and exits with status 1, signaling an error condition to the calling environment.

When dealing with nested control structures, the use of exit within these blocks abides by the same principles. It terminates the overall script execution, not just the current loop or conditional block.

```
{
    if (\$1 == "critical") {
        while (some_condition) {
            if (some_other_condition) {
                print "Critical error encountered."
                exit 2
            }
        }
    }
}
```

In this script, upon encountering a line with the first field as "critical", the script enters a while loop. If some_other_condition is true, the script prints "Critical error encountered." and exits with status 2, handling critical conditions urgently.

The exit statement's utility extends beyond signaling conditions and terminating processing—it informs debugging practices and controlled script behavior under different operational contexts, ensuring AWK scripts align with precise operational requirements.

5.7 Pattern Matching with Control Structures

In AWK, pattern matching is an essential feature that allows for the selection of specific records for processing based on patterns in their contents. Pattern matching can be seamlessly integrated with control structures to create powerful and efficient data processing scripts. This section will delve into how pattern matching can be combined with various control structures, providing detailed examples and explanations to enhance understanding.

One of the fundamental elements in AWK's pattern matching is the use of regular expressions. Regular expressions enable the specification of complex search patterns, which can be utilized in conditional statements and loops to control the flow of the program based on specific criteria.

Pattern Matching in Conditional Statements

The if statement in AWK can be combined with pattern matching to execute certain actions only when data matches a specified pattern. The syntax for incorporating pattern matching within an if statement is straightforward:

```
if ($0 ~ /pattern/) {
    # Actions to be executed if the pattern matches
}
```

In this snippet, $0 refers to the entire record, and the ~ operator checks if the record matches the specified regular expression /pattern/. If there is a match, the actions encapsulated within the braces are executed.

Consider the following example, which processes a list of names and prints those that contain the substring "Smith":

```
BEGIN { FS = "," }
{
    if ($0 ~ /Smith/) {
        print $0
    }
}
```

The if statement here checks each record ($0) for the presence of the substring "Smith". If a match is found, the entire record is printed.

Combining Pattern Matching with Loops

Pattern matching can also be integrated within loops, allowing for iterative processing until a condition is met. This is particularly useful when dealing with large datasets where specific patterns need to be identified repeatedly.

Consider the following example, which counts the number of records that match a certain pattern:

```
BEGIN { count = 0 }
{
    if ($0 ~ /pattern/) {
        count++
    }
}
END {
    print "Number of matching records: " count
}
```

In this example, the count variable is incremented each time a record matching the specified pattern is encountered. The result is printed at the end of the processing.

Using while and do-while Loops

The while loop can be used in conjunction with pattern matching to repeatedly execute a block of code as long as a certain condition holds true. Here is an example:

```
BEGIN { FS = " " }
{
    i = 1
    while (i <= NF) {
        if ($i ~ /pattern/) {
            print "Match found at field " i ": " $i
        }
        i++
    }
}
```

In this script, the while loop iterates through each field of the current record (NF contains the number of fields). The if statement inside the loop checks if the current field matches the specified pattern and prints a message if a match is found.

Similarly, the do-while loop performs the actions at least once before checking the condition:

```
BEGIN { FS = " " }
{
```

```
    i = 1
    do {
        if ($i ~ /pattern/) {
            print "Match found at field " i ": " $i
        }
        i++
    } while (i <= NF)
}
```

The for Loop with Pattern Matching

For loops provide another means to integrate pattern matching, especially when iterating over a known range. Here is a typical usage:

```
BEGIN { FS = " " }
{
    for (i = 1; i <= NF; i++) {
        if ($i ~ /pattern/) {
            print "Match found at field " i ": " $i
        }
    }
}
```

This example demonstrates iterating over each field within a record, checking for matches, and printing the matching fields.

Pattern Matching with switch Statements

AWK's switch statement also supports pattern matching. This can be especially useful when dealing with multiple patterns. Here is an example:

```
BEGIN { FS = " " }
{
    for (i = 1; i <= NF; i++) {
        switch ($i) {
            case /pattern1/:
                print $i " matches pattern1"
                break
            case /pattern2/:
                print $i " matches pattern2"
                break
            default:
                print $i " does not match any pattern"
        }
    }
}
```

This script checks each field against multiple patterns and executes corresponding actions based on the matched pattern.

Pattern matching within control structures significantly extends AWK's capability to handle complex text processing tasks. By combining conditional statements, loops, and the switch statement with pattern matching, it is possible to create robust scripts that can efficiently process and analyze large datasets.

5.8 Nested Control Structures

Nested control structures in AWK allow you to build complex logical flows by placing one control structure inside another. This technique expands the capability of your AWK scripts, enabling them to handle multifaceted scenarios through hierarchical logic. Nesting can be applied to conditional statements, loops, and even combinations of both. For clarity and consistency, understand the precedence and scope rules that govern these structures in AWK.

Consider the case of nested if statements. When you need to make multiple decisions based on different conditions, each subsequent if statement can be placed within the preceding one.

```
if (condition1) {
    if (condition2) {
        # actions to take if both conditions are true
    }
}
```

Here, condition2 is checked only if condition1 is true. Multiple levels of nesting can be employed, based on the complexity of the logic you wish to implement. Each if block must be properly enclosed within curly braces to maintain the correct scope.

Let's illustrate this with a more complex example involving a combination of nested if statements and loops. Assume we have a dataset where we need to check multiple conditions and perform specific actions based on those conditions.

```
{
    if ($1 > 100) {
        if ($2 == "yes") {
            for (i = 1; i <= NF; i++) {
                if ($i ~ /^[0-9]+$/) {
                    print $i " is a number"
                }
            }
        } else {
            print "Second field is not 'yes'"
        }
    } else if ($1 <= 100 && $1 > 50) {
        while ($1 < 75) {
            print "Value in the first field is between 51 and 75"
            break
        }
    } else {
        print "Value in the first field is 50 or less"
```

```
    }
}
```

In this example: - The outer if checks if the first field ($1) is greater than 100. - If $1 is greater than 100, the script checks if the second field ($2) equals "yes". - If $2 is "yes", the script enters a for loop to process each field in the record that contains only numbers. - If $2 is not "yes", it prints a message indicating this. - If $1 is between 51 and 100, it enters an else if block where a while loop checks if $1 is less than 75 and prints a statement before breaking out of the loop. - If $1 is 50 or less, it executes the final else block.

Nested loops are another common pattern. An outer loop contains an inner loop, allowing the inner loop to execute completely for each iteration of the outer loop. This structure is beneficial for tasks such as matrix operations or complex data parsing.

```
BEGIN {
    for (i = 1; i <= 3; i++) {
        for (j = 1; j <= 3; j++) {
            printf "i = %d, j = %d\n", i, j
        }
    }
}
```

In this code snippet, the inner for loop executes three times for each execution of the outer for loop, resulting in nine total iterations, demonstrating every combination of i and j from 1 to 3.

In real-world applications, nested control structures can be utilized to parse and process multi-dimensional data structures, such as JSON objects or nested CSV files. Consider a nested loop to process such hierarchical data:

```
{
    split($0, fields, ",")
    for (i in fields) {
        split(fields[i], subfields, ":")
        for (j in subfields) {
            print "field: " i ", subfield: " j " = " subfields[j]
        }
    }
}
```

This example demonstrates how to split each record into fields by commas, and then each field into subfields by colons, iterating over both levels to print each subfield value. Proper indentation and consistent brace usage are essential to maintaining readability when managing multiple levels of nesting.

The ability to nest control structures is pivotal in writing advanced AWK scripts. It permits the construction of intricate logic by combining simple, comprehensible parts. By properly employing nesting, you can tackle complex data processing tasks efficiently and effectively.

5.9 The switch Statement

The switch statement in AWK provides a structured and efficient way to handle multiple conditional branches based on the value of a single expression. This is particularly useful when the number of conditions becomes large, making the use of multiple if and else if statements cumbersome and error-prone.

The syntax of the switch statement is as follows:

```
switch (expression) {
    case value1:
        // code to execute if expression == value1
        break
    case value2:
        // code to execute if expression == value2
        break
    ...
    default:
        // code to execute if expression does not match any case
}
```

The expression is evaluated once, and its result is compared with each case value. When a match is found, the corresponding block of code executes until a break statement is encountered. If no match is found, and a default case is provided, the default block executes.

Consider the following AWK script that categorizes numeric grades into letter grades:

```
#!/usr/bin/awk -f

{
    grade = $1

    switch (grade) {
        case grade >= 90:
            print "A"
            break
        case grade >= 80:
            print "B"
            break
        case grade >= 70:
            print "C"
            break
        case grade >= 60:
            print "D"
```

```
            break
        default:
            print "F"
    }
}
```

In this script, the grade variable is evaluated, and the appropriate letter grade is printed based on the case conditions. Note that the conditions use relational operators; it is important that all cases are mutually exclusive, as earlier cases will preclude subsequent ones from being evaluated due to the presence of break statements.

If the script processes a file with the following grades:

```
95
87
72
65
54
```

The output will be:

```
A
B
C
D
F
```

One key consideration in using the switch statement is ensuring that cases are well-defined and ordered correctly, particularly when using ranges or relational operators, as shown above. Misordered cases can lead to incorrect results if a more general case precedes a more specific case.

Switch statements can be nested within other control structures, and vice versa. An example combining if-else with switch demonstrates handling multiple grade categories with additional conditions:

```
#!/usr/bin/awk -f

{
    grade = $1

    if (grade >= 0 && grade <= 100) {
        switch (grade) {
            case grade >= 90:
                if (grade > 95) {
                    print "A+"
                } else {
                    print "A"
                }
                break
            case grade >= 80:
                if (grade > 85) {
                    print "B+"
                } else {
                    print "B"
```

```
            }
            break
        case grade >= 70:
            if (grade > 75) {
                print "C+"
            } else {
                print "C"
            }
            break
        case grade >= 60:
            if (grade > 65) {
                print "D+"
            } else {
                print "D"
            }
            break
        default:
            print "F"
        }
    } else {
        print "Invalid grade"
    }
}
```

Here, the if statement first checks if the grade is in the valid range of 0 to 100. If true, the switch statement further refines the letter grade with distinctions like A+, B+, etc., using nested if statements within each case.

Switch statements can also be applied to string comparisons. Consider a script that categorizes fruits based on their names:

```
#!/usr/bin/awk -f
{
    fruit = $1

    switch (fruit) {
        case "apple":
        case "orange":
        case "banana":
            print fruit " is a common fruit."
            break
        case "kiwi":
        case "mango":
            print fruit " is an exotic fruit."
            break
        default:
            print fruit " is not categorized."
    }
}
```

For an input file containing:

```
apple
kiwi
blueberry
banana
```

The output would be:

```
apple is a common fruit.
kiwi is an exotic fruit.
blueberry is not categorized.
banana is a common fruit.
```

This script demonstrates how multiple case labels can share a single block of code, simplifying logical grouping. For example, "apple", "orange", and "banana" all lead to the same printf statement.

Proper combining and structuring of control flows with switch statements help in developing versatile and maintainable AWK scripts. Direct condition matching through well-organized case blocks reduces potential logical errors and enhances readability. The switch statement thereby becomes an indispensable tool for complex logical implementations in AWK programming, adding robustness and clarity to scripts.

5.10 Error Handling in AWK

Error handling is crucial in AWK programming, providing mechanisms to manage and respond to unusual conditions or runtime errors. Proper error handling ensures robustness and reliability in scripts by gracefully managing unexpected situations.

getline is central to error handling in AWK. This function is versatile, enabling reading lines of input, redirection of input and output, and reading data from commands executed by the system(). When getline encounters an issue, such as an end-of-file or error in reading, it sets the variable ERRNO to a string describing the error.

```
BEGIN {
    while ((getline < "data.txt") > 0) {
        print $0
    }
    if (ERRNO != "") {
        print "Error occurred:", ERRNO > "/dev/stderr"
    }
}
```

When the getline function fails, it returns -1, and ERRNO contains the description of the error. Checking the value of ERRNO immediately after calling getline enables the script to identify and handle specific errors effectively.

For error handling within patterns and actions, the system() function allows the execution of shell commands from within AWK. When system() executes a command, it returns the exit status of that command.

```
{
    command = "grep " $1 " file.txt"
    exit_status = system(command)
    if (exit_status != 0) {
        print "Command failed with exit status", exit_status > "/dev/stderr"
    }
}
```

Here, the system() function executes a command and captures its exit status. By checking this status, the script can determine if the command executed successfully or if it encountered an error.

Incorporating robust error handling requires understanding AWK's built-in functions such as exit, which can be used to terminate the AWK program prematurely.

```
{
    if ($1 == "ERROR") {
        print "Fatal error encountered. Terminating program." > "/dev/stderr"
        exit 1
    } else {
        print $0
    }
}
```

Using the exit function allows the script to terminate execution conditionally. This is particularly beneficial in scenarios where continuing execution may cause further errors or incorrect processing.

AWK's BEGIN and END patterns can be effectively utilized for initialization and cleanup processes, ensuring any necessary resource allocation or error logging occurs systematically.

```
BEGIN {
    error_count = 0
    print "Processing started."
}
{
    if ($1 == "ERROR") {
        error_count++
        print "Error on line", NR, $0 > "/dev/stderr"
    } else {
        print $0
    }
}
END {
    if (error_count > 0) {
        print "Processing completed with", error_count, "errors." > "/dev/stderr"
    } else {
        print "Processing completed successfully."
    }
}
```

In this script, error counts are tracked, and appropriate messages are logged at the beginning and end of processing. This approach ensures a holistic error handling and reporting mechanism.

Integrating AWK scripts into larger systems often necessitates debugging techniques. Setting FS and OFS strategically aids in pinpointing issues.

```
BEGIN {
   FS = ","
   OFS = ","
}
{
   if (NF != expected_fields) {
      print "Field count mismatch on line", NR > "/dev/stderr"
      next
   }
   print $0
}
```

Here, FS and OFS are set to commas, with a check added to ensure each record has the expected number of fields. If the field count does not match, an error message is printed, and the record is skipped.

Combining these techniques facilitates comprehensive error handling in AWK scripts. By leveraging getline, system(), exit, ERRNO, and strategically employing BEGIN and END patterns, error handling in AWK can be robust and effective. This meticulous approach ensures the reliability and maintainability of AWK programs under various conditions.

5.11 Combining Control Structures for Complex Logic

To effectively utilize AWK's full potential, combining various control structures is essential for managing complex logic within scripts. By strategically integrating conditional statements, loops, pattern matching, and more, scripts can handle a broad range of computational tasks in a robust and efficient manner.

Consider the use of nested conditional statements and loops for data validation. Imagine a scenario where you have a data file containing records and you need to validate certain fields before processing them. The following example demonstrates a situation where combining if, for loops, and switch statements lead to a solution for verifying and categorizing data.

```
BEGIN {
    FS = ","
}

{
    for (i = 1; i <= NF; i++) {
        if ($i ~ /^[0-9]+$/) { # Check if the field is numeric
            if ($i > 0 && $i <= 100) {
                print "Field", i, "is a valid percentage:", $i
            } else {
                print "Field", i, "is out of valid range:", $i
            }
        } else if ($i ~ /^[a-zA-Z]+$/) { # Check if the field is alphabetic
            switch ($i) {
                case "admin":
                    print "Field", i, "is admin category"
                    break
                case "user":
                    print "Field", i, "is user category"
                    break
                default:
                    print "Field", i, "has an unknown category:", $i
            }
        } else {
            print "Field", i, "is invalid:", $i
        }
    }
}

END {
    print "Validation complete."
}
```

In this AWK script, the BEGIN block initializes the field separator. The main block iterates over each field in the record to determine its type and validity. The combination of if statements and the switch statement facilitates checking whether the field is numeric, alphabetic, or invalid.

The for loop cycles through all fields in the record (from 1 to NF, the total number of fields). For each field $i, the script first checks if it consists only of digits (numeric) using the regular expression \^[0-9]+$. If the field is numeric, another if statement determines if it falls within the valid range (0-100). Fields outside this range are flagged as invalid percentages.

If a field contains only alphabetic characters (\^[a-zA-Z]+$), a switch statement categorizes the value. Known categories (e.g., "admin" and "user") are recognized, while unknown categories are handled by the default case. Finally, any field that does not meet the numeric or alphabetic criteria is marked as invalid.

The END block simply prints a completion message, signaling the end of the validation process.

Consider a more complex scenario involving nested loops and control transfer commands, break and continue. Suppose you need to process a log file where each entry contains a timestamp, user identifier, and action. The goal is to filter entries based on user activities for specific time ranges, skipping over specific actions, and terminating early when certain conditions are met.

```
BEGIN {
    FS = " "
}
{
    timestamp = $1
    user = $2
    action = $3

    if (timestamp >= "2023-01-01" && timestamp <= "2023-01-31") {
        if (user ~ /^user[0-9]+$/) {
            for (i = 4; i <= NF; i++) {
                if ($i == "SKIP_ACTION") {
                    continue
                }
                if ($i == "TERMINATE") {
                    print "Terminating due to action:", $i
                    break
                }
                print "Processing action for user", user, "at", timestamp, ":", $i
            }
        }
    }
}
END {
    print "Log processing complete."
}
```

In this example, the script processes log entries by validating the timestamp and user identifier, then iterates through subsequent fields representing user actions. The for loop scans actions starting from the fourth field to NF.

The continue command is used to skip over entries marked as SKIP_ACTION, while the break command terminates the loop upon encountering an entry marked as TERMINATE. This combination of commands ensures efficient actionable log entries are processed effectively.

By combining and nesting different control structures, AWK scripts can handle complex logic, ensuring versatility and flexibility in data processing tasks.

Chapter 6

Built-in Functions in AWK

This chapter provides an in-depth look at AWK's built-in functions, including string functions, mathematical functions, time functions, array functions, I/O functions, bitwise functions, and system functions. It explains how to use these functions effectively within AWK scripts and demonstrates combining them for complex tasks. The chapter also introduces user-defined functions, extending AWK's capabilities to meet specific requirements. Mastery of these functions is essential for efficient and powerful text processing.

6.1 Introduction to Built-in Functions

AWK is a powerful text processing language that provides a plethora of built-in functions to aid in various text manipulation and computational tasks. Understanding these functions is crucial for harnessing the full potential of AWK, enabling users to perform complex operations succinctly and efficiently.

Built-in functions in AWK can be categorized into several types: string functions, mathematical functions, time functions, array functions, input/output (I/O) functions, bitwise functions, and system functions. These functions allow users to perform a wide range of tasks, from simple string manipulations to sophisticated mathematical calculations and system interactions. This section introduces these categories, setting the stage for detailed discussions in subsequent sections.

String Functions in AWK handle operations related to string manipulation and examination. Common tasks include changing the case of characters, extracting substrings, and searching for patterns within strings. For instance, the toupper() and tolower() functions convert strings to upper and lower case, respectively:

```
BEGIN {
    text = "Hello World"
    print toupper(text) # Output: HELLO WORLD
    print tolower(text) # Output: hello world
}
```

```
HELLO WORLD
hello world
```

String functions are indispensable when dealing with text data, enabling precise and flexible manipulation of content.

Mathematical Functions provide fundamental mathematical operations including arithmetic, trigonometric, exponential, and logarithmic calculations. These functions are essential for performing numeric computations within AWK scripts. For example, the sqrt() function calculates the square root of a number, while the sin() and cos() functions return the sine and cosine of an angle measured in radians:

```
BEGIN {
    print sqrt(16) # Output: 4
    print sin(3.14159/2) # Output: 1 (approximately)
    print cos(0) # Output: 1
}
```

```
4
1
1
```

Mathematical functions allow for the integration of complex arithmetic and geometric calculations in data processing tasks.

Time Functions in AWK enable the handling of timestamps and time-related operations. They can be used to fetch the current time, format dates, and perform calculations with time intervals. For instance, the strftime() function formats the date and time according to the specified format:

```
BEGIN {
    current_time = systime()
    print strftime("%Y-%m-%d %H:%M:%S", current_time)
}
```

2023-01-01 12:34:56

Time functions are particularly useful in log file analysis and other applications that require date and time manipulations.

Array Functions facilitate operations on associative arrays, which are a unique feature of AWK. These functions can determine the number of elements in an array, check if an index exists, and more. For example, delete removes an element from an array, and length() returns the number of elements:

```
BEGIN {
    fruits["apple"] = 4
    fruits["banana"] = 6
    delete fruits["banana"]
    print length(fruits) # Output: 1
}
```

1

Understanding array functions is essential for managing data collections efficiently within AWK scripts.

Input/Output Functions manage file reading and writing operations. They allow users to open, read from, write to, and close files. The getline function is versatile for reading data from files, standard input, or pipelines:

```
BEGIN {
    while ((getline line < "data.txt") > 0) {
        print line
    }
    close("data.txt")
}
```

[data file content]

Input/Output functions are crucial for interacting with external data sources and destinations.

Bitwise Functions perform operations on the binary representations of integers. Although less commonly used than other function types, they are vital in specific applications such as low-level data manipulation or performance optimization. For example, and(), or(), and xor() functions perform bitwise AND, OR, and XOR operations, respectively:

```
BEGIN {
    print and(12, 10) # Output: 8
```

```
    print or(12, 10) # Output: 14
    print xor(12, 10) # Output: 6
}
```

```
8
14
6
```

Proficiency with bitwise functions is beneficial for tasks that require manipulation of individual bits within integers.

System Functions execute system-level commands and obtain system-level information within AWK scripts. These functions can interact with the operating system's environment, execute shell commands, and access system configuration. For example, system() allows the execution of shell commands:

```
BEGIN {
    system("echo Hello, AWK!")
}
```

```
Hello, AWK!
```

System functions are essential for extending the reach of AWK beyond text processing to broader system-level tasks and integrations.

Understanding and effectively utilizing these built-in functions provides a strong foundation for text processing and data analysis in AWK. As we explore each category in depth in subsequent sections, the examples provided will illustrate practical applications, showcasing the versatility and power of AWK's built-in functions.

6.2 String Functions

AWK provides a robust set of built-in string functions that enable users to perform a wide range of text processing tasks. Understanding and effectively utilizing these string functions is crucial for handling and manipulating text data efficiently within your AWK scripts.

textttlength: The length function returns the number of characters in a string. If no argument is provided, it returns the length of the current record ($0).

```
awk 'BEGIN {print length("AWK Programming")}'
```

15

texttsubstr: The substr function extracts a substring from a given string. It takes two mandatory arguments: the string and the starting position, and an optional third argument specifying the length of the substring. The position is 1-based.

```
awk 'BEGIN {print substr("AWK Programming", 5, 11)}'
```

Programming

textttindex: The index function returns the position of the first occurrence of a substring within a string. If the substring is not found, it returns 0.

```
awk 'BEGIN {print index("AWK Programming", "Prog")}'
```

5

textttmatch: The match function searches for a regular expression in a string and returns the position where the match starts. If the match is found, it sets the built-in variables RSTART and RLENGTH to the start position and the length of the match, respectively.

```
awk 'BEGIN {
    if (match("AWK Programming", "Prog")) {
        print "Match found at position:", RSTART
        print "Match length:", RLENGTH
    }
}'
```

Match found at position: 5
Match length: 4

textttsplit: The split function divides a string into an array based on a given delimiter. It returns the number of elements created. The default delimiter is the space character.

```
awk 'BEGIN {
    n = split("One,Two,Three,Four", array, ",")
    for (i = 1; i <= n; i++) {
        print array[i]
    }
}'
```

One
Two
Three
Four

textttolower: The tolower function converts all characters of a string to lowercase.

```
awk 'BEGIN {print tolower("AwK PrOGramMing")}'
```

```
awk programming
```

texttttoupper: The toupper function converts all characters of a string to uppercase.

```
awk 'BEGIN {print toupper("AwK PrOGramMing")}'
```

```
AWK PROGRAMMING
```

texttsprintf: The sprintf function formats and returns a string without printing it. The syntax is similar to the printf statement, with format specifiers.

```
awk 'BEGIN {formatted = sprintf("Number: %d, String: %s", 42, "AWK"); print
    formatted}'
```

```
Number: 42, String: AWK
```

texttgsub: The gsub function globally substitutes all occurrences of a regular expression with a replacement string in the given input string. It returns the number of substitutions made.

```
awk 'BEGIN {
    str = "red@green@blue"
    gsub("@", " and ", str)
    print str
}'
```

```
red and green and blue
```

texttsub: The sub function substitutes the first occurrence of a regular expression with a replacement string in the given input string. It returns 1 if a substitution was made, and 0 otherwise.

```
awk 'BEGIN {
    str = "red@green@blue"
    sub("@", " and ", str)
    print str
}'
```

```
red and green@blue
```

Employing these string functions effectively can greatly enhance the ability to handle text data within AWK scripts. Mastery of these functions allows for the efficient extraction, manipulation, and formatting of strings, paving the way for more complex text processing tasks. As you become more proficient, combining these functions will enable you to tackle sophisticated text processing challenges with ease.

6.3 Mathematical Functions

AWK provides a variety of built-in mathematical functions to perform arithmetic and transcendental operations efficiently within scripts. Mastery of these mathematical functions enhances the capability to manipulate and analyze numerical data. This section covers the most commonly used mathematical functions available in AWK and demonstrates their usage with examples.

The standard set of mathematical functions in AWK includes:

- $\sin(x)$: Computes the sine of x, where x is in radians.
- $\cos(x)$: Computes the cosine of x, where x is in radians.
- $\tan(x)$: Computes the tangent of x, where x is in radians.
- $\text{atan2}(y, x)$: Computes the arctangent of y/x, which is the angle in radians between the positive x-axis and the point (x, y).
- $\log(x)$: Computes the natural logarithm (base e) of x.
- $\log10(x)$: Computes the base-10 logarithm of x.
- $\exp(x)$: Computes the exponential function of x, e raised to the power x.
- $\text{sqrt}(x)$: Computes the square root of x.
- $\text{int}(x)$: Rounds x to the nearest integer towards zero.
- $\text{rand}()$: Generates a pseudo-random number between 0 and 1.
- $\text{srand}([x])$: Seeds the random number generator using x as the seed. If x is omitted, the current time is used.

Each mathematical function will be illustrated with examples to clarify its usage.

Example 1: Using $\sin()$ and $\cos()$

```
BEGIN {
    x = 1.5708 # approximately pi / 2
    print "sin (/2) =", sin(x)
    print "cos (/2) =", cos(x)
}
```

```
sin( /2) = 1
cos( /2) = 0
```

In the above example, x is set to approximately $\frac{\pi}{2}$. The sine of $\frac{\pi}{2}$ is 1, and the cosine is 0.

Example 2: Using atan2()

```
BEGIN {
    y = 1
    x = 1
    print "atan2(1, 1) =", atan2(y, x)
}
```

```
atan2(1, 1) = 0.785398
```

The atan2(y, x) function computes the arctangent of $\frac{y}{x}$, returning the angle in radians. Here, $\operatorname{atan2}(1, 1)$ equals $\frac{\pi}{4}$, approximately 0.785398 radians.

Example 3: Using log() **and** log10()

```
BEGIN {
    x = 10
    print "log(10) =", log(x)
    print "log10(10) =", log10(x)
}
```

```
log(10) = 2.302585
log10(10) = 1
```

The log(x) function computes the natural logarithm of x, while log10(x) computes the base-10 logarithm. For x = 10, the natural logarithm is approximately 2.302585 and the base-10 logarithm is precisely 1.

Example 4: Using exp()

```
BEGIN {
    x = 1
    print "exp(1) =", exp(x)
}
```

```
exp(1) = 2.718282
```

The exp(x) function calculates e^x. For x = 1, e^1 is approximately 2.718282.

Example 5: Using sqrt()

```
BEGIN {
    x = 9
    print "sqrt(9) =", sqrt(x)
}
```

```
sqrt(9) = 3
```

The sqrt(x) function computes the square root of x. For x = 9, the square root is 3.

Example 6: Using int()

```
BEGIN {
    x = 3.7
    y = -3.7
    print "int(3.7) =", int(x)
    print "int(-3.7) =", int(y)
}
```

```
int(3.7) = 3
int(-3.7) = -3
```

The int(x) function rounds x towards zero. Therefore, int(3.7) returns 3, and int(-3.7) returns -3.

Example 7: Using rand() **and** srand()

```
BEGIN {
    srand(1) # Seed the random number generator
    print "Random number 1:", rand()
    print "Random number 2:", rand()
}
```

```
Random number 1: 0.237532
Random number 2: 0.56634
```

The rand() function generates a pseudo-random number between 0 and 1. The srand([x]) function seeds the random number generator with x. If x is not provided, the current time is used as the seed. By using a fixed seed, 1, the sequence of random numbers becomes reproducible for testing and debugging purposes.

Understanding and leveraging these mathematical functions allows for robust numerical computations within AWK scripts, enabling advanced data analysis and manipulation capabilities.

6.4 Time Functions

Time functions in AWK facilitate the handling, manipulation, and formatting of date and time values, paying significant attention to system time. Particularly useful for log processing, data auditing, and temporal data management, these functions are designed to operate uniformly on various platforms.

The principal time-related functions in AWK include mktime(), systime(), and strftime(). Leveraging these functions effectively can significantly improve the efficiency of time-based data operations.

mktime() takes a date/time string as input and returns the corresponding epoch time (number of seconds since January 1, 1970, 00:00:00 UTC). The input format is specific: YYYY MM DD HH MM SS.

```
# Example usage of mktime()
BEGIN {
    datetime_str = "2023 10 15 12 30 00"
    epoch_time = mktime(datetime_str)
    print epoch_time
}
```

The output would be the epoch time corresponding to the provided date and time string.

```
1697371800
```

systime() fetches the current system time as an epoch time. This function is invaluable for time-stamping operations or calculating durations.

```
# Example usage of systime()
BEGIN {
    current_time = systime()
    print current_time
}
```

The output would be the current epoch time when this AWK script is executed.

```
1697371800
```

strftime() formats a given epoch time according to a specified format string, adhering to the conventions of the C library's strftime() function. The format string incorporates standard placeholders:

- %% - a literal %
- %a - abbreviated weekday name
- %A - full weekday name
- %b - abbreviated month name
- %B - full month name
- %d - day of the month (01-31)
- %m - month (01-12)
- %Y - year (e.g., 2023)

- %H - hour (00-23)
- %M - minute (00-59)
- %S - second (00-60)

An example showcasing the strftime() function:

```
# Example usage of strftime()
BEGIN {
    epoch_time = systime()
    formatted_time = strftime("%Y-%m-%d %H:%M:%S", epoch_time)
    print formatted_time
}
```

This script would output the current date and time in the format: YYYY-MM-DD HH:MM:SS.

```
2023-10-15 12:30:00
```

Combining these functions can address more complex scenarios. For instance, calculating the difference between two different time points:

```
# Calculate duration between two time points
BEGIN {
    start_time = mktime("2023 10 15 08 00 00")
    end_time = mktime("2023 10 15 12 30 00")
    duration = end_time - start_time
    print "Duration in seconds:", duration
}
```

Executing this script yields the duration in seconds between the specified start and end times.

```
Duration in seconds: 16200
```

Furthermore, to convert this duration into hours, minutes, and seconds:

```
# Convert duration to HH:MM:SS format
BEGIN {
    duration = 16200 # duration in seconds
    hours = int(duration / 3600)
    minutes = int((duration % 3600) / 60)
    seconds = duration % 60
    printf "Duration: %02d:%02d:%02d\n", hours, minutes, seconds
}
```

The expected output will be in HH:MM:SS format.

```
Duration: 04:30:00
```

Utilizing these time functions, AWK scripts can proficiently manage tasks involving time manipulation, comparison, and formatting essential in many text processing scenarios, such as log analysis or temporal data reporting.

6.5 Array Functions

AWK, an intricate pattern scanning and processing language, incorporates several built-in functions to handle arrays. These capabilities extend AWK's competence in efficient data manipulation and transformation. The ability to use array functions effectively is crucial for optimizing scripts that require handling complex data structures.

split function is fundamental in manipulating strings and placing them into arrays. It divides a given string using a specified delimiter, and the resultant segments are stored as elements in an array. The syntax for the split function is:

```
split(string, array, fieldsep)
```

Where string is the input string to be split, array is the name of the array to hold the divided parts, and fieldsep is the delimiter used. If fieldsep is omitted, the value of FS (field separator) is used.

```
awk 'BEGIN {
  split("a-b-c-d", arr, "-");
  for (i in arr)
    print i, arr[i];
}'
```

```
1 a
2 b
3 c
4 d
```

In this example, the string "a-b-c-d" is split into individual elements of the arr array using the hyphen "-" as the delimiter.

The asort function sorts the elements of an array. It is particularly useful when dealing with data that needs to be ordered. The function's syntax is:

```
asort(source, dest)
```

Here, source is the array to be sorted, while dest is the array where the sorted elements are stored. If the dest parameter is omitted, the sorting is done in place.

```
awk 'BEGIN {
  arr[1] = "orange"; arr[2] = "apple"; arr[3] = "banana";
  asort(arr);
  for (i in arr)
    print i, arr[i];
}'
```

```
1 apple
2 banana
3 orange
```

The sorted values replace the original values in arr.

asort can also be applied for numerical sorting, as demonstrated below:

```
awk 'BEGIN {
  arr[1] = 22; arr[2] = 12; arr[3] = 34;
  asort(arr);
  for (i in arr)
    print i, arr[i];
}'
```

```
1 12
2 22
3 34
```

The asorti function, similarly structured to asort, sorts array indices instead of values. Its syntax is:

```
asorti(source, dest)
```

This function sorts the indices of source array and stores in dest array. If dest is omitted, the indices in source are replaced by the sorted indices.

```
awk 'BEGIN {
  arr["apple"]=1; arr["orange"]=2; arr["banana"]=3;
  asorti(arr, newArr);
  for (i in newArr)
    print i, newArr[i];
}'
```

```
1 apple
2 banana
3 orange
```

A crucial point when sorting arrays in AWK is that sorting criteria cannot be modified. The asort and asorti functions sort arrays in ascending order, and built-in modifications to this behavior involve creating custom sorting algorithms.

The length function, well-known for its use with strings, also applies effectively on arrays. When called with an array argument, it returns the count of the number of elements in the array.

```
awk 'BEGIN {
  arr[1] = "one"; arr[2] = "two"; arr[3] = "three";
  print length(arr);
}'
```

```
3
```

This illustrates the array's element count being returned by the length function.

Deep understanding and correct utilization of these array functions empower the creation of efficient and powerful AWK scripts tailored for complex data processing needs.

6.6 I/O Functions

AWK offers several built-in functions specifically designed for handling input and output operations. These I/O functions provide enhanced control over how data flows into and out of AWK scripts, enabling efficient data processing and manipulation. Understanding and using these functions proficiently can dramatically extend the applicability and power of your AWK scripts.

The most commonly used I/O functions in AWK are getline, print, and printf. Each serves a distinct purpose and can be leveraged in various scenarios to improve the script's performance and readability.

getline is a versatile function that reads input from files, pipes, or standard input. It can be used in several ways:

- getline: Reads the next line from the standard input or the current input file.
- getline var: Reads the next line into the variable var and returns the number of fields read.
- getline < "filename": Reads the next line from the specified file.
- command | getline: Executes the command and reads the next line of output.
- command | getline var: Executes the command and reads the next line of output into var.

Here are code examples demonstrating the usage of getline:

```
# Reading standard input
echo "Hello, World!" | awk '{ getline line; print line }'
```

```
Hello, World!
```

```
# Reading from a file
awk 'BEGIN { getline < "file.txt"; print }'
```

Output will be the first line from file.txt

```
# Executing a command and reading its output
awk 'BEGIN { "ls" | getline; print }'
```

Output will be the first line of the 'ls' command

The print and printf functions are essential for outputting data.

print is straightforward and prints the specified expressions to the standard output, with a space separating each expression and a newline character at the end. The print function can also print to files and pipes.

- print expr1, expr2, ...: Prints the expressions to standard output.
- print expr1, expr2, ... > "filename": Prints the expressions to the specified file.
- print expr1, expr2, ... | "command": Pipes the expressions output to the specified command.

Examples of print usage:

```
# Basic print to standard output
echo "Hello, World!" | awk '{ print "AWK says:", $0 }'
```

AWK says: Hello, World!

```
# Print to a file
echo "Hello, File!" | awk '{ print "File Output:" > "output.txt" }'
```

output.txt will contain "File Output:"

```
# Pipe to a command
echo "Hello, Pipe!" | awk '{ print "Piped Output:" | "cat" }'
```

Piped Output: Hello, Pipe!

printf offers more control over formatting the output. It follows the same syntax as printf in C, allowing precise specification of how the output should appear.

```
# Basic printf usage
echo "123" | awk '{ printf "%s %04d\n", "Number:", $1 }'
```

Number: 0123

```
# Printf to a file
echo "123" | awk '{ printf "Formatted Number: %03d\n", $1 > "formatted_output.txt"
    }'
```

```
# formatted_output.txt will contain "Formatted Number: 123"
```

For advanced I/O handling, combining these functions in AWK scripts allows you to manage large datasets, perform complex text processing, and interact programmatically with system commands. Understanding the intricate details of these functions, such as how they handle file descriptors and buffer management, is crucial for crafting efficient scripts.

6.7 Bitwise Functions

Bitwise functions in AWK provide low-level access to data manipulation at the bit level, enabling complex operations on binary data. These functions are essential when dealing with tasks that require direct bit manipulation, such as implementing custom encryption algorithms, optimizing performance-critical sections of code, and interfacing with hardware devices where operations at the byte or bit level are necessary.

AWK supports several bitwise functions and operators, including bitwise AND (&), bitwise OR (|), bitwise XOR ^(), bitwise NOT (~), and bitwise shift operators (left shift « and right shift »). To make efficient use of these operators, it is crucial to understand their behavior and the precise manipulation they perform on the bits of integer operands.

Below are detailed explanations of each bitwise operator in AWK:

Bitwise AND (&): The bitwise AND operator compares each bit of its two operands. If both corresponding bits are 1, the result in that position is set to 1. Otherwise, it is set to 0.

```
# Example of bitwise AND operator
BEGIN {
    a = 5 # 5 = 0101 in binary
    b = 3 # 3 = 0011 in binary
    result = a & b # result = 0001 in binary
    print result # Output will be 1
}
```

1

Bitwise OR (|): The bitwise OR operator compares each bit of its two operands. If at least one corresponding bit is 1, the result in that position is set to 1. Otherwise, it is set to 0.

```
# Example of bitwise OR operator
BEGIN {
    a = 5 # 5 = 0101 in binary
    b = 3 # 3 = 0011 in binary
    result = a | b # result = 0111 in binary
```

```
    print result # Output will be 7
}
```

7

Bitwise XOR (^): The bitwise XOR operator compares each bit of its two operands. The result in each position is set to 1 if and only if exactly one of the corresponding bits is 1. Otherwise, it is set to 0.

```
# Example of bitwise XOR operator
BEGIN {
    a = 5 # 5 = 0101 in binary
    b = 3 # 3 = 0011 in binary
    result = a ^ b # result = 0110 in binary
    print result # Output will be 6
}
```

6

Bitwise NOT (~): The bitwise NOT operator inverts each bit of its operand (changes 1s to 0s and 0s to 1s). This operation is also known as a bitwise complement.

```
# Example of bitwise NOT operator
BEGIN {
    a = 5 # 5 = 0101 in binary
    result = ~a # result = -6 (if considering 32-bit integers)
    print result # Output will be -6
}
```

-6

Note: The result can vary based on the architecture and how negative numbers are represented in the machine (typically using two's complement representation).

Left Shift («): The left shift operator shifts the bits of its operand to the left by the specified number of positions. Bits shifted out on the left are discarded, and zero bits are shifted in from the right.

```
# Example of left shift operator
BEGIN {
    a = 5 # 5 = 0101 in binary
    result = a << 1 # result = 1010 in binary = 10
    print result # Output will be 10
}
```

10

Right Shift (»): The right shift operator shifts the bits of its operand to the right by the specified number of positions. Bits shifted out on the right are discarded, and the sign bit is shifted in from the left, meaning it can perform sign extension if the number is negative.

```
# Example of right shift operator
BEGIN {
    a = 8 # 8 = 1000 in binary
    result = a >> 1 # result = 0100 in binary = 4
    print result # Output will be 4
}
```

4

Combining these bitwise operators allows for more complex manipulations. Understanding these fundamental operations empowers programmers to perform efficiently a variety of tasks that would be cumbersome using arithmetic operations alone. By mastering these bitwise functions in AWK, programmers can develop high-performance solutions to problems requiring precise control of binary data.

6.8 System Functions

System functions in AWK provide mechanisms to interact with the underlying operating system. These functions can be employed to execute shell commands, handle process IDs, and access environment variables. Understanding these functions allows you to integrate AWK scripts with system-level operations, achieving advanced automation and control.

system():

The system() function is used to execute a shell command from within an AWK script. The function takes a command string as its argument, which it passes to the system shell. The return value of system() is the exit status of the command executed.

```
BEGIN {
    status = system("ls -l")
    print "The exit status of the 'ls -l' command is:", status
}
```

The above script executes the ls -l command using the system shell and prints its exit status. A return value of 0 indicates successful execution, while any non-zero value signifies an error.

ENVIRON:

The ENVIRON array in AWK provides access to the environment variables available to the shell. Each element of ENVIRON is a key-value pair where the key is the name of the environment variable, and the value is its corresponding value.

```
BEGIN {
    print "Home directory:", ENVIRON["HOME"]
    print "Shell in use:", ENVIRON["SHELL"]
}
```

This example prints the user's home directory and the shell that is being used. The ENVIRON array can be particularly useful for retrieving configuration details or passing data between shell and AWK scripts.

getenv():

The getenv() function is an alternative to accessing environment variables directly through the ENVIRON array. getenv() takes the name of the environment variable as its argument and returns its value. This function can be useful in situations where the direct access via ENVIRON might seem cumbersome.

```
BEGIN {
    homeDir = getenv("HOME")
    shellInUse = getenv("SHELL")
    print "Home directory:", homeDir
    print "Shell in use:", shellInUse
}
```

Executing the above script would yield the same results as the previous example, thereby demonstrating the flexibility of using getenv().

close():

The close() function is used to close a file or a pipe that was opened by an AWK script. This function is essential for resource management, especially when dealing with many files or executing numerous system commands.

```
{
    print | "sort > sorted.txt"
}
END {
    close("sort > sorted.txt")
}
```

In this script, the print command pipes the current record to the sort command, which sorts the data and writes it to sorted.txt. The close() function ensures that the pipe is properly closed at the end of processing.

Exec() Functionality Absence:

Unlike some other scripting languages, AWK does not provide a built-in exec() function to replace the current process with a new one. The system() function should suffice for most tasks that might require execution of another program within an AWK script.

Together, these system functions and features empower advanced integration between AWK scripts and the operating system. Leveraging these capabilities allows for complex and efficient workflows that seamlessly combine data processing and system commands.

6.9 Using Functions in AWK Scripts

When using functions in AWK scripts, it is vital to understand how to effectively integrate built-in and user-defined functions to perform sophisticated data manipulations and computations. This section demonstrates practical applications and techniques for leveraging AWK functions within scripts, enhancing both simplicity and efficiency in text processing.

Consider a dataset representing employee information stored in a file named employees.txt:

```
John Doe,Software Engineer,75000
Jane Smith,Data Scientist,85000
Emily Johnson,Web Developer,78000
Michael Brown,System Administrator,82000
```

An AWK script may be employed to process this dataset. The following example calculates the total salary of all employees using built-in mathematical functions and prints the result formatted as currency:

```
BEGIN {
    FS = ","
    total_salary = 0
}
{
    total_salary += $3
}
END {
    printf("Total Salary: $%.2f\n", total_salary)
}
```

Executing this script produces the following output:

```
Total Salary: $320000.00
```

This example demonstrates initialization in the BEGIN block, accumulation within the main processing block, and final output formatting in the END block. The printf function is used to control the numerical format, providing a clear and neatly formatted final result.

In addition to mathematical functions, AWK's string functions allow intricate manipulations of text data. Suppose we want to extract and display only the first names of all employees. The script below utilizes the split function to accomplish this task:

```
BEGIN {
    FS = ","
}
{
    split($1, name, " ")
    print name[1]
}
```

The output of this script will be:

```
John
Jane
Emily
Michael
```

Here, the split function divides the full name into an array using space as the delimiter, allowing the extraction of the first name by accessing the first element of the resulting array.

AWK scripts also excel in handling date and time data through time functions like strftime and systime. Suppose we want to append the current date to each record in our dataset. We would employ the following script:

```
BEGIN {
    FS = ","
    OFS = ","
    current_date = strftime("%Y-%m-%d", systime())
}
{
    print $0, current_date
}
```

The anticipated output might look like this (assuming the current date is 2023-10-31):

```
John Doe,Software Engineer,75000,2023-10-31
Jane Smith,Data Scientist,85000,2023-10-31
Emily Johnson,Web Developer,78000,2023-10-31
Michael Brown,System Administrator,82000,2023-10-31
```

This example demonstrates initializing current_date with the formatted current date and appending it to each record by modifying the output field separator OFS.

Array functions in AWK, such as delete and asort, allow for powerful data manipulations. If we aim to sort the employees based on their salary in ascending order and then print the sorted list, the script might look like this:

```
BEGIN {
    FS = ","
}
{
    employees[$3] = $0
}
END {
    n = asort(employees, sorted_employees)
    for (i = 1; i <= n; i++) {
        print sorted_employees[i]
    }
}
```

After execution, the resulting output will display the sorted records:

```
John Doe,Software Engineer,75000
Emily Johnson,Web Developer,78000
Michael Brown,System Administrator,82000
Jane Smith,Data Scientist,85000
```

By using the asort function, we sorted the array employees and printed the elements in ascending order of salaries.

Finally, integrating system functions like getline enables reading external data within an AWK script. For example, reading a file containing department information and merging it with our employee data:

Contents of departments.txt:

```
Software Engineer,Engineering
Data Scientist,Analytics
Web Developer,Design
System Administrator,IT
```

AWK script to merge employee data with department data:

```
BEGIN {
    FS = ","
    while ((getline < "departments.txt") > 0) {
        dept[$1] = $2
    }
    FS = ","
    OFS = ","
}
{
    print $0, dept[$2]
}
```

Expected output:

```
John Doe,Software Engineer,75000,Engineering
Jane Smith,Data Scientist,85000,Analytics
Emily Johnson,Web Developer,78000,Design
Michael Brown,System Administrator,82000,IT
```

This script demonstrates using getline to read department data into an associative array dept, which is then used to append department information to each employee record.

Effective use of built-in functions in AWK scripts allows for highly flexible and powerful data processing capabilities, streamlining text manipulation and computation tasks.

6.10 Combining Functions for Complex Tasks

Combining built-in functions in AWK allows for the creation of scripts capable of handling complex text processing tasks. By leveraging multiple functions together, we can solve intricate problems efficiently. This section explores several scenarios where combining functions yields powerful results, demonstrating the practical application of theoretical knowledge discussed so far.

We will start by revisiting some of the built-in functions and how they interact together within an AWK script. The key focus will be to understand the synergy between different functions to achieve the desired outcome.

To illustrate the concepts, consider a scenario where we process a log file to extract specific information. The log file entries follow this format:

```
IP_ADDRESS - - [TIMESTAMP] "REQUEST" STATUS_CODE SIZE
```

We aim to:

- Extract and count occurrences of each IP address.
- Calculate the average size of requests.
- Identify the most common status code.

Here is a sample AWK script achieving the above tasks:

```
BEGIN {
    FS = " ";
    print "Processing log file...";
}

{
    # Extract IP address
    ip = $1;
    ip_count[ip]++;

    # Add to total size for average calculation
    total_size += $10;
```

```
    count++;

    # Count status codes
    status_code = $9;
    status_count[status_code]++;
}

END {
    # Print IP address count
    print "IP Address Occurrences:";
    for (ip in ip_count) {
        print ip, ip_count[ip];
    }

    # Calculate average size
    average_size = total_size / count;
    print "Average Request Size:", average_size;

    # Find the most common status code
    max_count = -1;
    for (code in status_count) {
        if (status_count[code] > max_count) {
            max_count = status_count[code];
            common_status = code;
        }
    }
    print "Most Common Status Code:", common_status;
}
```

Explanation

BEGIN Block:

- FS = " " sets the field separator to a space, which is typical for log files with fixed format.
- print "Processing log file..." provides a simple start message.

Main Block:

- ip = $1; extracts the IP address which is the first field.
- ip_count[ip]++; tracks the count for each IP address using an associative array.
- total_size += $10; accumulates the sizes from the tenth field to calculate the average later.
- count++; increments the record count, useful for average calculation.
- status_code = $9; extracts the status code from the ninth field.

- status_count[status_code]++; keeps a count of each status code using another associative array.

END Block:

- The loop for (ip in ip_count) iterates over the ip_count array to print occurrences of each IP.
- average_size = total_size / count; computes the average request size.
- Another loop for (code in status_count) finds the most common status code by tracking the maximum count.

Advanced Combination Example

Assume we now need to identify and report the top 3 IP addresses causing failed requests (status codes 4xx and 5xx). To do this, additional filtering and sorting are required.

Here is the enhanced script:

```
BEGIN {
    FS = " ";
    print "Processing log file...";
}
{
    # Extract fields
    ip = $1;
    status_code = $9;
    size = $10;

    # Only process records with 4xx or 5xx status codes
    if (status_code ~ /^4/ || status_code ~ /^5/) {
        failed_ip_count[ip]++;
        failed_size[ip] += size;
    }
}

END {
    # Create arrays for sorting
    n = 0;
    for (ip in failed_ip_count) {
        n++;
        ip_list[n] = ip;
        size_list[n] = failed_size[ip];
        count_list[n] = failed_ip_count[ip];
    }

    # Bubble sort based on count
    for (i = 1; i <= n-1; i++) {
        for (j = i+1; j <= n; j++) {
            if (count_list[i] < count_list[j]) {
                # Swap
                tmp = count_list[i];
```

```
                count_list[i] = count_list[j];
                count_list[j] = tmp;

                tmp = ip_list[i];
                ip_list[i] = ip_list[j];
                ip_list[j] = tmp;

                tmp = size_list[i];
                size_list[i] = size_list[j];
                size_list[j] = tmp;
            }
        }
    }

    # Print top 3 IP addresses
    print "Top 3 IP addresses causing failed requests:";
    for (i = 1; i <= 3 && i <= n; i++) {
        print ip_list[i], "Count:", count_list[i], "Total Size:", size_list[i];
    }
}
```

Explanation

Main Block:

- The status code is checked using regular expressions status_code ~ /4/ || status_code ~ /5/; to filter 4xx and 5xx codes.
- For filtered records, both failed_ip_count and failed_size associative arrays are updated.

END Block:

- IP addresses and their counts and sizes are transferred into regular arrays ip_list, size_list, count_list to facilitate sorting.
- A bubble sort algorithm organizes the IP addresses based on the count of failed requests in descending order.
- The top three IP addresses are printed with their corresponding counts and total sizes.

Combining AWK's built-in functions synergistically enables handling of complex text processing and data analysis tasks effectively. This structured approach exemplifies the practical application and power of AWK, fostering a deeper understanding and mastery of the language.

6.11 Extending AWK with User-defined Functions

AWK provides powerful built-in functions that significantly enhance its text processing capabilities. However, there are scenarios where built-in functions may not meet specific requirements, necessitating the creation of user-defined functions. These custom functions allow for modular programming, code reusability, and more manageable and readable scripts.

Syntax for User-defined Functions

The syntax for defining a function in AWK is straightforward. A function is declared using the function keyword, followed by the function name, a list of arguments enclosed in parentheses (even if there are no arguments, parentheses are required), and a block of statements enclosed in curly braces.

```
function function_name(arguments) {
    statements
}
```

Arguments and Local Variables

Arguments in AWK functions are treated as local variables within the function. Additional local variables can be declared inside the function to store intermediate results. Here is an example of a user-defined function that calculates the factorial of a number, illustrating the use of arguments and a local variable.

```
function factorial(n) {
    # Local variable to store the result
    result = 1

    # Calculating factorial using a for loop
    for (i = 1; i <= n; i++) {
        result *= i
    }

    return result
}

# Example usage of the factorial function within an AWK script
BEGIN {
    print "Factorial of 5 is:", factorial(5)
}
```

```
Factorial of 5 is: 120
```

Returning Values from Functions

Functions can return values using the return statement. If a function does not explicitly return a value, AWK returns an empty string by default. The returned value can be used directly in expressions, printed, or assigned to variables.

```
function max(a, b) {
    if (a > b) {
        return a
    } else {
        return b
    }
}

# Example usage of the max function
BEGIN {
    x = 10
    y = 20
    print "The maximum value is:", max(x, y)
}
```

```
The maximum value is: 20
```

Function Scope and Recursion

Variables declared inside a function are local to that function and do not affect variables outside the function. AWK also supports recursion, allowing a function to call itself. However, caution is advised to avoid infinite recursion and stack overflow errors. The following example demonstrates a recursive factorial function.

```
function recursive_factorial(n) {
    if (n <= 1) {
        return 1
    } else {
        return n * recursive_factorial(n-1)
    }
}

# Example usage of the recursive_factorial function
BEGIN {
    print "Factorial of 5 is:", recursive_factorial(5)
}
```

```
Factorial of 5 is: 120
```

Passing Arrays to Functions

Arrays in AWK can also be passed to functions. Arrays are typically passed by reference, meaning that changes made to an array inside a function will affect the original array. Here is an example of a function that calculates the sum of elements in an array.

```
function array_sum(arr, n) {
    sum = 0
    for (i = 1; i <= n; i++) {
```

```
        sum += arr[i]
    }
    return sum
}

# Example usage of the array_sum function
BEGIN {
    my_array[1] = 1
    my_array[2] = 2
    my_array[3] = 3
    my_array[4] = 4
    my_array[5] = 5

    print "Sum of array elements is:", array_sum(my_array, 5)
}
```

```
Sum of array elements is: 15
```

Example: Complex Function Combining String and Math Operations

Consider a more complex scenario where we need to normalize a list of numbers (i.e., subtract the mean and divide by the standard deviation). This can be done by combining string and mathematical operations within a user-defined function.

```
function normalize(numbers, n, result, mean, sd, sum, sq_sum) {
    sum = 0
    sq_sum = 0

    # Calculate mean
    for (i = 1; i <= n; i++) {
        sum += numbers[i]
    }
    mean = sum / n

    # Calculate standard deviation
    for (i = 1; i <= n; i++) {
        sq_sum += (numbers[i] - mean) * (numbers[i] - mean)
    }
    sd = sqrt(sq_sum / n)

    # Normalize values
    for (i = 1; i <= n; i++) {
        result[i] = (numbers[i] - mean) / sd
    }

    return result
}

# Example usage of the normalize function
BEGIN {
    numbers[1] = 10
    numbers[2] = 20
    numbers[3] = 30
    numbers[4] = 40
    numbers[5] = 50

    result = normalize(numbers, 5)
```

```
    for (i = 1; i <= 5; i++) {
        print "Normalized value", i, ":", result[i]
    }
}
```

```
Normalized value 1 : -1.26491
Normalized value 2 : -0.632456
Normalized value 3 : 0
Normalized value 4 : 0.632456
Normalized value 5 : 1.26491
```

User-defined functions in AWK improve code clarity by encapsulating complex operations and fostering code reuse across different scripts. They are instrumental in creating robust and maintainable AWK programs suitable for a wide range of text processing tasks.

Chapter 7

Advanced Text Processing with AWK

This chapter delves into advanced text processing techniques with AWK, including sophisticated field manipulation, text substitution, and formatting. It covers working with multi-line records, splitting and joining lines, and handling special characters. Additionally, readers will learn about data validation, cleansing, report generation, file merging, comparison, and error handling. The chapter also explores integrating AWK with shell scripting to enhance its functionality. These advanced techniques enable efficient handling of complex data processing tasks.

7.1 Introduction to Advanced Text Processing

In this section, we delve deep into the advanced capabilities of AWK for text processing tasks that go beyond basic pattern matching and field manipulation. Mastery in these advanced techniques provides the ability to efficiently handle increasingly complex data processing tasks with AWK.

AWK is adept at manipulating text through a variety of built-in functions and constructs. This section will explore sophisticated methods for extracting, transforming, and presenting data, as well as techniques to ensure data integrity and facilitate error handling.

We will begin by reviewing several critical concepts that are foundational to advanced text processing:

- Complex Field Manipulation
- Text Substitution and Formatting
- Multi-Line Record Handling
- Line Splitting and Joining
- Managing Special Characters
- Data Validation and Cleansing
- Report Generation
- File Merging and Comparison
- Error Handling
- Integration with Shell Scripting

By integrating these capabilities, users can leverage AWK to attain exceptional proficiency in text processing, enhancing their workflow and productivity in handling varied data formats.

Complex Field Manipulation: AWK allows intricate operations on fields within a record. Users can perform mathematical operations, text transformations, and conditional modifications. For instance, consider the following AWK script that doubles the value in the second field if it exceeds 100:

```
awk '{ if ($2 > 100) $2 = $2 * 2; print $0 }' input_file.txt
```

The above code demonstrates the use of conditional statements to modify data based on specific criteria.

Text Substitution and Formatting: AWK is equipped with powerful substitution functions that can be used to replace or reformat text. The gsub function in AWK is used to globally substitute all occurrences of a regex pattern within a string:

```
awk '{ gsub(/foo/, "bar", $0); print $0 }' input_file.txt
```

The above script replaces every instance of foo with bar in each record of the input file.

Multi-Line Record Handling: AWK typically processes text line-by-line, but there are scenarios where records may span multiple lines. By setting the RS (Record Separator) and ORS (Output Record Separator) variables appropriately, AWK can be configured to handle multi-line records:

```
awk 'BEGIN { RS="\n\n"; ORS="\n\n" } { print $0 }' input_file.txt
```

Here, each record is separated by a blank line.

Line Splitting and Joining: AWK provides the flexibility to split lines into multiple records or combine multiple lines into a single record. This is particularly useful in transforming data formats:

```
awk '{ printf "%s ", $0 } END { print "" }' input_file.txt
```

The above script concatenates all lines in the input file into a single line.

Managing Special Characters: Special characters such as newline (\n) and tab (\t) can be managed efficiently in AWK. The use of escape sequences allows for precise text formatting and handling:

```
awk 'BEGIN{ FS="\t"; OFS="|"} { print $1, $2, $3 }' input_file.txt
```

In this example, input fields separated by tabs are output with a pipe (|) delimiter.

Data Validation and Cleansing: Ensuring data integrity is a critical task in text processing. AWK can validate and cleanse data by incorporating patterns and conditions to filter out erroneous data:

```
awk '{ if ($2 !~ /^[0-9]+$/) { print "Invalid data in line:", NR; next } print $0 }'
    input_file.txt
```

This script checks if the second field contains only numeric values and flags invalid data.

Report Generation: AWK is capable of generating detailed reports by aggregating and summarizing data. The use of arrays and built-in functions like sum, count, and average can facilitate effective report generation:

```
awk '{ sum+=$2; count++ } END { print "Total:", sum, "Average:", sum/count }'
    input_file.txt
```

This script calculates and prints the total and average of values in the second field.

File Merging and Comparison: AWK can merge multiple files and compare their contents, aiding in the consolidation and comparison of datasets. By using getline, records from multiple files can be read and processed:

```
awk 'NR==FNR { a[FNR]=$0; next } { print a[FNR], $0 }' file1.txt file2.txt
```

In this example, records from file1.txt are printed alongside corresponding records from file2.txt.

Error Handling: Efficient text processing includes robust error handling to ensure smooth execution. AWK scripts can incorporate error handling by using condition checks and informative messages to guide the user:

```
awk '{ if (NF != 3) { print "Error: Incorrect number of fields at line", NR; next } print
      $0 }' input_file.txt
```

This script checks if each record has exactly three fields and prints an error message if not.

Integration with Shell Scripting: AWK's true power is realized when integrated with shell scripts. This combination allows for complex workflows, where AWK handles text manipulation and the shell manages file operations and process control. An example shell script using AWK is:

```
#!/bin/bash
for file in *.txt; do
    awk '{ sum+=$1 } END { print sum }' "$file"
done
```

In this shell script, AWK calculates the sum of the first field for each text file in the directory.

Mastering these advanced techniques in AWK will significantly enhance your capabilities in text processing and data management tasks, enabling you to handle the most challenging scenarios with precision and efficiency.

7.2 Advanced Field Manipulation

In this section, we will explore advanced techniques for field manipulation in AWK. We will cover operations such as reordering fields, creating new fields, and modifying existing field content. These techniques are crucial when dealing with data that require complex restructuring or cleaning.

Reordering Fields

Reordering fields is fundamental when generating custom reports or transforming data into a required format. AWK allows us to specify fields in any order using the print statement. For instance, consider a sample data file data.txt:

```
John,Doe,28,New York
Jane,Smith,32,California
```

To swap the first and second fields:

```
awk -F"," '{ print $2, $1, $3, $4 }' data.txt
```

Output:

```
Doe John 28 New York
Smith Jane 32 California
```

Creating New Fields

Sometimes, it is necessary to create new fields based on existing data. This can be achieved using string concatenation or arithmetic operations. For instance, if you need to create a full name field by combining the first and last names from the previous data file:

```
awk -F"," '{ $5 = $1 " " $2; print $5, $3, $4 }' data.txt
```

Output:

```
John Doe 28 New York
Jane Smith 32 California
```

Here, a fifth field is created which concatenates the first and second fields with a space.

Modifying Existing Fields

Modifying fields involves changing the contents of a field based on certain criteria. For example, to convert all names to uppercase:

```
awk -F"," '{ $1 = toupper($1); $2 = toupper($2); print $1, $2, $3, $4 }' data.txt
```

Output:

```
JOHN DOE 28 New York
JANE SMITH 32 California
```

The function toupper() is used here to convert the first and second fields to uppercase.

Advanced Field Separation

By default, AWK uses any whitespace (spaces or tabs) as the field separator. However, more complex field separations can be achieved using the -F option with regular expressions. For example, consider a data file advanced_data.txt:

```
Name: John Age: 28 Location: New York
Name: Jane Age: 32 Location: California
```

To extract fields based on a colon and a space as delimiters:

```
awk -F": " '{ print $2, $4, $6 }' advanced_data.txt
```

Output:

```
John 28 New York
Jane 32 California
```

Here, -F": " sets the field separator to a colon followed by a space.

Field Manipulation with Conditions

Applying conditions to field manipulations allows for more dynamic data processing. Consider a scenario where you want to increment the age by one only if the location is "California":

```
awk -F"," '{ if ($4 == "California") $3 += 1; print $1, $2, $3, $4 }' data.txt
```

Output:

```
John Doe 28 New York
Jane Smith 33 California
```

In this example, the age of Jane Smith is incremented by one as her location is California.

Using Built-in Variables for Field Manipulation

AWK provides several built-in variables that facilitate field manipulation. Among them, NF (Number of Fields) is particularly useful. For example, to print records that have more than three fields:

```
awk 'NF > 3 { print $0 }' data.txt
```

Output:

```
John,Doe,28,New York
Jane,Smith,32,California
```

Here, NF > 3 is a condition that prints only those records which have more than three fields.

The advanced field manipulation techniques covered in this section equip you with the ability to handle various sophisticated data transformation tasks using AWK efficiently. By mastering these techniques, you can perform complex data restructuring and cleansing operations with ease.

7.3 Text Substitution and Formatting

Text substitution and formatting are pivotal operations in advanced text processing with AWK. These techniques enable the transformation of text data, making it suitable for diverse applications such as data analysis, report generation, and system monitoring. The substitution modifies text patterns within a record, while formatting adjusts the presentation of text according to specific requirements.

Text Substitution

At the core of text substitution is the gsub function, which globally substitutes all instances of a pattern with a replacement string within a record. The syntax for gsub is straightforward:

```
gsub(regexp, replacement, target)
```

Here, regexp denotes the regular expression pattern to be matched, replacement is the string to replace the matched pattern, and target is the string or field in which the replacement occurs. If the target is omitted, the entire record is considered the target.

Consider a scenario where the input file, data.txt, contains the following records:

```
Name: John Doe, Position: Developer
Name: Jane Smith, Position: Designer
Name: Jack White, Position: Manager
```

To substitute the colon (:) with an equal sign (=) across the records, an AWK script can be structured as follows:

```
awk '{gsub(":", "=", $0); print}' data.txt
```

Executing the script will produce the output:

```
Name= John Doe, Position= Developer
Name= Jane Smith, Position= Designer
Name= Jack White, Position= Manager
```

In many scenarios, it's beneficial to perform selective substitutions within specific fields. For instance, to replace the word **Position** with **Role** only in fields containing the job designation, the script may be adjusted:

```
awk '{gsub("Position", "Role", $3); print}' data.txt
```

This command modifies only the third field, leading to the following output:

```
Name: John Doe, Role: Developer
Name: Jane Smith, Role: Designer
Name: Jack White, Role: Manager
```

Text Formatting

Formatting involves aligning and structuring text to achieve a specific layout. AWK provides several built-in functions and capabilities to format text effectively.

A fundamental function for text formatting is printf. Unlike print, which adds a newline by default, printf offers more control over the output format. Its usage resembles that of the C programming language:

```
printf format, argument1, argument2, ...
```

The format string can include placeholders such as %d for integers, %s for strings, and %f for floating-point numbers. Consider formatting the records in data.txt into a neatly aligned table:

```
awk 'BEGIN { printf "%-15s %-15s\n", "Name", "Role" }
    {
        name = $2 " " $3
        role = $5
        printf "%-15s %-15s\n", name, role
    }' data.txt
```

The output of this script will be:

```
Name            Role
John Doe        Developer
Jane Smith      Designer
Jack White      Manager
```

Here, %-15s ensures that each string occupies a minimum width of 15 characters, left-justified. This alignment is particularly useful for producing readable and structured reports.

Another crucial aspect of formatting is manipulating the appearance of numbers. Consider a data file, sales.txt, with monthly sales figures:

```
January 12345.67
February 23456.78
March 34567.89
```

To format these figures into a currency format with comma separation and two decimal places, AWK can employ the following script:

```
awk '{printf "%-10s %\'12.2f\n", $1, $2}' sales.txt
```

This will yield the output:

```
January     12,345.67
February    23,456.78
March       34,567.89
```

The format specifier %12.2f includes a comma (locale's thousands separator) for every thousand units and restricts the floating-point number to two decimal places.

Additionally, AWK can handle date and time formatting. For a record containing a timestamp, such as 2023-04-25 10:30:00, one can use strftime function to reformat the date-time string. For example,

```
awk '{ timestamp=$1 " " $2;
    formatted_time=strftime("%B %d, %Y %I:%M %p", mktime(gensub(/[-:]/, " ", "g
        ", timestamp)))
    print formatted_time }' datetime.txt
```

If datetime.txt contains:

```
2023-04-25 10:30:00
```

The output, after reformatting, will be:

```
April 25, 2023 10:30 AM
```

In this section, we discussed sophisticated techniques for text substitution using gsub and detailed formatting using printf and strftime. These methods are essential for converting raw text data into structured and user-friendly formats, which are applicable in multiple domains of data processing and report generation. The practicality of these techniques in real-world scenarios cannot be overstated, as they form the foundation for efficient text data handling and presentation.

7.4 Working with Multi-line Records

In text processing with AWK, a significant challenge can arise when dealing with multi-line records. Standard AWK operations generally assume that each record is a single line, delimited by the newline character. To extend AWK's functionality for multi-line records, we can manipulate the RS and ORS variables. These variables, which stand for Record Separator and Output Record Separator respectively, control how AWK reads and outputs records.

Modifying the RS variable allows AWK to treat a different character, or a regular expression pattern, as the record delimiter. This functionality is particularly useful when dealing with data formats where records span multiple lines. By changing the record separator, we enable AWK to treat blocks of lines as single records.

```
awk 'BEGIN { RS = ""; FS = "\n" } { print "Record:", $0 }' filename
```

In this example, setting RS to an empty string (") makes AWK treat blank lines as separators between records. This allows it to read multiple lines grouped by blank lines as single records. The FS variable is set to newline characters, which makes each line within the multi-line record a separate field.

When manipulating fields within multi-line records, consider the following AWK script:

```
awk 'BEGIN { RS = ""; FS = "\n" }
{
    for (i = 1; i <= NF; i++) {
        print "Field", i, ":", $i
    }
}' filename
```

Here, NF provides the number of fields in the current record, and the script iterates through each field within the multi-line record, printing it. This handling is crucial for advanced text processing tasks requiring multi-line record manipulation.

To delve deeper into practical applications, let's consider processing log files where entries for each event span multiple lines. Assume a log entry is separated by a unique delimiter 'END'.

```
awk 'BEGIN { RS = "END"; FS = "\n" }
{
    print "Event start:";
    for (i = 1; i <= NF; i++) {
        print " -", $i
```

```
    }
    print "Event end.\n"
}' logfile
```

This script sets RS to the string 'END', allowing AWK to treat each event as a record, irrespective of its length in lines. The FS variable remains the newline character, making each line within the event a field.

For tasks where you need to combine lines into single records based on patterns, consider using a regular expression for RS. For instance, if entries start with a timestamp and the goal is to group each entry into a record for processing:

```
awk 'BEGIN { RS = "\n[0-9]{4}-[0-9]{2}-[0-9]{2} "; FS = "\n" }
{
    print "Log Entry starts:";
    for (i = 1; i <= NF; i++) {
        print " -->", $i
    }
    print "Log Entry ends.\n"
}' logfile
```

In this example, RS is set to match a newline followed by a date stamp in 'YYYY-MM-DD' format, allowing each log entry starting with a date to be read as a complete record.

To transform multi-line records into single-line records for further processing, adjust the ORS variable. Suppose preprocessing is required to collapse multiline entries into a single line.

```
awk 'BEGIN { RS = ""; FS = "\n"; ORS = " " }
{
    for (i = 1; i <= NF; i++) {
        print $i
    }
    print "\n"
}' filename
```

This script sets ORS to a space, causing AWK to print fields of each multi-line record separated by a space on a single line. After looping through all fields, a newline is printed to start a new record.

Comprehensive multi-line record manipulation can significantly enhance data processing efficiency and accuracy, addressing complex text structuring within files. By utilizing AWK's record and field separator features effectively, even the most intricately formatted data can be processed seamlessly.

Advanced usage involves dynamically setting RS and FS within the script. Such flexibility proves advantageous when processing varying data formats or dynamically adapting to different record structures. This dynamic capability underscores AWK's powerful versatility for handling multi-line records proficiently.

7.5 Splitting and Joining Lines

When working with text files in AWK, there are frequent occasions where the functionality of splitting lines into more manageable parts or joining lines together is essential. In this section, we will explore advanced techniques for these operations, enabling efficient text processing and data manipulation.

Splitting lines in AWK is often necessary when dealing with large records that need to be broken down into smaller, more digestible pieces. Conversely, joining lines is useful when data spans multiple lines, and a unified record is required. These operations enhance flexibility and control over the input records, making AWK a powerful tool for various data processing tasks.

The simplest approach to split a line is by utilizing the built-in split() function. This function divides a string into an array based on a specified delimiter. The syntax for split() is as follows:

```
split(string, array, fieldsep)
```

Here, string is the input text, array is the target array where the split parts are stored, and fieldsep is the delimiter defining where the splits occur.

```
$ echo "apple,banana,cherry" | awk '{
    split($0, fruits, ",");
    for (i in fruits) {
        print fruits[i]
    }
}'
```

The output of this code would be:

```
apple
banana
cherry
```

This example reads a comma-separated string and splits it into an array called fruits. Each element of the array is then printed on a new line. Using the split() function is highly effective when lines contain structured delimiters and a straightforward split is needed.

In more complex scenarios, such as splitting a line with multiple delimiters or specific conditions, regular expressions can be utilized as field separators. For instance, consider a text where fields are separated by a mix of commas and semicolons. The following AWK command handles such a situation:

```
$ echo "apple,banana;cherry,grape" | awk '{
    split($0, fruits, /[,;]+/);
    for (i in fruits) {
        print fruits[i]
    }
}'
```

Output:

```
apple
banana
cherry
grape
```

In this case, the regular expression /[;,]+/ serves as the delimiter in the split() function, ensuring that both commas and semicolons are considered splitting points.

Joining lines involves concatenating multiple lines into a single record. One can achieve this by reading successive lines and appending their content. The approach retains each line's original sequencing while combining them into a single output line. The following example demonstrates how to join lines in AWK:

```
awk '{
    if (NR > 1)
        printf "%s ", $0
    else
        printf "%s", $0
}' file.txt
```

This code fragment appends a space between lines and prints the result as a continuous string. The NR variable represents the current record number, allowing for conditional logic to handle the first line differently (without preceding it with a space).

To join lines based on a specific condition, such as presence or absence of a certain pattern, we can harness AWK's pattern matching capabilities. Consider a scenario where lines that begin with a hash (#) are comments in a configuration file, and those comments should remain separate while non-comment lines are concatenated:

```
awk '{
    if ($0 ~ /^#/) {
        if (result != "") {
            print result;
            result = "";
        }
```

```
        print $0;
    } else {
        result = (result == "") ? $0 : result " " $0;
    }
}
END {
    if (result != "") {
        print result;
    }
}' config.txt
```

Output:

```
# Comment 1
data line 1 data line 2 data line 3
# Comment 2
data line 4 data line 5
```

This script checks if the current line matches a pattern (starting with #). If it does, any previously accumulated data lines (result) are printed, and the comment line is printed as a separate entity. Non-comment lines are concatenated into the result variable.

Efficient line splitting and joining are crucial in text processing tasks, enabling refined control over input and output data formats. Whether parsing complex logs, transforming datasets, or preparing data for further analysis, these techniques underpin numerous advanced AWK operations.

7.6 Dealing with Special Characters

When processing text data with AWK, special characters often play a crucial role and require careful handling. Special characters can include whitespace characters (spaces, tabs, newlines), delimiters, and various punctuation marks. Properly managing these characters ensures accurate data extraction and manipulation.

Special characters must often be escaped or handled differently to prevent misinterpretation by AWK's pattern matching and field separation mechanisms. This section will cover techniques for dealing with these characters effectively, including escaping special characters, using character classes, and employing built-in AWK functions.

Escaping Special Characters:

In AWK, certain characters like the backslash (\), double quotes ("), and dollar sign ($) have special meanings and must be escaped with a backslash if they are to be interpreted literally. For example, to match a literal dollar sign in a pattern, use \$.

```
# Escape the dollar sign to match literal '$' character
awk '/\$[0-9]+/' prices.txt
```

This example matches lines in prices.txt that contain a dollar sign followed by one or more digits, such as \$5 or \$100.

Using Character Classes:

Character classes in AWK allow you to define a set of characters to match in a pattern. Character classes are specified by enclosing the set in square brackets. For instance, to match any punctuation mark, you can use the character class [:punct:].

```
# Match lines containing any punctuation
awk '/[[:punct:]]/' textfile.txt
```

This command prints all lines in textfile.txt that contain at least one punctuation character.

Whitespace Handling:

Whitespace characters, such as spaces and tabs, are commonly used as field separators. AWK's default field separator (FS) is any whitespace, meaning it splits records into fields based on spaces or tabs. However, if your data contains multiple consecutive spaces that should be treated as a single separator, you can adjust the FS variable accordingly.

```
# Set field separator to a space to handle multiple consecutive spaces
awk 'BEGIN { FS = " " } { print $1, $2 }' datafile.txt
```

If a single space is desired as the delimiter even when data contains multiple consecutive spaces:

```
# Remove consecutive spaces using gsub before splitting
awk '{ gsub(/ +/, " "); $1=$1; print $1, $2 }' datafile.txt
```

In this example, gsub(/ +/, " ") replaces multiple consecutive spaces with a single space.

Handling Newlines and Multi-line Records:

AWK processes input line by line, but certain cases might require processing multi-line records, especially when records are separated by a blank line or a specific pattern. To handle such cases, the RS and ORS (record separator and output record separator) can be redefined.

If records are separated by blank lines:

```
# Set record separator to blank lines
awk 'BEGIN { RS = "" } { print $1 }' multilinefile.txt
```

This command treats each paragraph as a single record, allowing AWK to process multi-line records seamlessly.

Built-in String Functions:

AWK provides several built-in functions to manipulate strings that include special characters. Functions like index, length, substr, and match can be useful in these scenarios.

For example, to find the position of a special character within a string:

```
awk '{ pos = index($0, "#"); if (pos > 0) print "Found # at position", pos }' file.txt
```

This script searches for the presence of the # character in each line of file.txt and prints its position if found.

By incorporating these techniques, you can handle special characters in text data with precision and ease, allowing for more robust text processing tasks in AWK.

7.7 Data Validation and Cleansing

Data validation and cleansing are critical components of any data processing workflow. Ensuring the accuracy and consistency of data is essential for producing reliable results. When working with AWK, we can leverage its powerful pattern matching and text manipulation capabilities to perform sophisticated validation and cleansing tasks.

Data validation involves checking the data against specific criteria to determine its validity. Common validation tasks include verifying numeric ranges, checking string formats, and ensuring data consistency across records. Data cleansing, on the other hand, involves correcting or removing invalid data, handling missing values, and standardizing formats.

Validating Numeric Fields

A common validation requirement is to ensure that certain fields contain numeric values within a specified range. Consider a dataset where the second field should contain ages between 0 and 120. We can write an AWK script to validate this:

```
awk '{
```

```
    if ($2 >= 0 && $2 <= 120) {
        print $0
    } else {
        print "Invalid age:", $2
    }
}' data.txt
```

The script uses a simple conditional statement to check if $2 (the second field) lies between 0 and 120. Valid records are printed as-is, while invalid records are flagged with an error message.

Validating String Formats

Another typical validation task is ensuring that text fields follow a specific format. For example, suppose we need to validate email addresses in the third field. An email address should contain an "@" symbol, and the domain part should include at least one dot. Here is a script to perform this validation:

```
awk '{
    if ($3 ~ /^[a-zA-Z0-9._%+-]+@[a-zA-Z0-9.-]+\.[a-zA-Z]{2,}$/) {
        print $0
    } else {
        print "Invalid email:", $3
    }
}' data.txt
```

In this script, the `$3 ~ /^[a-zA-Z0-9._%+-]+@[a-zA-Z0-9.-]+[a-zA-Z]{2,}$/` expression uses a regular expression to match valid email formats. Records with valid emails are printed, while invalid emails are reported.

Handling Missing Values

Missing values are a common issue in real-world datasets. We can identify and handle missing fields using AWK. The following script prints records where the first field is missing:

```
awk '{
    if ($1 == "") {
        print "Missing value in field 1:", $0
    } else {
        print $0
    }
}' data.txt
```

The condition `$1 == ""` checks for empty values in the first field. Records with missing values are flagged, while valid records are printed normally.

Standardizing Data Formats

Consistent data formats are crucial for accurate analysis. We often need to standardize date formats, phone numbers, or other field types. Consider a dataset with dates in various formats. We can use AWK to convert them to a standard format (e.g., YYYY-MM-DD):

```
awk '{
    if ($4 ~ /^[0-9]{2}\/[0-9]{2}\/[0-9]{4}$/) {
        split($4, a, "/")
        printf("%s-%s-%s %s\n", a[3], a[1], a[2], $0)
    } else if ($4 ~ /^[0-9]{4}-[0-9]{2}-[0-9]{2}$/) {
        print $0
    } else {
        print "Invalid date format:", $4
    }
}' data.txt
```

In this script, dates in the format MM/DD/YYYY are converted to YYYY-MM-DD using the split function, while already standardized dates are printed as-is. Invalid dates are flagged.

Removing Duplicate Records

Duplicate records can skew analysis and must be removed. AWK can easily identify and remove duplicates. Consider a dataset where records are considered duplicates if the first field is identical:

```
awk '!seen[$1]++' data.txt
```

The !seen[$1]++ idiom uses an associative array seen to track unique occurrences of the first field. Only the first occurrence of each unique value is printed.

Combining Validation and Cleansing

In practice, combining multiple validation and cleansing steps in a single AWK script is often necessary. Here is an example script that performs several tasks sequentially:

```
awk 'BEGIN {
    FS = ","
    OFS = ","
}
{
    valid = 1

    if ($2 < 0 || $2 > 120) {
        print "Invalid age:", $2
        valid = 0
    }

    if ($3 !~ /^[a-zA-Z0-9._%+-]+@[a-zA-Z0-9.-]+\.[a-zA-Z]{2,}$/) {
        print "Invalid email:", $3
        valid = 0
    }
```

```
    if ($4 ~ /^[0-9]{2}\/[0-9]{2}\/[0-9]{4}$/) {
        split($4, a, "/")
        $4 = sprintf("%s-%s-%s", a[3], a[1], a[2])
    } else if ($4 !~ /^[0-9]{4}-[0-9]{2}-[0-9]{2}$/) {
        print "Invalid date format:", $4
        valid = 0
    }

    if ($1 == "") {
        print "Missing value in field 1:", $0
        valid = 0
    }

    if (valid && !seen[$1]++) {
        print $0
    }
}' data.txt
```

This comprehensive script:

- Sets both field separator (FS) and output field separator (OFS) to a comma.
- Initializes a boolean flag, valid, to track the validity of each record.
- Validates the age in the second field ($2).
- Checks the email format in the third field ($3).
- Standardizes the date format in the fourth field ($4).
- Verifies that the first field ($1) is not missing.
- Prints only valid, non-duplicate records.

These methods provide a robust framework for data validation and cleansing using AWK, ensuring that datasets are accurate, consistent, and ready for analysis.

7.8 Generating Reports with AWK

AWK excels at generating well-formatted reports from textual data due to its powerful text manipulation features and built-in formatting capabilities. This section focuses on leveraging AWK to create diverse types of reports by summarizing and presenting data in a clear and structured manner.

To begin, consider a scenario where we have a file, sales.txt, containing sales data with the following format:

```
Date,Salesperson,Region,Amount
2023-01-01,John Doe,North,1500
2023-01-01,Jane Smith,South,1800
2023-01-02,John Doe,North,1600
2023-01-02,Jane Smith,South,1700
...
```

We aim to generate a summary report that provides the total sales amount per salesperson. This can be achieved using the following AWK script:

```
awk -F, '
NR > 1 {
    sales[$2] += $4
}
END {
    print "Salesperson,Total Sales"
    for (person in sales) {
        print person "," sales[person]
    }
}
' sales.txt
```

In this script:

- -F, sets the field separator to a comma.
- NR > 1 skips the header line of the input file.
- The sales array accumulates the sales amounts by Salesperson.
- The END block iterates over the sales array to print the report.

Executing this script produces:

```
Salesperson,Total Sales
John Doe,3100
Jane Smith,3500
```

AWK's ability to format its output enables the generation of more elaborate reports. Suppose we want to enhance readability by formatting the output into columns. We can use the printf function:

```
awk -F, '
NR > 1 {
    sales[$2] += $4
}
END {
    printf "%-15s %10s\n", "Salesperson", "Total Sales"
    for (person in sales) {
        printf "%-15s %10.2f\n", person, sales[person]
    }
}
' sales.txt
```

This script formats the output into aligned columns:

```
Salesperson          Total Sales
John Doe                3100.00
Jane Smith              3500.00
```

To further customize the report, consider adding sub-totals per region. Given our data, we can extend the script to include this feature:

```
awk -F, '
NR > 1 {
    sales[$2] += $4
    region_sales[$3] += $4
}
END {
    printf "%-10s %-15s %10s\n", "Region", "Salesperson", "Total Sales"
    for (region in region_sales) {
        for (person in sales) {
            printf "%-10s %-15s %10.2f\n", region, person, sales[person]
        }
        printf "%-25s %10.2f\n", "Region Subtotal", region_sales[region]
    }
}
' sales.txt
```

This adaptation introduces the region_sales array to accumulate sales amounts by region. The output now includes regional sub-totals:

```
Region     Salesperson     Total Sales
North      John Doe          3100.00
North      Jane Smith        3500.00
Region Subtotal             4600.00
South      John Doe          3100.00
South      Jane Smith        3500.00
Region Subtotal             3500.00
```

To further exemplify AWK's reporting capabilities, assume we want to create a monthly summary report from a simplified input file, monthly_-sales.txt:

```
Month,Sales
2023-01,5000
2023-02,6200
2023-03,7000
...
```

The following AWK script generates a summary of the total sales per quarter:

```
awk -F, '
NR > 1 {
    quarter = substr($1, 6, 2)
    if (quarter == "01" || quarter == "02" || quarter == "03") {
        Q1 += $2
    } else if (quarter == "04" || quarter == "05" || quarter == "06") {
        Q2 += $2
    } else if (quarter == "07" || quarter == "08" || quarter == "09") {
        Q3 += $2
    } else if (quarter == "10" || quarter == "11" || quarter == "12") {
        Q4 += $2
    }
}
```

```
END {
    printf "Quarterly Sales Summary\n"
    printf "Q1: %.2f\nQ2: %.2f\nQ3: %.2f\nQ4: %.2f\n", Q1, Q2, Q3, Q4
}
' monthly_sales.txt
```

The script calculates quarterly sales by extracting the month part from the Month field and categorizing it into the relevant quarter. The output presents the quarterly sales summary:

```
Quarterly Sales Summary
Q1: 18200.00
Q2: 0.00
Q3: 0.00
Q4: 0.00
```

AWK's versatility also allows for the generation of more specialized reports, such as those including conditional fields or derived metrics. For instance, if we want to generate a report that highlights salespersons who have exceeded a specific sales threshold, this script demonstrates how:

```
awk -F, '
NR > 1 {
    sales[$2] += $4
}
END {
    threshold = 3000
    printf "Salespersons with Sales Exceeding %d\n", threshold
    for (person in sales) {
        if (sales[person] > threshold) {
            printf "%-15s %10.2f\n", person, sales[person]
        }
    }
}
' sales.txt
```

This script includes a conditional test to filter and report only those salespersons whose total sales exceed the threshold. The corresponding output shows:

```
Salespersons with Sales Exceeding 3000
Jane Smith        3500.00
```

These examples highlight the flexibility and power of AWK in generating customized, structured, and informative reports. By mastering these techniques, the user can efficiently transform raw data into meaningful information suitable for analysis and decision-making processes.

7.9 Merging and Comparing Files

Efficiently merging and comparing files is a critical aspect of advanced text processing with AWK. This section will explore techniques to combine data from multiple sources, perform record comparisons, and check for discrepancies between files. We assume familiarity with basic AWK operation modes and principles discussed in preceding chapters.

To merge files, the NR == FNR idiom is frequently employed, which is an effective method to handle multiline records from multiple files. When processing files with AWK, NR represents the total number of input lines read so far, while FNR denotes the number of lines read from the current file.

The following code snippet demonstrates merging the content of two files, file1.txt and file2.txt, on a common key field:

```
awk 'NR == FNR { data[$1] = $0; next }
{
    if ($1 in data)
        print data[$1], $0
}' file1.txt file2.txt
```

In this code, the initial NR == FNR condition holds true while reading file1.txt. The action block following retrieves the first field ($1), and stores the entire line in the associative array data. Upon entering file2.txt, the condition fails, triggering the print statement for records where the key exists in the data array. The result is a merged file with aligned data rows.

If preprocessing or postprocessing is required, AWK's ability to handle multiple actions across multiple files allows for streamlined workflow configuration. For instance, consider the scenario where fields from file2.txt not present in file1.txt need to be appended and processed:

```
awk 'NR == FNR { data[$1] = $0; next }
{
    if (!($1 in data))
        print $0 > "outputfile.txt"
    else
        print data[$1], $0 > "outputfile.txt"
}' file1.txt file2.txt
```

This script builds on the previous example by ensuring unmatched records from file2.txt are also included in outputfile.txt, preserving comprehensive data integrity.

For the advanced task of file comparison, AWK's robust pattern-matching capabilities excel. Take, for example, a scenario where the objective is to list discrepancies between two files:

```
awk 'NR == FNR { data[$0]++; next }
{
    if ($0 in data)
        data[$0]--;
    else
        print "Only in file2.txt:", $0
}
END {
    for (line in data)
        if (data[line] > 0)
            print "Only in file1.txt:", line
}' file1.txt file2.txt
```

Here, while reading file1.txt, each line is stored in the data associative array with a count. As file2.txt is processed, the script decrements the count for lines present in both files. The END block subsequently identifies and prints lines unique to each file, aiding in efficient file comparison.

Using AWK with additional shell scripting can further enhance its functionality. For more intricate file-merging operations involving multiple criteria or extensive datasets, integrating external tools or commands is often suitable. Consider the combined use of AWK and sort for sorted file mergers:

```
sort file1.txt file2.txt | awk 'BEGIN {prev=""}
{
    if ($0 != prev)
        print;
    prev = $0
}'
```

This script first sorts the contents of file1.txt and file2.txt, feeding the result into an AWK process that eliminates duplicate lines (under the assumption that sorting ensures adjacent duplicates).

Additionally, precise control can be obtained via AWK's scripting flexibility, thus handling myriad edge cases encountered in real-world scenarios. For instance, if field-specific conditions govern the merging process and data from multiple files needs to be carefully integrated, conditional checks and corresponding actions can be implemented:

```
awk 'NR == FNR { key[$1] = $2; next }
{
    if ($1 in key && $2 == key[$1])
        print "Match:", $0
    else if ($1 in key)
        print "Mismatched:", $0, "Expected:", key[$1]
    else
        print "Only in file2.txt:", $0
```

```
}' file1.txt file2.txt
```

This approach ensures only pertinent data is processed based on specific field criteria, offering nuanced control over file handling operations.

Leveraging these advanced AWK capabilities enables robust, efficient, and automated file merging and comparison operations, critical for complex data management tasks.

7.10 Error Handling in Text Processing

Error handling is a crucial aspect of text processing with AWK, particularly when processing large datasets or automating workflows where manual intervention is impractical. Effective error handling ensures that your AWK scripts can gracefully manage unexpected input and runtime errors, maintaining smooth operation and providing informative feedback to the user.

Types of Errors in AWK:

- **Syntax Errors:** These occur when the AWK script contains invalid syntax. AWK typically detects these errors before execution.
- **Run-time Errors:** These occur during the execution of the script and may be due to invalid data, file I/O problems, or command failures.
- **Logical Errors:** These errors arise from incorrect logic in the script, producing unintended results despite correct syntax and run-time settings.

Identifying and Handling Syntax Errors:

AWK provides error messages that help pinpoint syntax errors. For instance:

```
awk '{ print $1, $2 }' inputfile
awk: syntax error at source line 1
 context is
    { >>> print <<< $1, $2
awk: illegal statement at source line 1
```

The message specifies the source line and highlights the problematic code portion. Correcting syntax errors involves carefully reviewing the code against AWK's syntax rules.

Handling Run-time Errors:

Run-time errors often require dynamic checks within the script. Incorporating conditions and error messages can mitigate issues:

```
awk '
BEGIN { if (ARGC < 2) { print "Usage: awk -f script.awk inputfile"; exit 1; } }
{
    if ($1 == "") { print "Error: Missing value in column 1 at line " NR; exit 2; }
    print $1, $2
}' inputfile
```

In this example:

- The BEGIN block checks for the correct number of command line arguments.
- The code within the main block checks for missing values in column 1 and prints an error message, then exits with a non-zero status.

Handling File I/O Errors:

File I/O errors are common when reading from or writing to files. Using the getline function for file handling requires careful error checking:

```
awk '
BEGIN {
    filename = "datafile.txt"
    if ((getline < filename) < 0) {
        print "Error: Unable to read from " filename; exit 3;
    }
}
{
    print $0
}' inputfile
```

The error handling here ensures that any issue in opening datafile.txt results in an appropriate error message and program termination.

Using AWK's Built-in exit Statement:

AWK's exit statement allows for graceful termination of scripts, optionally returning a status code:

```
{
    # Process the record
    if ($1 < 0) {
        print "Negative value in column 1, line " NR; exit 4;
    }
    print $1, $2, $3
}
END {
    if (NR == 0) {
        print "No records processed."; exit 5;
```

```
    }
    print "Processing completed successfully.";
}' inputfile
```

Logical Errors and Debugging:

Logical errors are not flagged by AWK but require thorough testing and debugging to identify. Techniques include:

- **Print Statements:** Use print statements to trace variable values and program flow.

```
{
    print "Debug: Processing line " NR ", value = " $1
    # Further processing
}
```

- **Conditional Breakpoints:** Insert conditions to halt execution under specific circumstances.

```
{
    if (NR == 10) { print "Debug: Reached line 10"; exit 6; }
}
```

Error Codes and Exit Status:

Using consistent error codes facilitates handling errors in shell scripts or higher-level programs. For example:

```
{
    # Some processing
    if (error_condition) {
        print "Specific error message"; exit 7;
    }
    # More processing
}
```

A standard mapping of exit status codes to error types ensures coherent error handling across different scripts and automated systems.

Incorporating robust error handling strategies into your AWK scripts significantly enhances their reliability and maintainability, especially when dealing with critical data processing tasks. This practice ensures that potential issues are detected and addressed promptly, maintaining the integrity and accuracy of the outputs.

7.11 AWK and Shell Scripting Integration

Integrating AWK with shell scripting extends its capabilities and allows for more complex and flexible data processing tasks. By combining the power of AWK with the versatility of shell scripts, it is possible to automate complex workflows, involve multiple data sources, and enhance error handling mechanisms. This section outlines how to effectively use AWK within shell scripts and demonstrates practical examples to elucidate these principles.

To execute an AWK command within a shell script, the basic syntax involves embedding the AWK command inside a shell script file, typically with the extension '.sh'. Here is a basic example illustrating how to use AWK within a shell script to process a text file:

```
#!/bin/bash
# Example Shell Script Using AWK
input_file="data.txt"
awk 'BEGIN {FS=","} {print $1, $2}' "$input_file"
```

The above script sets the input field separator to a comma and prints the first two fields of each line from the file data.txt. The input_file variable stores the filename, which can easily be changed to process different files without modifying the AWK command.

output_example

Shell variables can be passed to AWK commands to make the scripts more dynamic. This is achieved by using the -v option in AWK to assign shell variables to AWK variables:

```
#!/bin/bash
# Script to pass shell variables to AWK
input_file="data.txt"
search_term="pattern"
awk -v term="$search_term" 'BEGIN {FS=","} $0 ~ term {print $1, $2}' "$input_file
"
```

In this example, the shell variable search_term is passed to the AWK variable term. The AWK script then searches each line of data.txt for term and prints the first two fields if the pattern matches.

Complex AWK scripts can be embedded into shell scripts using multiple lines and loops. Consider a scenario where multiple files need to be processed in a loop:

```
#!/bin/bash
# Script to process multiple files with AWK
for file in *.txt
do
  echo "Processing $file..."
  awk 'BEGIN {FS=","; OFS="|"}
     { for (i=1; i<=NF; i++) {
        $i = toupper($i)
      }
      print $0
```

```
    }' "$file"
done
```

This script iterates over all text files in the current directory, converting each field to uppercase and changing the output field separator to a pipe (|). The nested for loop in the AWK command processes each field of the current record.

AWK and shell scripts can also interact with each other by using pipelines for reading input and redirecting output. An example of this is using the ls command to list files and then processing the filenames with AWK:

```
#!/bin/bash
# Script using a pipeline with AWK
ls -l | awk 'BEGIN {print "Permissions\tUser\tFilename"}
             {print $1, $3, $9}'
```

The output of the ls -l command is piped to AWK, which formats the permissions, user, and filenames into a tab-separated format with headers.

It is crucial to handle errors and unexpected scenarios when integrating AWK with shell scripts. Implementing error handling within the script ensures robustness and reliability:

```
#!/bin/bash
# Script with error handling
input_file=$1
if [[ ! -f "$input_file" ]]; then
  echo "Error: File '$input_file' not found!"
  exit 1
fi

awk 'BEGIN {FS=","}
     {
       if (NF < 2) {
         print "Warning: Line " NR " has less than 2 fields" > "/dev/stderr"
       } else {
         print $1, $2
       }
     }' "$input_file"
```

This script checks if the input file exists before processing. During the AWK execution, if any line has fewer than two fields, a warning message is sent to the standard error stream, informing the user of a potential data issue.

In summary, integrating AWK with shell scripting enables enhanced data processing capabilities and automation. Utilizing shell script constructs, variables, and error handling features, along with the powerful text processing abilities of AWK, results in robust and flexible solutions for complex data manipulation tasks. By mastering these techniques, one can significantly improve the efficiency and efficacy of text processing workflows.

Chapter 8

Working with Files in AWK

This chapter focuses on file handling in AWK, covering reading, writing, and appending data to files. It discusses processing multiple files, file redirection, handling file errors, and using AWK with piped input and output. The chapter also addresses temporary files, data streams, file permissions, security, and advanced file management techniques. Mastering these topics is crucial for effectively managing and manipulating files using AWK.

8.1 Introduction to File Handling in AWK

File handling in AWK is essential for automating data processing tasks and efficiently managing file-based data. AWK's ability to read from and write to files extends its usefulness beyond line-by-line text processing, enabling it to operate as a powerful scripting language for various tasks requiring file manipulation. This section provides a foundational understanding of how AWK handles files, setting the stage for more advanced concepts covered later in the chapter.

AWK incorporates built-in functions and operators to facilitate file operations seamlessly. The primary constructs used in file handling include reading, writing, and appending to files, which are facilitated by redirection mechanisms. Understanding these constructs is crucial for efficiently utilizing AWK in practical applications.

```
# Example of reading from a file
awk '{ print $0 }' input_file.txt
```

In this basic example, awk reads the file input_file.txt line by line and prints each line to the standard output. The pattern-action statement {} specifies that the action should be performed on each line without a specific pattern match.

Reading from files in AWK is most commonly performed by providing the filename as an argument. This method exemplifies AWK's functionality for quickly and efficiently processing textual data files.

To write to files, AWK uses the output redirection operator >. This operator directs the output of a print or printf statement to a specified file.

```
# Example of writing to a file
awk 'BEGIN { print "Hello, World!" > "output_file.txt" }'
```

In this example, awk writes the string "Hello, World!" to output_file.txt. The BEGIN block ensures the action is executed before any input is processed. Note that using the > operator in this manner will create the file if it does not exist or overwrite the file if it already exists.

Appending data to a file is similar to writing, but it uses the » operator. This operator appends the output to the file instead of overwriting it.

```
# Example of appending to a file
awk 'BEGIN { print "Appending this line." >> "output_file.txt" }'
```

This will append the string "Appending this line." to the existing text in output_file.txt.

AWK also supports processing multiple input files, enabling the aggregation and analysis of data spread across several files. When multiple filenames are provided as arguments, AWK processes each file one after the other.

```
# Example of processing multiple files
awk '{ print $0 }' file1.txt file2.txt file3.txt
```

In this instance, awk processes file1.txt, file2.txt, and file3.txt sequentially, printing each line from each file to the standard output.

File redirection in AWK also allows for more complex data manipulations by combining input and output redirection, as seen in examples where input is taken from one or more files and output is directed to another file. This capability simplifies the workflow in data processing tasks.

Error handling is a significant aspect of file operations. AWK provides mechanisms to handle errors gracefully when dealing with file I/O operations, such as checking the status of file opening and closing operations.

Using pipes in conjunction with AWK expands its versatility, enabling AWK to read input from the output of other commands or sending AWK's output to other commands or scripts.

```
# Example of using pipe with AWK
ls -l | awk '{ print $9 " (" $5 " bytes)" }'
```

Here, the output of ls -l is piped into AWK, which processes and formats it to display filenames along with their sizes in bytes. Using AWK with pipelines facilitates the integration of AWK within larger shell scripts and command-line workflows.

These foundational concepts of file handling in AWK—reading, writing, appending, processing multiple files, redirection, error handling, and piped input/output—enable users to manipulate files effectively, thereby leveraging AWK's full potential for text processing and data management. This section serves as an introduction to these fundamental operations, essential for any subsequent advanced file management techniques discussed later in the chapter.

8.2 Reading Files with AWK

Reading files is a fundamental operation in AWK that allows users to process data line by line, perform text manipulation, and extract pertinent information based on specific criteria. The ability to effectively read and manage files is essential for any script that aims to automate text processing tasks.

To read a file with AWK, one typically uses the following general syntax:

```
awk 'script' filename
```

Here, script is the portion of AWK code that defines how the input data should be processed, and filename is the name of the file to be read. AWK reads the input file line by line and applies the script to each line.

```
awk '{print $0}' input.txt
```

In this example, the script {print $0} prints every line of input.txt to the standard output.

$0 refers to the entire line of text. AWK splits each line into fields based on a delimiter (by default, whitespace). Fields are accessed using $1 for the first field, $2 for the second, and so on.

```
awk '{print $1, $3}' input.txt
```

In this command, AWK prints the first and third fields of each line in input.txt.

Using Pattern Matching

Pattern matching is a powerful feature in AWK that allows scripts to process only those lines that match a specific pattern.

```
awk '/pattern/ {print $0}' input.txt
```

This expression prints all lines in input.txt that contain the string pattern. Regular expressions can be used for more complex pattern matching.

Reading Multiple Files

AWK has the capability to read multiple files sequentially. The files are processed in the order they are listed on the command line. Each line from each file is considered independently.

```
awk '{print $1}' file1.txt file2.txt
```

This command prints the first field of each line from file1.txt and file2.txt. The files are processed in sequence, with AWK switching from one to the next automatically.

FS - Field Separator

The field separator variable FS defines how AWK splits lines into fields. The default field separator is whitespace, but it can be changed to any character or regular expression.

```
awk 'BEGIN {FS=","} {print $1, $2}' input.csv
```

In the above command, the field separator is set to a comma, making it suitable for processing CSV files. The script prints the first and second fields of each line.

NR - Number of Records

NR is a built-in variable in AWK that keeps track of the number of input records (lines) processed so far. It is useful for applying actions to specific lines.

```
awk 'NR==3 {print $0}' input.txt
```

This command prints the third line of input.txt.

Handling Empty Lines

When reading files, it is common to encounter empty lines. AWK handles these lines gracefully, allowing scripts to either skip or process them as needed.

```
awk 'NF > 0 {print $0}' input.txt
```

In this example, NF (number of fields) is used to check if the line is empty. Only non-empty lines are printed.

Built-in Functions for Reading Files

AWK provides several built-in functions to facilitate the processing of input files.

- getline - Reads the next record from the input.

The getline function can be used to read from files within an AWK script.

```
awk '{
    while ((getline line < "input.txt") > 0) {
        print line
    }
    close("input.txt")
}' dummy.txt
```

This script reads lines from input.txt within the context of processing another file, dummy.txt. The close function closes the file after processing.

AWK's flexibility in reading and processing files makes it a robust tool for text manipulation and data extraction tasks. The seamless handling of multiple input files, pattern matching, and custom field delimiters empowers users to perform complex data processing with ease.

8.3 Writing to Files

In AWK, writing to files is a crucial operation that allows for the recording and manipulation of processed data. This operation is integral in data pipelines and report generation. AWK provides several mechanisms for directing output to files, leveraging the print and printf statements along with redirection operators. Understanding these mechanisms is paramount for effective file management in AWK.

Basic File Writing in AWK

To write to a file, the > redirection operator is used. The print statement is combined with the redirection operator to direct the output to a specific file. If the file does not exist, AWK will create it. If the file exists, AWK will overwrite its contents. The syntax is as follows:

```
print output > "filename"
```

For instance, consider a simple AWK script that processes an input file data.txt and writes selected fields to output.txt:

```
awk '{print $1, $2 > "output.txt"}' data.txt
```

In this example, the values of the first and second fields from each record in data.txt are written to output.txt.

Retaining Control with printf

The printf function provides more precise control over the formatting of the output to files. The syntax for redirecting printf output is similar to print:

```
printf format, values > "filename"
```

For example, to write formatted output to a file:

```
awk '{printf "%-10s %s\n", $1, $2 > "output.txt"}' data.txt
```

Here, printf formats the output with the first field left-aligned in a 10-character wide field and the second field following.

Appending Data to Files

Appending data to an existing file without overwriting its contents requires the » operator. This operator ensures that new content is added to the end of the file:

```
print output >> "filename"
```

Consider an example where additional records are to be appended to output.txt:

```
awk '{print $3, $4 >> "output.txt"}' data.txt
```

This command appends the third and fourth fields from each record in data.txt to output.txt.

Conditional File Writing

Writing to files conditionally based on the content of the input record is a powerful feature. You can direct output to different files by evaluating conditions within the print or printf statements:

```
awk '{if ($3 > 50) print $1, $2 > "high.txt"; else print $1, $2 > "low.txt"}' data.txt
```

This script directs records with a third field value greater than 50 to high.txt and others to low.txt.

Handling File Descriptors

Managing multiple files efficiently involves handling file descriptors. AWK allows the use of a file descriptor variable to simplify file operations, especially when writing to the same file in different parts of the script:

```
awk 'BEGIN {file = "output.txt"} {print $0 > file}' data.txt
```

In the above example, the file descriptor file is initialized in the BEGIN block and used throughout the script to write to output.txt.

Closing Files in AWK

Closing files is an important practice to free up system resources, especially when dealing with numerous files. Use the close function to explicitly close a file after writing to it:

```
awk '{print $1, $2 > "output.txt"; close("output.txt")}' data.txt
```

Explicitly closing files ensures that AWK does not exceed system limits on open file descriptors and avoids potential data corruption or loss.

Error Handling During File Writing

Error handling during file operations is critical to ensure data integrity and robust script execution. AWK provides the system function to capture the exit status of file operations. This can be leveraged to log errors or take corrective action:

```
awk '{print $1, $2 > "output.txt"; status = system("echo $?")}' data.txt
```

Here, the exit status of the print command is captured and can be checked to detect errors.

The multifaceted capabilities of AWK for writing to files equip users with the tools needed for sophisticated file manipulation and data storage strategies. Through comprehensive understanding and application of these techniques, efficient and effective file management is achievable in AWK programming.

8.4 Appending Data to Files

Appending data to files is a common task in AWK scripting, allowing the addition of new data to the end of an existing file. This section delves into the mechanisms and best practices for appending data, ensuring consistency, integrity, and efficiency in file manipulations.

File Handle for Append Mode

In AWK, files are opened in different modes using file handles. To append data to a file, use the » operator. This operator ensures that the content is added at the end of the file, preserving any existing data.

```
awk '{ print $0 >> "output.txt" }' input.txt
```

In this example, the file output.txt is opened in append mode. Each line from input.txt is appended to output.txt.

Managing File Handles

It's prudent to manage file handles explicitly, especially when appending to files inside loops or conditional statements. This can be achieved using the close function to avoid potential file handle exhaustion or unintended file locking.

```
awk '
  {
    print $0 >> "output.txt";
    close("output.txt");
  }
' input.txt
```

By calling close("output.txt") after each append operation, the file handle is released, and subsequent operations will re-open the file afresh. This is crucial when appending content conditionally or within iterative structures.

Example: Appending Selective Data

Consider a scenario where only specific lines from input.txt need to be appended to output.txt based on a condition.

```
awk '
  /pattern/ {
    print $0 >> "output.txt";
    close("output.txt");
  }
' input.txt
```

In this script, only lines matching pattern are appended to output.txt.

Each matching line results in closing the file, ensuring the handle does not stay open unnecessarily.

Efficiency Considerations

Repeated opening and closing of files can introduce overhead, particularly for large files or numerous append operations. When possible, minimize the number of open/close operations:

```
awk '
  BEGIN { to_append = 0 }
  /pattern/ {
    buffer[to_append++] = $0;
  }
  END {
    for (i = 0; i < to_append; i++) {
      print buffer[i] >> "output.txt";
    }
    close("output.txt");
  }
' input.txt
```

This approach collects all lines to be appended in an array and performs a single append operation in the END block, closing the file afterward.

Handling Large Data Volumes

For extremely large datasets, consider chunking data to avoid excessive memory usage. This can be done by periodically flushing appended content to the file.

```
awk '
  BEGIN { buffer_count = 0; buffer_limit = 1000 }
  /pattern/ {
    buffer[buffer_count++] = $0;
    if (buffer_count == buffer_limit) {
      for (i = 0; i < buffer_count; i++) {
        print buffer[i] >> "output.txt";
      }
      buffer_count = 0;
      close("output.txt");
    }
  }
  END {
    for (i = 0; i < buffer_count; i++) {
      print buffer[i] >> "output.txt";
    }
    close("output.txt");
  }
' input.txt
```

This script appends data in chunks of 1000 lines, thereby managing memory more efficiently and ensuring the file is intermittently closed.

Error Handling When Appending

It is crucial to handle potential errors during file operations. AWK's error-handling mechanisms can capture and log errors during file append operations.

```
awk '
  function append_data(line, file) {
    if (system("echo " line " >> " file) != 0) {
      print "Error appending to " file > "/dev/stderr";
    }
  }
  /pattern/ {
    append_data($0, "output.txt");
  }
' input.txt
```

Here, the append_data function uses system to invoke shell commands for appending, checking for non-zero exit statuses to detect failures.

Understanding these concepts and practices for appending data to files in AWK ensures robust and efficient file handling, even in complex scenarios.

8.5 Processing Multiple Files

When working with multiple files in AWK, the capability to process several files within a single AWK script is instrumental. This section will delve into the techniques for handling multiple files efficiently, exploring command line arguments, internal file iteration methods, and useful practices to avoid common pitfalls.

To illustrate processing multiple files, consider the following example where two data files, file1.txt and file2.txt, need to be processed together. Each file contains tabular data, and our objective is to combine this data for analysis. First, let's take a look at how to specify multiple files in the command line and then proceed to handle the data within the AWK script.

```
awk 'BEGIN { FS=" " } { print $0 }' file1.txt file2.txt
```

In this command, awk processes file1.txt and file2.txt sequentially. The BEGIN block sets the field separator to a space, and the main block prints each record from both files. AWK treats data from each file as if it were concatenated into one long stream of records.

To distinguish the current file being processed, the built-in variable FILENAME can be leveraged. FILENAME stores the name of the current file AWK is reading. For example:

```
awk '{
    print FILENAME ": " $0
}' file1.txt file2.txt
```

In this example, each printed record is prefixed with the name of the originating file. This is particularly useful when performing file-specific operations based on the source of the data.

Sometimes, it becomes necessary to perform initialization or cleanup tasks when transitioning between files. AWK provides the special patterns BEGINFILE and ENDFILE for this purpose. These patterns execute actions at the start and end of each file, respectively:

```
awk 'BEGIN { FS=":" }
BEGINFILE {
    print "Processing file: " FILENAME
}
{
    print $1, $2
}
ENDFILE {
    print "Finished processing file: " FILENAME
}' file1.txt file2.txt
```

Here, every file's beginning is marked by printing a message, and a concluding message is printed at the end. The BEGINFILE and ENDFILE ensure these tasks are executed at the correct junctures.

Often, it is necessary to generate reports aggregated from multiple files. This is where FNR, a built-in variable indicating the current record number in the current file, becomes advantageous. To reset computations at the start of each file, FNR can be utilized:

```
awk '{
    sum += $1
    count++
}
END {
    print "Overall Average:", sum / count
}
ENDFILE {
    print "File Average for " FILENAME ":", sum / FNR
    sum = 0; count = 0
}' file1.txt file2.txt
```

In this script, FNR ensures each file's average is computed separately, while the END block calculates the overall average across both files.

It is equally critical to handle scenarios where files may not exist or fail to open. AWK does not provide built-in error handling for file operations, so this needs to be managed externally:

```
for file in file1.txt file2.txt
do
    if [ ! -f $file ]; then
        echo "Error: $file not found."
        continue
    fi
    awk '... your script ...' $file
done
```

The shell script wraps around the AWK call, verifying each file's existence before processing. If a file does not exist, an error message is printed, and the loop continues to the next file.

Enabling robust data processing across multiple files necessitates understanding and judicious use of AWK variables and patterns. By leveraging FILENAME, FNR, BEGINFILE, and ENDFILE, users can craft sophisticated scripts capable of handling complex file-processing workflows efficiently.

8.6 Using AWK with File Redirection

AWK provides powerful capabilities for file redirection, allowing you to direct output not just to the standard output (which is typically the terminal), but also to files or even as input to other programs. This functionality leverages the shell's redirection capabilities and AWK's special syntax to achieve complex data processing workflows.

Output Redirection

The simplest form of file redirection is output redirection. Using the > operator, you can redirect the output of an AWK script to a file.

```
awk '{print $0}' input.txt > output.txt
```

In this example, the content of input.txt is read and printed line by line to output.txt. The > operator overwrites the file if it exists.

For appending to a file rather than overwriting it, the » operator is used.

```
awk '{print $0}' input.txt >> output.txt
```

Here, the output is appended to output.txt if it already exists, retaining its previous content.

File Redirection within AWK Scripts

AWK also allows file redirection within the script itself using the print and printf statements. This approach is particularly useful when you need to conditionally redirect output based on certain criteria in the data.

```
awk '{
    if ($3 > 50) {
        print $0 > "high_values.txt";
    } else {
        print $0 > "low_values.txt";
    }
}' input.txt
```

In this script, lines where the third field ($3) is greater than 50 are redirected to high_values.txt, while the others are redirected to low_values.txt.

It is important to note that each usage of > opens the file in write mode, which erases its previous content. To append to files from within the AWK script, use the » operator.

```
awk '{
    if ($3 > 50) {
        print $0 >> "high_values.txt";
    } else {
        print $0 >> "low_values.txt";
    }
}' input.txt
```

Input Redirection

While output redirection steers the output to files, input redirection allows AWK to read from files specified by the redirection operator, instead of being limited to the command line-specified files.

```
awk '{print $0}' < input.txt
```

This command reads from input.txt just as it would if the file were specified directly in the command line. The usage of input redirection within the script is less common but equally powerful, allowing you to open and read files based on scripting logic.

```
awk 'BEGIN {
    while ("cat filelist.txt" | getline file) {
        while ((getline line < file) > 0) {
            print line;
        }
        close(file);
    }
}'
```

In this example, AWK first reads a list of filenames from filelist.txt. For each filename, it subsequently opens the file and processes its content, printing each line to the standard output.

Piped Input and Output

Another powerful feature is the use of pipes to direct output to other commands. This is particularly useful for creating pipelines of commands for complex data processing scenarios.

```
awk '{print $1}' input.txt | sort
```

This command extracts the first field ($1) from each line of input.txt and sorts the result. The output of the AWK command is piped directly into the sort command.

Similarly, within AWK scripts, pipes can be used to send output to other commands.

```
awk '{print $1 | "sort"}' input.txt
```

This script sends the first field of each input line to the sort command through a pipe. This approach is functionally similar to using shell pipes but is more integrated into the AWK script execution.

Pipes can also be used to read input from other commands.

```
awk 'BEGIN {
    while ("ls" | getline filename) {
        print filename;
    }
}'
```

Here, AWK executes the ls command and uses the getline function to read its output line by line, printing each filename to the standard output.

Managing these processes and files accurately is critical for efficient AWK scripting. Paying attention to detail in file naming, ensuring correct paths, and handling file or command execution errors can avert common pitfalls. Use the close() function in AWK to close files or pipes to prevent resource leaks, particularly in looping constructs.

Redirection enriches AWK's already robust text processing capability, allowing developers to integrate AWK scripts seamlessly into larger workflows and systems. This enhanced versatility makes mastering redirection an indispensable skill for effective file management and data processing in AWK.

8.7 Handling File Errors

Error handling in file operations is a critical aspect of programming with AWK. When working with files, various issues can arise, such as non-existent files, lack of permissions, full disk space, or other I/O errors. To ensure robustness in your AWK scripts, it is necessary to anticipate and manage these possibilities effectively. AWK provides several mechanisms to handle file errors, leveraging its built-in functions, special variables, and control structures. In this section, we will explore these tools to handle file errors comprehensively.

Redirection Error Handling

When redirecting input or output to files, errors can occur due to reasons like permission issues or non-existent directories. AWK's built-in getline function can be used to handle errors during file opening. For example, attempting to read from a file:

```
BEGIN {
    if ((getline < "inputfile.txt") < 0) {
        print "Error: Cannot open file 'inputfile.txt'" > "/dev/stderr";
        exit 1;
    }
}
```

In this block of code, getline tries to read from "inputfile.txt". If getline returns a value less than zero, it indicates an error, and the script prints an error message to the standard error stream and exits with a status code of 1.

Output Redirection Errors

Errors in output redirection can be similarly handled. For instance, when attempting to write to a file:

```
BEGIN {
    outputFile = "outputfile.txt";
    if (!(print "Sample Output" > outputFile)) {
        print "Error: Cannot write to file 'outputfile.txt'" > "/dev/stderr";
        exit 2;
    }
}
```

Here, if the redirection fails, the script prints an error message to standard error and exits, ensuring the issue is immediately addressed.

Handling write and append errors

AWK scripts may need to write or append large amounts of data to files. Disk full errors or permission problems can hinder these operations. To illustrate error checking during file writes or appends:

```
{
    if (!(print $0 > "output.txt")) {
        print "Error: Cannot write data to 'output.txt'" > "/dev/stderr";
        exit 3;
    }
    if (!(print $0 >> "appendfile.txt")) {
        print "Error: Cannot append data to 'appendfile.txt'" > "/dev/stderr";
        exit 4;
    }
}
```

In both cases, using conditional checks ensures that file write and append operations are validated, preventing potential loss of data or silent failures.

Using ERRNO Variable

The special variable ERRNO can be used to retrieve the error message corresponding to the last system error encountered in I/O operations:

```
BEGIN {
    if ((getline tmp < "nonexistentfile.txt") < 0) {
        print "Error: " ERRNO > "/dev/stderr";
        exit 1;
    }
}
```

In this example, if an error occurs during the getline operation, ERRNO holds the system error message, which can be printed for more detailed diagnostic information.

Comprehensive Error Checking

A thorough error handling strategy involves checking for potential errors at every point where file I/O is performed. This kind of approach ensures maximum robustness:

```
BEGIN {
    inputFile = "input.txt";
    if ((getline < inputFile) < 0) {
        print "Input file error: " ERRNO > "/dev/stderr";
        exit 1;
    }

    outputFile = "output.txt";
    if (!(print "Sample output" > outputFile)) {
        print "Output file error: " ERRNO > "/dev/stderr";
        exit 2;
    }

    appendFile = "append.txt";
    if (!(print "Appending data" >> appendFile)) {
        print "Append file error: " ERRNO > "/dev/stderr";
        exit 3;
    }
```

```
}
{
    if (!(print $0 > outputFile)) {
        print "Error during file write: " ERRNO > "/dev/stderr";
        exit 4;
    }

    if (!(print $0 >> appendFile)) {
        print "Error during file append: " ERRNO > "/dev/stderr";
        exit 5;
    }
}
```

In this comprehensive example, each file operation is checked meticulously, and corresponding error messages are printed, with script termination upon encountering an error.

Handling file errors effectively in AWK scripts requires incorporating these checks and balances into your code. This approach ensures that file-related operations are executed reliably, with appropriate feedback whenever an issue arises.

8.8 Using AWK with Piped Input and Output

AWK is a powerful text processing tool, capable of handling not only static file inputs but also dynamic streams of data through pipes. This functionality allows AWK scripts to process real-time data feed and integrate seamlessly with other command-line utilities. Understanding how to use AWK with piped input and output enhances its utility in versatile scripting environments.

Pipes can direct the output of one command into the input of another, and AWK is particularly adept at processing these streams. This section provides a detailed explanation of these concepts and demonstrates practical examples of their usage.

To start, consider a simple example where the output of the UNIX ls command (used to list files and directories) is piped into an AWK script to print file names and their sizes.

```
ls -l | awk '{print $9, $5}'
```

In this command, ls -l produces a list of files in long format, providing detailed information for each file. The output is then piped into AWK. The AWK script awk '{print $9, $5}' extracts and prints the file name ($9) and file size ($5). Here, the fields of each line of the ls output are separated into different columns, and the AWK script processes these columns accordingly.

The interaction between commands through pipes offers extensive capabilities for data manipulation. For instance, combining grep with AWK can filter and process data in a two-step manner.

1. Use grep to filter lines.
2. Use AWK to process the filtered lines.

Consider the following command that finds lines containing the word "error" in a log file and then prints the timestamp and error message:

```
grep "error" logfile.txt | awk '{print $1, $3, $4, $5, $6, $7, $8, $9}'
```

Here, grep "error" logfile.txt filters all lines mentioning "error". Piped to AWK, the command awk '{print $1, $3, $4, $5, $6, $7, $8, $9}' extracts and prints the timestamp and relevant error message components.

AWK can also chain together multiple commands using pipelines, enabling complex data processing workflows. For example, you can compute the total size of files within a directory that were modified within the last 7 days:

```
find . -type f -mtime -7 -exec ls -l {} \; | awk '{sum += $5} END {print sum}'
```

In this example, find is used to list files modified within the last 7 days. The -exec ls -l {} executes the ls -l command for each file found. The resulting output, piped into AWK, is processed by the script awk '{sum += $5} END {print sum}}', which sums the sizes of the files and prints the total.

Pipelines are not limited to input; AWK can also pipe its output to other commands. This feature is particularly useful when AWK's processed data needs further handling by other tools.

```
awk '{print $1}' datafile.txt | sort | uniq -c | sort -nr
```

Here, AWK extracts the first column of datafile.txt. This output is then piped into sort to sort the data, uniq -c to count unique occurrences, and sort -nr to sort by count in descending order. This command sequence provides a frequency histogram of values in the first column of the data file.

It is also possible to capture the output of an AWK script into a variable within a shell script. This can be done using command substitution.

```
max_size=$(ls -l | awk '{if($5 > max) max=$5} END {print max}')
echo "The largest file size is: $max_size"
```

In this script, the largest file size within the output of ls -l is computed using AWK and stored in the shell variable max_size. The echo command then prints the result.

Piping with AWK enables effective interleaving of multiple text-processing tools such as sed, cut, and tr, facilitating sophisticated data processing pipelines.

```
cat data.txt | sed 's/foo/bar/g' | cut -d' ' -f2 | tr 'a-z' 'A-Z' | awk '{print $1}'
```

In this command sequence, cat data.txt reads the content of data.txt. The sed command then performs a substitution, replacing "foo" with "bar". The cut command selects the second field, and tr converts lowercase characters to uppercase. Finally, AWK prints the first field of the processed data.

Understanding and applying these techniques makes AWK an indispensable tool for robust data stream pipeline creation, streamlining complex data processing tasks.

8.9 Temporary Files and Data Streams

Temporary files and data streams play a significant role in data processing and file handling tasks in AWK. They facilitate efficient data manipulation and inter-process communication, especially when working with large datasets or when intermediate data needs to be temporarily stored and processed.

Temporary files are used for storing transient data that is needed only during the execution of a program. These files are typically removed after their purpose has been served, thus freeing the system resources. Data streams, on the other hand, allow for the communication of data between processes, enabling AWK to read from or write to other programs directly.

Creating and Using Temporary Files

In AWK, temporary files can be created using the standard UNIX/Linux utilities such as mktemp. The mktemp utility generates unique temporary filenames, ensuring that the temporary files do not conflict with existing files. Once a temporary file is created, the typical process involves writing data to the file, reading data from the file, and then deleting the file.

Here is an example of creating and using a temporary file in AWK:

```
BEGIN {
    # Generate a unique temporary filename
    "mktemp" | getline tmpfile
    close("mktemp")

    # Write to the temporary file
    print "This is temporary content" > tmpfile

    # Read from the temporary file
    while ((getline line < tmpfile) > 0) {
        print line
    }
    close(tmpfile)

    # Remove the temporary file
    system("rm " tmpfile)
}
```

In this example, the script creates a temporary file, writes a line of text to it, reads the content back, and then deletes the temporary file.

Data Streams in AWK

Data streams enable AWK to interact with other commands by using pipes. AWK can read from standard input or another command's output, process the data, and then write the output to standard output or another command's input.

Using data streams, one can achieve efficient real-time data processing. For instance, AWK can process the data generated by another command and immediately use it without needing to store it temporarily.

Here is an example of using data streams with AWK:

```
# Using a pipeline to process the output of 'ls' command with AWK
ls -l | awk '
BEGIN {
    print "Filename\tSize"
}
{
    if (NR > 1) {
        print $9 "\t" $5
    }
}'
```

In this example, the 'ls -l' command lists files in a directory. The output is then piped to AWK, which processes and formats the file names and their sizes.

Combining Temporary Files and Data Streams

Combining temporary files and data streams can be beneficial for complex data manipulation tasks. One such scenario is when intermediate results need to be cached temporarily before further processing.

The following example demonstrates this combination:

```
BEGIN {
    # Generate a unique temporary filename
    "mktemp" | getline tmpfile
    close("mktemp")

    # First data processing: Filter and write filtered data to the temporary file
    "ls -l" | getline && getline # Skip the total line and the headers
    while ((getline < "-") > 0) {
        if ($5 > 1000) {
            print $0 > tmpfile
        }
    }
    close("-")
    close(tmpfile)

    # Second data processing: Read from the temporary file and process further
    while ((getline line < tmpfile) > 0) {
        print "Filtered file:", line
    }

    close(tmpfile)

    # Remove the temporary file
    system("rm " tmpfile)
}
```

In this example, the ls -l command's output is filtered to include only files larger than 1000 bytes. The filtered data is written to a temporary file, which is then read back and further processed.

Best Practices for Handling Temporary Files and Data Streams

When using temporary files and data streams, consider the following best practices to ensure efficient and error-free operations:

- Always ensure temporary files are deleted after use to prevent cluttering the filesystem.
- Handle errors when creating, reading, or writing to temporary files by checking the command execution status.
- Use unique temporary filenames to avoid conflicts, which can be achieved using utilities like mktemp.
- Secure temporary files by setting appropriate permissions, preventing unauthorized access.

- Prefer data streams for real-time data processing to reduce the system overhead associated with file I/O operations.

By adhering to these best practices, one can effectively utilize temporary files and data streams for robust and efficient file handling and data processing in AWK. The integration of these techniques significantly enhances the flexibility and capabilities of AWK scripts.

8.10 File Permissions and Security

In UNIX-like operating systems, file permissions are a fundamental aspect of file security, defining who can read, write, or execute a file. AWK, while primarily a text processing language, operates within an environment where understanding and correctly handling file permissions is crucial. Incorrect permissions can lead to security vulnerabilities or operational malfunctions, especially when writing to or reading from files.

Understanding File Permissions

File permissions in UNIX and UNIX-like systems are managed at three levels:

- Owner: The user who owns the file.
- Group: Users who are part of a group associated with the file.
- Others: All other users.

Permissions are denoted using a combination of read (r), write (w), and execute (x) access, represented by a triplet for each level. For example, rw-r–r– means that the owner has read and write permissions, the group has read-only permission, and others also have read-only permission.

Changing File Permissions with chmod

The chmod command is used to change file permissions. It can be invoked from within an AWK script using the system function. The system function executes a command in the shell and returns the exit status of that command.

```
awk 'BEGIN { system("chmod 644 /path/to/file") }'
```

Checking File Permissions

Before accessing a file, it is prudent to check its permissions to ensure it can be read or written as required. This can be done using the stat command in combination with AWK.

```
stat -c "%A %n" /path/to/file
\begin{FittedVerbatim}
-rw-r--r-- /path/to/file
\end{FittedVerbatim}
```

The -c option of the stat command allows customizing the output format to display file permissions in a symbolic form.

File Ownership with chown

Changing the ownership of files can be necessary to ensure the correct user or group has control over file modifications and executions. The chown command is used for this purpose and can also be invoked from within an AWK script.

```
awk 'BEGIN { system("chown user:group /path/to/file") }'
```

Using ls to List Permissions

AWK scripts can also parse the output of the ls -l command to dynamically check permissions. This is useful for scripting purposes where conditional actions might be necessary based on the file's current state.

```
ls -l /path/to/file
\begin{FittedVerbatim}
-rw-r--r-- 1 user group 4096 Apr 12 12:34 /path/to/file
\end{FittedVerbatim}
```

This command reveals detailed information, including file permissions, number of links, owner, group, size, modification date, and time.

Security Implications of File Permissions

Incorrectly set file permissions can lead to vulnerabilities, enabling unauthorized users to read, modify, or execute sensitive files. Files intended solely for reading by specific users should not have world-write permissions. Conversely, executable scripts should have the execute permission removed if they are not intended to be run by others.

For example, a configuration file that only the owner should modify and no one else should read or execute might have the following permissions:

```
chmod 600 /path/to/config.cfg
```

This command ensures that the configuration file is secure, limiting access only to the owner.

Using umask to Set Default Permissions

The umask command sets the default file creation permissions. AWK scripts can set umask to control the default permissions of files created within the script.

```
awk 'BEGIN { system("umask 077") }'
```

Setting umask 077 ensures that new files are created with permissions 600 by default, which is read and write for the owner, and no permissions for group and others.

Practical Example: Secure File Handling in AWK

A comprehensive approach to secure file handling in AWK involves checking permissions, modifying them if necessary, and always ensuring the script does not inadvertently expose sensitive data.

```
# AWK Script to secure file handling
BEGIN {
  file = "/path/to/file"

  # Ensure the file is writable before proceeding
  if (system("test -w " file) != 0) {
    print "Error: File is not writable"
    exit 1
  }

  # Change file permissions if insecure
  if (system("stat -c \"%a\" " file) != 600) {
    system("chmod 600 " file)
  }

  # Proceed with file operations
  # Your file processing code goes here
}
```

This script performs a series of checks and modifications to ensure secure handling of the file. It checks if the file is writable, then ensures that the file has the permissions 600 before proceeding with any file operations.

8.11 Advanced File Management Techniques

In this section, we delve into advanced file management techniques utilizing AWK. This involves sophisticated operations such as conditional file processing, dynamic file creation based on input data, and utilizing system calls within AWK scripts.

To effectively manage and manipulate files at an advanced level, it is crucial to understand how to integrate AWK programming with the broader system environment.

Conditional File Processing

Conditional file processing allows for selective reading from or writing to multiple files based on the content and format of input data. Consider the case where different types of records must be written to different files. This can be achieved using conditional statements within the AWK script.

```
# Define the pattern-action pairs
awk '{
    if ($2 == "error")
        print $0 > "error_log.txt"
    else if ($2 == "info")
        print $0 > "info_log.txt"
    else
        print $0 > "general_log.txt"
}' inputfile.txt
```

In this script, records are classified based on the second field ($2) in the input file inputfile.txt. Depending on whether the second field is "error", "info", or another value, records are routed to "error_log.txt", "info_log.txt", or "general_log.txt" respectively. This approach uses AWK's pattern-action model for filtering and directing records.

Dynamic File Creation

Dynamic file creation involves generating output files based on data content dynamically. By employing variables and formatted strings, AWK can construct filenames at runtime.

```
# Creating filenames dynamically based on input fields
awk '{
    output_file = "log_" $1 ".txt"
    print $0 > output_file
}' inputfile.txt
```

Here, the output filename is constructed using the first field ($1) from each input record. The resulting filename (log_$1.txt) ensures that records are written to files named according to their category or identifier present in the first field.

Utilizing System Calls

AWK allows the execution of system commands directly from within the script. This feature can be leveraged for advanced file operations that are beyond the scope of AWK's built-in functionality. System calls are typically performed using the system() function.

```
# Backup older logs and then create new log
BEGIN {
    if (system("mv log.txt log_backup.txt") != 0) {
        print "Error: Unable to create a backup file." > "/dev/stderr"
        exit 1
    }
}

# Append new data to log
{
    print $0 >> "log.txt"
}
```

In this example, a system call is used to move an existing log file (log.txt) to a backup location (log_backup.txt). The script then appends new data to the fresh log file. It is essential to handle the return value of the system() function to ensure that the command runs successfully and to provide error feedback if it fails.

File Descriptors and Special Files

AWK scripts often need to interact with file descriptors and special files such as standard input (/dev/stdin), standard output (/dev/stdout), and standard error (/dev/stderr). These special files can be utilized to manage data flow effectively.

```
# Redirect errors to standard error
{
    if (NF < 3) {
        print "Error: Incomplete record found on line " NR > "/dev/stderr"
    } else {
        print $0 > "/dev/stdout"
    }
}
```

This script checks for records with fewer than three fields ($NF < 3$). If an incomplete record is found, an error message is printed to the standard error output. Otherwise, the complete record is printed to the standard output. This approach ensures that error messages do not interfere with standard output data.

Handling Temporary Files

Temporary files are often used for intermediate storage and processing. AWK can interact with temporary files created by the system's mktemp utility or similar.

```
# Create a temporary file and pass its name to an AWK script
temp_file=$(mktemp)
```

```
awk -v temp_file="$temp_file" '
BEGIN { print "Temporary file created: " temp_file > "/dev/stderr" }

# Write processed data to the temporary file
{
    print $0 > temp_file
}

END { print "Processed data saved to: " temp_file > "/dev/stderr" }
' inputfile.txt
```

In this example, a temporary file is created using the mktemp command and its name is passed to the AWK script through the -v option. The AWK script writes processed data to this temporary file, and also provides informational messages to the standard error.

These advanced file management techniques leveraging AWK provide robust tools for efficient and dynamic file handling, enabling sophisticated data manipulation workflows tailored to various application needs.

Chapter 9

Debugging and Optimization

This chapter addresses debugging and optimization techniques for AWK scripts. It covers common errors and their solutions, the use of print statements for debugging, and utilizing GAWK's debugger. Further, it explores profiling AWK programs, optimizing script performance, managing memory efficiently, and handling data effectively. The chapter also provides best practices to avoid pitfalls and enhance the robustness and speed of AWK scripts.

9.1 Introduction to Debugging in AWK

Effective debugging of AWK scripts is a crucial skill for any programmer seeking to develop robust and efficient programs. This section delves into the fundamental aspects of debugging within the AWK language, providing a detailed examination of the techniques and tools available to identify and resolve errors in AWK scripts. Understanding these core concepts will significantly enhance your proficiency in troubleshooting and refining your code.

The process of debugging in AWK involves identifying, isolating, and rectifying both syntactical and logical errors. One of the primary methods for initiating this process is the utilization of print statements. Print statements allow the programmer to monitor the values of variables and the flow of execution within the script, thereby facilitating a step-by-step analysis.

Consider the following AWK script, which contains a logical error:

```
BEGIN {
    count = 0;
    total = 0;
}
{
    total += $2;
    count++;
}
END {
    average = total / count
    print "The average is", average
}
```

To debug this script, we can insert print statements to trace the values of total and count at various points. For example:

```
BEGIN {
    count = 0;
    total = 0;
}
{
    total += $2;
    count++;
    print "Current total:", total, "Current count:", count
}
END {
    average = total / count;
    print "The average is", average
}
```

Running this script with an input file containing several lines of data produces the following output in the terminal:

```
Current total: 5 Current count: 1
Current total: 15 Current count: 2
Current total: 30 Current count: 3
...
The average is 10
```

By examining the output, it is possible to verify the values assigned to total and count at each iteration, confirming their correctness. This method provides a straightforward yet powerful avenue for validating the logic of your script.

In addition to print statements, AWK supports more sophisticated debugging mechanisms, particularly through GNU AWK (GAWK). GAWK extends the functionality of standard AWK by incorporating an inbuilt debugger. The GAWK debugger provides a more controlled environment for code inspection, including breakpoints, stepping through code line by line, and inspecting variable states.

To invoke the GAWK debugger, utilize the –debug option when executing your script:

```
gawk --debug -f script.awk datafile.txt
```

This command initiates the debugger, enabling detailed control over the execution of your script. You can set breakpoints to halt execution at specific lines, examine the values of variables, and resume execution as needed. To set a breakpoint, use the b command followed by the line number:

```
gawk> b 5
```

To continue execution until the next breakpoint or the end of the script, use the c command:

```
gawk> c
```

Another useful feature is the p command, which prints the value of a specified variable or expression:

```
gawk> p total
```

These debugging methods are illustrated in the following example session with the GAWK debugger:

```
gawk> b 5
Breakpoint 1 set at line 5
gawk> c
Breakpoint 1, at line 5
5:     total += $2;
gawk> p total
total = 0
gawk> c
Breakpoint 1, at line 5
5:     total += $2;
gawk> p total
total = 5
gawk> c
...
```

The GAWK debugger allows precise control over code execution, facilitating thorough inspection and troubleshooting. By leveraging these debugging techniques, programmers can systematically resolve errors, optimize performance, and enhance the reliability of their AWK scripts.

Understanding how to effectively debug AWK scripts is paramount for any programmer aiming to create efficient, error-free code. By mastering the use of print statements and the GAWK debugger, you can significantly enhance your ability to troubleshoot and optimize your AWK programs.

9.2 Common Errors and Their Solutions

Errors in AWK scripts are inevitable, especially as the complexity of your scripts increases. Understanding common errors and their solutions is crucial for efficient debugging and optimization. This section discusses frequent issues encountered in AWK programming and provides solutions to each.

Syntax Errors A syntax error occurs when the structure of the AWK script doesn't conform to the language rules. Common causes include missing braces, incorrect statement termination, or mismatched parentheses.

Consider the following script with a syntax error:

```
BEGIN {
    print "Start of the program"
    print "Another line"
}
```

The above script will generate a syntax error because statements within a BEGIN or END block must be terminated by a semicolon.

```
BEGIN {
    print "Start of the program";
    print "Another line";
}
```

By adding the semicolons, the syntax error is resolved.

Uninitialized Variables AWK initializes all variables to the empty string or zero, depending on context. However, using variables without proper initialization can lead to unexpected behavior.

```
{
    total = total + $1
    print total
}
```

If total is not initialized, it implicitly starts at zero. Explicitly initializing total can make the script more readable and avoid potential logical errors:

```
BEGIN {
    total = 0
}
{
    total = total + $1
    print total
}
```

Incorrect Field Separators If the input data uses a different field separator, the FS variable must be set accordingly. Failure to do so can disrupt data parsing.

For instance, given a comma-separated input file:

```
name,age,grade
Alice,21,A
Bob,22,B
```

The following AWK script will not parse the fields correctly:

```
{
    print $1, $2, $3
}
```

Setting the FS variable to a comma resolves this issue:

```
BEGIN {
    FS = ","
}
{
    print $1, $2, $3
}
```

This will correctly output:

```
Alice 21 A
Bob 22 B
```

Array Indexing Errors Improperly handling associative arrays can lead to errors. For example, AWK associative arrays use strings as keys, which may lead to unintentional overwrites if keys are not carefully assigned.

```
{
    arr[$1] = $2
}
END {
    for (key in arr)
        print key, arr[key]
}
```

Ensure consistent and careful assignment of keys to avoid overwriting issues.

Off-by-One Errors Loop constructs, particularly those dealing with record counts (NR) or field counts (NF), are prone to off-by-one errors.

Consider iterating over all fields in a record:

```
{
    for (i = 1; i <= NF; i++)
        print $i
}
```

This loop correctly starts at the first field and iterates to the last field. Omitting the initialization or end condition can lead to off-by-one errors.

Logical Errors and Conditionals Errors in conditional statements often result from misplaced operators or incorrect logic.

```
{
    if ($1 = "specific_value")
        print $2
}
```

The correct equality operator in AWK is ==, not =. The above should be:

```
{
    if ($1 == "specific_value")
        print $2
}
```

Misuse of Regular Expressions Regular expressions in AWK are powerful but can also be a source of errors if used incorrectly. Ensure the regular expression syntax is correct and properly delimited by slashes.

```
{
    if ($1 ~ /pattern/)
        print $1
}
```

Always validate the regular expression and test it against sample input to confirm it captures the intended matches.

Division by Zero Similar to other programming languages, dividing by zero in AWK will result in runtime errors or even undefined behavior:

```
{
    result = $1 / $2
    print result
}
```

Proper checks should be in place to handle or avoid division by zero:

```
{
    if ($2 != 0) {
        result = $1 / $2
        print result
    } else {
        print "Division by zero error"
    }
}
```

A thorough understanding of these common errors and their respective solutions aids in developing more robust and error-free AWK scripts.

Applying these corrective measures meticulously contributes to the overall stability and effectiveness of your scripts.

9.3 Using Print Statements for Debugging

To effectively debug AWK scripts, utilizing print statements is an invaluable and straightforward method. This technique offers insights into program execution, variable contents, and overall script logic. By strategically placing print statements within the code, one can track the flow of execution and diagnose issues efficiently. This section delves into implementing print statements for debugging, focusing on various practical scenarios.

The primary form of the print statement in AWK is:

```
print item1, item2, ..., itemN
```

Each item can be a string, variable, computed value, or even the output of a function. AWK concatenates the output items, separated by a space by default.

Consider an AWK script intended to process a data file and calculate the sum of a specific field. Below is an example of a faulty script:

```
awk 'BEGIN { sum = 0 }
{ sum += $2 }
END { print "Total:", sum }' datafile.txt
```

To debug this script, one can insert print statements to examine the values of sum and field 2 ($2) at different points during execution:

```
awk 'BEGIN { sum = 0 }
{
  print "Current Record:", $0
  print "Field 2:", $2
  sum += $2
  print "Updated Sum:", sum
}
END { print "Total:", sum }' datafile.txt
```

Through this approach, one can observe the intermediate values of $2 and sum for each record. For instance, if the input data file contains:

```
a 1
b 2
c x
d 4
```

The debugging output might be:

```
Current Record: a 1
Field 2: 1
Updated Sum: 1
Current Record: b 2
Field 2: 2
Updated Sum: 3
Current Record: c x
Field 2: x
Updated Sum: 3
Current Record: d 4
Field 2: 4
Updated Sum: 7
Total: 7
```

It becomes apparent that the third record contains x instead of a numeric value, which disrupts the sum calculation. Correcting the script to handle non-numeric data can proceed based on this insight.

Another scenario involves checking the conditions within conditional statements. Consider an AWK script to filter and process data from a file conditionally:

```
awk '{ if ($3 > 100) { process($1, $2); sum += $2 } }' datafile.txt
```

Here, one can insert print statements to verify the condition and the values of the involved variables:

```
awk '{
  print "Processing Record:", NR
  print "Field 3:", $3
  if ($3 > 100) {
    print "Condition Met for Record:", NR
    process($1, $2)
    sum += $2
  }
  print "Sum so far:", sum
}' datafile.txt
```

The intermediate print outputs reveal each step's conditions and accumulated results, enabling the identification of logical errors or data anomalies.

One must be cautious with placement and frequency of print statements. Excessive print statements can produce overwhelming output, making it difficult to discern useful information. Ideally, limit print statements to critical checkpoints and summary values.

The flexibility of print can be enhanced by incorporating context-specific information. For example, prefixing debug messages with custom text strings, such as:

```
print "DEBUG: Checking Field 2:", $2
```

Using formatted strings via the printf function allows for more controlled and readable debug outputs, especially for numerical precision or aligning values neatly in columns. For example:

```
awk '{
  printf "Record %d: Field 1: %s, Field 2: %d\n", NR, $1, $2
  sum += $2
  printf "Sum after record %d: %d\n", NR, sum
}' datafile.txt
```

This output format, by aligning fields precisely, simplifies visual inspections.

Effective debugging with print statements not only aids in error diagnosis but also provides a method to understand and verify the logic and flow of AWK scripts. Utilizing this technique, along with disciplined application and clarity in output messages, ensures efficient identification and rectification of issues within AWK programs.

9.4 Debugging with GAWK's Debugger

The GNU implementation of AWK, known as GAWK, includes a powerful built-in debugger that facilitates the identification and resolution of complex bugs in AWK scripts. The debugger provides functionality for stepping through code, examining variables, and managing breakpoints. Understanding how to effectively leverage these features is crucial for advanced debugging in AWK.

To start the GAWK debugger, use the –debug flag when invoking the interpreter:

```
gawk --debug -f script.awk
```

Upon execution, the GAWK debugger enters an interactive mode where the user can utilize various commands to inspect and control the execution of the script.

A fundamental aspect of debugging is setting breakpoints to pause execution at specified lines or functions, allowing the inspection of the script's state at that point. Use the break command to set a breakpoint:

```
break file.awk:line_number
```

or

```
break @function_name
```

For example, setting a breakpoint at line 12 of my_script.awk would be done as follows:

```
break my_script.awk:12
```

To set a breakpoint at the beginning of a function named process_data:

```
break @process_data
```

Once breakpoints are set, the run command initiates script execution:

```
run
```

When execution hits a breakpoint or stops, several commands allow inspection and control. The print command is used to display the value of variables:

```
print var_name
```

This command can also display complex expressions and array elements:

```
print var_name[i]
```

Stepping through the code line by line is achieved with the step and next commands. The step command executes the next line and enters any called functions:

```
step
```

The next command executes the next line but does not enter functions, making it useful for skipping over function calls:

```
next
```

The continue command resumes execution from the current position until the next breakpoint or termination:

```
continue
```

When complex variables such as arrays are involved, the info command provides detailed information. To display all elements in an array named data, use:

```
info array data
```

To list all breakpoints currently set, the command is:

```
info break
```

For deleting a breakpoint, the delete command followed by the breakpoint number is used:

```
delete 1
```

The exploration of functions in the script can be more structured by listing them via:

```
info functions
```

This lists all functions defined in the script, aiding in the identification of where to set function breakpoints or focus debugging efforts.

Commands can be abbreviated to their initial letters for convenience. For instance, step can be abbreviated to s, and print to p, reducing keystrokes during interactive debugging.

Here's an example session using GAWK's debugger on a fictional script with an array processing function:

```
BEGIN {
    print "Starting script"
    data[1] = "one"
    data[2] = "two"
}

function process_data() {
    for (i in data) {
        print data[i]
    }
}

END {
    process_data()
    print "Ending script"
}
```

To debug the above script, the following session provides an illustration:

```
$ gawk --debug -f script.awk
(gawk) break @process_data
Breakpoint 1 at function 'process_data'
(gawk) run
Starting script
Breakpoint 1, process_data at script.awk:12
(gawk) step
(gawk) print i
uninitialized
(gawk) continue
one
two
Ending script
```

This session sets a breakpoint at the process_data function, runs the script up to that point, steps into the function, inspects the variable i, and then continues execution to completion. Through steps like these, debugging with GAWK's debugger becomes efficient and directed, ultimately allowing for the precise identification and rectification of script errors.

Debugging features provided by GAWK are instrumental in maintaining high-quality, reliable AWK scripts, especially as scripts grow in complexity and size. Effective use of these tools can substantially reduce development and debugging time, making efficient debugging a vital skill for any AWK programmer.

9.5 Profiling AWK Programs

Profiling an AWK program involves analyzing its execution to understand the program's performance characteristics. This process identifies which parts of the program consume the most resources such as time and memory. Profiling helps in diagnosing performance bottlenecks, and can guide optimization efforts to enhance overall efficiency. This section delves into the profiling tools and techniques available for AWK scripts, with a primary focus on GNU AWK (GAWK).

Using gawk for Profiling

GAWK includes built-in profiling capabilities that generate detailed reports of program execution. To profile an AWK program with GAWK, the –profile or -p flag is used. This flag instructs GAWK to generate a profile report, which is typically output to a file with the extension .awkprof.

To use the profiling feature, execute the AWK script with the –profile option:

```
gawk --profile -f script.awk inputfile
```

The above command will produce a profile report named script.awkprof.

Understanding the Profile Report

The profile report generated by GAWK consists of several sections:

- Statement Counters
- Execution Time
- Memory Usage

Each section provides specific insights into the behavior of the script.

1. Statement Counters

The statement counters section lists each pattern-action pair from the AWK script and the number of times each statement has been executed. This information is useful to identify which parts of the script are frequently executed, and hence, are potential targets for optimization.

2. Execution Time

The execution time section displays the time spent in each part of the script. It allows users to pinpoint which statements or blocks of code consume the most time. This section of the profile report is crucial for identifying performance bottlenecks.

```
BEGIN {
    ...
}
{
    ...
}
END {
    ...
}
```

3. Memory Usage

The memory usage section provides data on the amount of memory consumed during the execution of the script. High memory usage can be indicative of inefficiencies in data handling or the need for more optimal data structures.

Enhanced Profiling Techniques

Apart from the built-in profiling option, there are several techniques to manually profile segments of an AWK script:

- **Divide and Conquer**: Split the script into smaller segments, and evaluate the performance of each segment individually. This technique helps in isolating performance-critical sections.
- **Time Functions**: Use the built-in systime() function to measure the execution time of specific sections of the script. This manual timing can supplement the automated profiling report.

To measure the time taken by a specific block of code, use the following structure:

```
BEGIN {
    start_time = systime()
```

```
}
{
    # Code block
    ...
}
END {
    end_time = systime()
    print "Elapsed time: " end_time - start_time, " seconds"
}
```

This code snippet calculates the total execution time of the entire script. Adjust the placement of start_time and end_time variables to profile specific sections of the code.

Optimizing Based on Profile Data

Once you have access to detailed profiling data, optimization efforts can be focused on the sections of the script that consume the most resources. Possible optimization strategies include:

- **Reducing the Number of Executions**: Minimize the frequency of executions for resource-heavy parts of the script.
- **Streamlining Loops**: Optimize loops by reducing overhead or refactoring them to fewer iterations.
- **Efficient Data Handling**: Employ more efficient data structures or algorithms to handle data-intensive parts.

Consider the following example to illustrate optimization:

```
{
    for (i = 1; i <= NF; i++) {
        sum += $i
    }
    print sum
}
```

An optimized version might precompute the sum where possible, or use more efficient looping constructs if applicable.

Example of Profiling and Optimization

Given a simple AWK script that processes a large dataset, the following example demonstrates how to profile and optimize the script:

Original Script:

```
{
    for (i = 1; i <= NF; i++) {
```

```
        if ($i ~ /^[0-9]+$/) {
            num_sum += $i
        } else {
            str_concat = str_concat $i
        }
    }
    print num_sum, str_concat
}
```

Execute with profiling:

```
gawk --profile -f original_script.awk datafile
```

After examining the profile, assume the bottleneck lies in the repeated string concatenation within the loop. The optimized version might look like:

```
{
    num_sum = 0
    str_concat = ""
    for (i = 1; i <= NF; i++) {
        if ($i ~ /^[0-9]+$/) {
            num_sum += $i
        } else {
            str_concat = sprintf("%s%s", str_concat, $i)
        }
    }
    print num_sum, str_concat
}
```

In this optimized version, using sprintf for string concatenation may offer performance improvements.

Effective profiling and subsequent optimization can significantly enhance the performance and efficiency of AWK scripts, ensuring they run faster and consume fewer resources. Profiling should be an essential step in the development cycle of complex AWK scripts to achieve optimal performance.

9.6 Optimizing AWK Script Performance

When considering the optimization of AWK scripts, it is essential to focus on both code efficiency and execution speed. This section provides a comprehensive understanding of several optimization techniques that can be applied to AWK to enhance its performance. We will discuss efficient coding practices, the effective use of built-in functions, and the minimization of computational overhead.

Firstly, it is important to write concise and legible code. Long, convoluted scripts can slow down execution and make future maintenance more difficult. Here are some strategies for optimizing AWK scripts:

- Avoid unnecessary computations.
- Use built-in functions.
- Optimize regular expressions.
- Minimize the use of external commands.
- Reduce input/output (I/O) operations.

Avoid Unnecessary Computations

Reducing redundant calculations within the script can significantly enhance execution speed. For instance, if a computation can be performed outside of a loop, it should be moved.

```
# Before Optimization
{
    for (i = 1; i <= NF; i++) {
        if ($i > max) {
            max = $i;
        }
    }
}

# After Optimization
BEGIN {
    max = -INF;
}
{
    for (i = 1; i <= NF; i++) {
        if ($i > max) {
            max = $i;
        }
    }
}
```

Here, by initializing max in the BEGIN block, we avoid reinitializing it with every input record.

Use Built-in Functions

Using AWK's built-in functions is typically faster than writing custom code to perform the same operations because they are highly optimized.

```
# Before Optimization
{
    result = sqrt($1^2 + $2^2)
}
```

```
# After Optimization
{
    result = sqrt(($1 * $1) + ($2 * $2))
}
```

While trivial in small examples, for large scripts, optimized arithmetic expressions can save substantial computational time.

Optimize Regular Expressions

Regular expressions are powerful but can be computationally expensive. Compiling simpler and more specific regular expressions reduces processing workload. Consider the following example:

```
# Before Optimization
{
    if ($0 ~ /error|ERROR|Error/) {
        print "Error found"
    }
}

# After Optimization
{
    if ($0 ~ /[eE]rror/) {
        print "Error found"
    }
}
```

In this instance, simplifying the regular expression to match case-insensitively with [eE] reduces backtracking and improves performance.

Minimize Use of External Commands

Calling external programs within AWK scripts incurs additional system calls which slow down the overall process. If equivalent AWK functions are available, use them.

```
# Before Optimization
{
    cmd = "date -d " $1
    cmd | getline date
    close(cmd)
    print date
}

# After Optimization (assuming $1 is in 'YYYY-MM-DD' format)
{
    split($1, arr, "-")
    print arr[3] "/" arr[2] "/" arr[1]
}
```

By avoiding the external date command, the script executes faster and consumes fewer resources.

Reduce Input/Output (I/O) Operations

I/O operations are generally the most time-consuming part of any script execution. Minimizing the number of read/write operations can significantly boost performance.

```
# Before Optimization
{
    print $0 > "output.txt"
}

# After Optimization
{
    if (NR == 1) {
        print $0 > "output.txt"
    } else {
        print $0 >> "output.txt"
    }
}
```

By appending subsequent records, the optimized version avoids re-opening the file with each record.

Through these techniques, it is possible to achieve substantial performance gains in AWK scripts, making them more efficient and responsive for large data processing tasks.

9.7 Memory Management in AWK

Memory management is a crucial aspect of writing efficient and robust AWK scripts. In AWK, memory usage is directly influenced by how data structures like arrays and strings are utilized. Understanding and managing memory efficiently can significantly enhance the performance and reliability of your scripts.

AWK dynamically allocates memory for variables and data structures, which provides flexibility but also requires attention to detail. Proper memory management in AWK involves recognizing how memory is allocated, modified, and freed during script execution.

Dynamic Memory Allocation: AWK automatically manages memory for variables and arrays, without requiring explicit allocation by the user. For instance, when you assign a value to a variable or an array element that did not previously exist, AWK allocates memory for it. Consider the following example:

```
BEGIN {
    a = "Hello, world!"
    myArray[1] = 42
```

```
}
```

Here, a and $\mathrm{myArray}[1]$ are automatically allocated memory when they are assigned values.

Array Management: Arrays in AWK can be associative, meaning they are indexed by strings rather than just integers. This provides powerful capabilities but can lead to increased memory consumption if not used carefully. For example:

```
BEGIN {
    myArray["name"] = "John Doe"
    myArray["age"] = 25
}
```

It's important to monitor the size of your arrays, especially if they grow dynamically based on input data. Large arrays can consume significant memory, leading to potential performance bottlenecks.

Garbage Collection: AWK performs garbage collection automatically, freeing memory that is no longer needed. However, it's essential to ensure that unused variables and data structures are not left lingering. Resetting variables when they are no longer needed can aid in efficient memory usage:

```
BEGIN {
    a = "Temporary data"
    # Some operations
    a = "" # Free memory by resetting the variable
}
```

a is freed from its original data once it is reset to an empty string.

Managing Large Datasets: Handling large datasets efficiently necessitates careful memory management. When processing large files, consider techniques such as dividing the data into smaller chunks or streaming data through the script to minimize memory footprint. Examine the following script that processes input line-by-line without holding all data in memory:

```
{
    # Process each line as it is read
    print $0
}
```

Processing data line-by-line ensures that memory usage remains constant regardless of the input file size.

Memory Usage Monitoring: GAWK provides built-in functions for monitoring memory usage, enabling you to track and optimize your script's memory footprint. The PROCINFO array can provide useful information:

```
BEGIN {
    print "Maximum memory used:", PROCINFO["maxmem"]
}
```

PROCINFO["maxmem"] gives the maximum memory used by the GAWK process, which can be helpful to understand memory peaks during execution.

Efficient String Handling: Strings being prone to frequent changes can potentially lead to high memory consumption. When generating large strings or performing multiple string operations, consider intermediate results and careful concatenation practices:

```
BEGIN {
    largeString = "First part"
    for (i = 1; i <= 1000; i++) {
        largeString = largeString " additional data"
    }
    print largeString
}
```

Instead of appending repeatedly within loops, it may be more efficient to construct required parts and concatenate them judiciously.

Avoiding Memory Leaks: Although AWK has automatic garbage collection, improper use of global variables or overextended scope of variables can lead to pseudo memory leaks where memory is not released timely. Keeping the scope of variables as narrow as possible can help in better memory release.

```
{
    localVar = $1
    # Perform operations
}
```

Using localVar within the scope of the main action ensures it is discarded after each record is processed.

Proper memory management in AWK involves a combination of monitoring, efficient coding practices, and understanding how AWK handles memory. Employing these strategies can significantly improve both the performance and reliability of your AWK scripts.

9.8 Efficient Data Handling

Efficient data handling in AWK scripts is essential for optimizing performance and ensuring that the scripts can scale with the input size. This section delves into methods and best practices for managing data effectively in AWK.

1. Using Arrays for Data Management:

Arrays in AWK are associative, which means they can be indexed by strings as well as numbers. This feature is powerful but needs to be used judiciously to prevent memory bloat and inefficient lookups.

```
BEGIN {
  data["Alice"] = 30
  data["Bob"] = 25
  data["Charlie"] = 35
}

# Accessing data
{ print data[$1] }
```

This script creates an array data with names as keys. While efficient for small datasets, arrays can become a memory concern with larger data. It is crucial to delete unnecessary elements to save memory.

```
delete data["Bob"]
```

2. Utilizing Built-in Functions for String Operations:

AWK provides several built-in functions for string handling, such as split(), substr(), and match(). Using these functions effectively can save processing time and simplify script logic.

split() divides a string into a number of fields and stores them in an array, allowing for efficient parsing and processing of data.

```
{
  split($1, fields, "-")
  print fields[1], fields[2]
}
```

substr() extracts substrings, which can be useful for manipulating strings without the overhead of regular expressions.

```
{
  prefix = substr($1, 1, 3)
  print prefix
}
```

3. Efficient Use of Regular Expressions:

Regular expressions in AWK are a powerful tool but can be computationally expensive. Using them judiciously is key for efficient data handling. Precompiled regular expressions can yield savings in complex scripts.

```
BEGIN {
  regex = "^[a-zA-Z0-9]+@example\\.com$"
}

{
  if ($1 ~ regex) {
    print $1, "is a valid email"
  }
}
```

match() is another useful function that returns the position of the matching string and allows for substring extraction.

```
{
  if (match($0, /pattern/, arr)) {
    print arr[0] # Full match
  }
}
```

4. Streamlined Input and Output:

Handling input and output efficiently can significantly impact the performance of AWK scripts. Reading large files line-by-line, processing data with minimal intermediate storage, and writing outputs in the required format are crucial steps.

Reading data once and storing it in arrays for manipulation can reduce redundant I/O operations.

```
NR == 1 { header = $0; next }
{ data[NR] = $0 }

END {
  print header
  for (line in data) {
    print data[line]
  }
}
```

It is also advisable to avoid print statements within loops that iteratively process large datasets unless necessary. Accumulate results in a variable and print them once processing is complete.

5. Optimizing Field and Record Separators:

Customizing the field separator (FS) and the record separator (RS) can lead to more efficient parsing of input data. Setting appropriate separators as per the input file structure allows AWK to parse the data correctly without additional processing.

```
BEGIN {
  FS = ","
  RS = "\n\n"
}
```

Using RS as a multiple-character string enables AWK to read records that are separated by multiple lines.

6. Leveraging External Commands and Pipelining:

AWK can execute external commands and use their output as input. This can be leveraged to offload complex tasks to more specialized utilities, thus enhancing efficiency.

```
"sort data.txt" | awk '{print $1}'
```

Pipelining in this manner ensures that AWK scripts remain efficient and focused on the aspects of data handling they are best suited for.

7. Memory Management Practices:

Efficient memory usage is a cornerstone of handling large datasets in AWK. Always delete array elements that are no longer needed to free up memory.

```
for (key in data) {
  if (some_condition) {
    delete data[key]
  }
}
```

Arrays should be kept as small as necessary, and local variables should be used within functions to manage scope and memory usage effectively.

By adhering to these practices, AWK scripts can handle data more efficiently, thereby enhancing their performance and scalability.

9.9 Avoiding Common Pitfalls

When developing and running AWK scripts, some common pitfalls can lead to bugs, degraded performance, or unexpected behavior. Understanding and avoiding these pitfalls can significantly improve the robustness and efficiency of your scripts. This section addresses several frequent issues and provides practical solutions to mitigate them.

Uninitialized Variables

In AWK, all variables are automatically initialized to empty string or zero depending on context. However, relying on this implicit initialization can sometimes lead to logical errors. To enhance readability and maintainability of your scripts, always explicitly initialize variables.

```
# Implicit Initialization
{
    count += 1
    print count
}

# Explicit Initialization
BEGIN {
    count = 0
}
{
    count += 1
    print count
}
```

String and Numeric Contexts

AWK variables can hold both strings and numbers, and it determines the context based on the operation being performed. However, inappropriate handling of contexts can lead to confusing behavior.

```
a = "10"
b = 2
print a + b # Outputs 12, numeric addition
print a b # Outputs 102, string concatenation
```

To avoid unexpected results, ensure you are clear about when AWK is treating variables as strings or numbers. Use explicit type conversions when necessary.

```
a = "10"
b = 2
print (a + 0) + b # Force numeric context
print a "" b # Force string context
```

Incorrect Field Separators

AWK parses records based on field separators which are by default whitespaces. Misunderstanding or forgetting to set the proper FS (Field Separator) can cause incorrect field parsing, leading to unexpected script behavior.

```
# Using default FS (whitespace)
{
    print $1
}
```

```
# Setting FS explicitly
BEGIN {
    FS = ","
}
{
    print $1
}
```

Always set the FS appropriately, especially when dealing with non-standard delimiters.

Ignoring Exit Status

AWK scripts return an exit status which can be crucial for understanding whether the script ran successfully or encountered errors. Neglecting the exit status can hide issues in script execution.

```
awk '{print $1}' inputfile
if [ $? -ne 0 ]; then
    echo "AWK script failed"
fi
```

Incorporate checks for exit status in your shell scripts to ensure you capture and handle any errors during the execution of AWK scripts.

Mismanaging BEGIN and END Blocks

The BEGIN and END blocks execute before and after processing all input lines, respectively. Misplacement or misunderstanding of these blocks can cause their code to be executed at the wrong times.

```
# Incorrect usage, will execute print before processing input
BEGIN {
    print "Start processing"
}
{
    # Process input
}
END {
    print "Finished processing"
}
```

Always ensure that operations meant to initialize state or finalize processing are correctly placed within BEGIN and END blocks.

Avoiding Hard-coded Values

Hard-coding values, such as file paths and constants, can reduce the flexibility and reusability of AWK scripts. Using variables or passing values as arguments improves script portability.

```
# Hard-coded VALUE
{
    if ($1 == 5)
```

```
        print $0
}

# Using variable
BEGIN {
    threshold = 5
}
{
    if ($1 == threshold)
        print $0
}
```

Overusing Print Statements in Loops

While print statements are useful for debugging, excessive use within loops can drastically reduce performance, especially with large datasets.

```
# Inefficient
{
    for (i = 1; i <= NF; i++) {
        print $i
    }
}

# More efficient
{
    output = ""
    for (i = 1; i <= NF; i++) {
        output = output $i " "
    }
    print output
}
```

Minimize the frequency of print statements inside loops or batch the outputs to improve script performance.

Failing to Use Proper Indentation and Comments

AWK scripts can become difficult to read and maintain without proper code indentation and comments. Ensure your code is well-structured and annotated with comments explaining non-trivial logic.

```
# Poorly formatted script
{print$1+$2}

# Well-structured script
{
    # Sum first two fields
    sum = $1 + $2
    print sum
}
```

Adhering to these guidelines will not only avoid common pitfalls but also aid in producing more readable, maintainable, and efficient AWK scripts.

9.10 Best Practices for Debugging and Optimization

Debugging and optimization are critical skills for developing efficient and robust AWK scripts. They aim to ensure that the script performs its intended function correctly while consuming minimal resources. Effective debugging can save significant time, and thoughtful optimization can enhance script performance. This section presents key best practices to help achieve these goals, focusing on proven techniques and strategies to debug and optimize AWK programs effectively.

Utilize Descriptive Variable Names

Variables with descriptive names improve code readability and maintainability. For instance, use recordCounter instead of rc to make it clear the variable counts records. This practice simplifies debugging as the purpose of each variable is evident, reducing the likelihood of confusion.

Apply Consistent Indentation and Formatting

Consistent indentation and formatting improve the readability of AWK scripts, making it easier to spot logical errors. Adhere to a uniform style for indentation, whether it's spaces or tabs, and ensure that each code block is properly aligned. This consistency helps in visually parsing the code structure quickly.

Print Statements for Debugging

Inserting print statements is a straightforward debugging technique that offers insights into the script's internal state at various stages. For instance, adding:

```
print "Current record:", $0
```

can help monitor the data being processed and verify that it matches expectations. Use print statements to display variable values, loop counters, and other critical information to trace the script's execution flow.

Use AWK's Built-in Error Reporting

AWK provides several built-in variables that can aid in debugging. Use NR (number of records) and FNR (file number of records) to track the number of records processed. For example:

```
print "Processing record number:", NR
```

This practice helps identify where, within the script, the error is occurring by allowing you to trace the progress through the input files.

Debugging with GAWK

GAWK offers a debugger that can set breakpoints, watch variables, and step through code execution. Invoking the debugger:

```
gawk --dbg -f script.awk
```

The debugger facilitates a deeper inspection, providing commands to set breakpoints and evaluate expressions. Utilize commands like b {condition} to break on specific conditions and print variable to display variable values without inserting print statements into the code.

Profile to Identify Performance Bottlenecks

Profiling can reveal the most time-consuming parts of a script. GAWK's –profile option generates a performance report:

```
gawk --profile -f script.awk inputfile
```

The resulting profile file details execution times for various parts of the script. Focus optimization efforts on the areas consuming the most time, ensuring that performance improvements target the actual bottlenecks.

Optimizing Loops and Conditional Statements

Loops and conditional statements are common sources of inefficiency. Here are strategies to optimize them:

- **Reduce loop overhead:** Minimize work inside loops by computing values outside the loop if they are constant. For instance:

  ```
  for (i = 1; i <= 100; i++) {
      total += i
  }
  ```

  can be simplified using mathematical formulas when applicable.

- **Break early:** Utilize break statements to exit loops as soon as the objective is achieved, reducing unnecessary iterations.

  ```
  for (i = 1; i <= 100; i++) {
      if (total > threshold) {
          break
      }
      total += i
  }
  ```

Efficient Memory Management

Managing memory efficiently is essential for script performance, especially when dealing with large datasets:

- **Avoid unnecessary variable creation:** Reuse variables when appropriate instead of creating new ones. This practice conserves memory and reduces garbage collection overhead.
- **Clear arrays:** If arrays are used, clear them when no longer needed to free up memory:

```
delete myArray
```

Test with Representative Data

Testing scripts with a dataset that closely mirrors the production environment ensures the correctness and performance of the script under realistic conditions. This practice helps uncover edge cases and performance issues that may not be apparent with smaller or contrived datasets.

Document Code Thoroughly

Thoroughly documenting code is crucial for future maintenance and debugging. Include comments explaining the purpose of complex sections and the role of key variables. Proper documentation aids in understanding the script's logic and expedites debugging when issues arise.

These practices, when diligently applied, can substantially enhance the debugging and optimization process. They offer a structured approach to identifying and resolving issues, ensuring that AWK scripts run correctly and efficiently.

Chapter 10

Real-world Applications of AWK

This chapter explores practical applications of AWK in various real-world scenarios. Topics include system administration, log file analysis, data extraction, and reporting. Additionally, it covers text data transformation, processing CSV and TSV files, network monitoring, automating tasks, and AWK's role in bioinformatics. The chapter concludes with case studies that showcase successful projects using AWK, demonstrating its versatility and efficiency in solving real-world problems.

10.1 Introduction to Real-world Applications

AWK, a powerful text-processing and pattern-matching language, has continually proven its utility in a multitude of practical scenarios across various industries. Leveraging its concise and expressive syntax, users can effortlessly manipulate data, analyze logs, extract pertinent information, and automate repetitive tasks. This section delves into the myriad of real-world applications where AWK's capabilities can provide significant advantages, particularly in system administration, log file analysis, data extraction, reporting, software development, text data transformation, and more.

A foundational aspect of AWK's versatility lies in its ability to process structured and unstructured data seamlessly. Unlike other languages that may require extensive boilerplate code for handling textual input, AWK operates efficiently with minimal setup. The language's inherent design favors rapid development and execution, making it an attractive choice for tasks that demand quick turnaround times.

To illustrate AWK's applicability, let us consider a common scenario in system administration. Administrators often face the challenge of parsing and analyzing system logs to monitor performance, detect anomalies, and ensure security compliance. AWK can be employed to extract specific fields from log entries, aggregate data over defined periods, and generate meaningful summaries. For instance, the following code snippet demonstrates how AWK can be used to parse an Apache HTTP server access log to count the number of requests per IP address:

```
awk '{count[$1]++} END {for (ip in count) print ip, count[ip]}' access.log
```

The command above iterates through each line of the access.log file, using the first field (IP address) as the key in the count associative array. Upon reaching the END block, AWK prints each IP address along with its corresponding count, providing a concise summary of request distribution.

Another prevalent application of AWK is in log file analysis, where it excels in filtering and transforming log records to uncover actionable insights. By applying regular expressions and pattern matching, AWK can isolate log entries that match specific criteria, perform calculations, and output formatted results. Consider the task of finding all error messages in a log file and calculating the frequency of each error type:

```
awk '/ERROR/ {errors[$3]++} END {for (error in errors) print error, errors[error]}'
    system.log
```

Here, AWK filters lines containing the keyword "ERROR" and increments the count for each unique error type found in the third field. The END block subsequently prints the error types alongside their frequencies, highlighting the prevalence of each error.

AWK's prowess extends beyond log analysis to data extraction and reporting tasks. In settings where structured data resides in CSV or TSV files, AWK can efficiently parse these files, extract relevant fields, and compute statistics. For example, parsing a CSV file to calculate the average value of a specific column can be accomplished with the following AWK command:

```
awk -F, '{sum += $2; count++} END {print "Average:", sum/count}' data.csv
```

By specifying a comma as the field separator with the -F option, AWK reads the second field from each record, accumulates the sum, and counts the number of records processed. The END block then computes and prints the average value.

AWK's role in software development is multifaceted, ranging from preprocessing source code files to automating build processes. Developers can harness AWK to generate code snippets, perform static analysis, and enforce coding standards. For instance, generating a list of function names and their line numbers from a C source file can be achieved with:

```
awk '/^void|int|char|float|double/ {print NR, $0}' source.c
```

This command searches for lines beginning with common data type keywords and prints the line number (NR) along with the matching line, aiding in code navigation and review.

Transforming text data is another domain where AWK's utility is evident. Users can reformat and reassemble textual content to meet specific requirements without resorting to complex scripting. For instance, converting a space-separated file to a tab-separated format is straightforward with AWK:

```
awk '{OFS="\t"; $1=$1; print}' input.txt > output.tsv
```

By setting the output field separator (OFS) to a tab character and reassigning the first field to itself, AWK ensures that subsequent print statements produce tab-separated output, facilitating data exchange and further processing.

As we progress through subsequent sections, we will explore these applications in greater detail, showcasing AWK's practical implementations through comprehensive examples and case studies. From network monitoring to bioinformatics, the wide array of real-world applications demonstrates AWK's integral role in streamlining workflows, enhancing data insights, and automating complex tasks.

10.2 AWK in System Administration

AWK is a highly versatile programming language that is particularly effective for system administration tasks. This section discusses its applications in various aspects of system administration, including user management, disk usage monitoring, and configuration file parsing. Mastering these concepts allows system administrators to automate repetitive tasks, enhance system performance, and maintain greater control over system resources.

User Management: AWK can be employed to handle tasks related to user management, such as listing active users, extracting specific user details, and monitoring user activity. For instance, to display a list of all users on a UNIX-like operating system, one can use the /etc/-passwd file. The following AWK script extracts usernames and their corresponding user IDs:

```
awk -F':' '{ print $1, $3 }' /etc/passwd
```

This script uses the colon : as the field separator (specified by -F':') and prints the first ($1) and third ($3) fields, which correspond to the username and user ID, respectively.

Disk Usage Monitoring: Disk space is a critical resource in system administration, and monitoring it is essential to prevent system failures. AWK can be used to process the output of the df command, which reports file system disk space usage. The following example demonstrates how to format and summarize the disk usage information:

```
df -h | awk 'NR==1 || /\/dev/{ printf "%-25s %-8s %-8s %-8s %s\n", $1, $2, $3, $4,
    $5 }'
```

In this script, NR==1 ensures that the header row is printed, and /dev/ filters the output to include only lines that contain /dev, which usually denotes actual storage devices. The printf function is used for formatted output, with each field properly aligned.

Configuration File Parsing: Configuration files often contain key-value pairs separated by spaces or specific delimiters. AWK is adept at extracting and analyzing these pairs. Consider a configuration file where each line consists of a setting name and its value separated by a space. The following AWK script retrieves the value of a given setting:

```
awk '$1 == "setting_name" { print $2 }' config_file.conf
```

In this example, "setting_name" should be replaced with the actual setting name one is looking for, and config_file.conf with the actual configuration file. The script searches for lines where the first field ($1) matches the specified setting name and prints the second field ($2), which is the value.

Log File Analysis: System administrators often need to analyze log files to troubleshoot issues and monitor system health. AWK can be used to extract and summarize data from logs. For instance, to count the number of occurrences of each type of error in a log file, one can use the following AWK script:

```
awk '{ errors[$3]++ } END { for (error in errors) print error, errors[error] }' /var/log/
    syslog
```

This script reads a log file, treating the third field ($3) as the error type. It increments a counter in the errors array for each occurrence of an error type. After processing all lines, it prints the error type and the corresponding count.

Performance Monitoring: Monitoring system performance can involve tracking CPU usage, memory usage, and network activity. AWK can help parse various system monitoring tools' outputs. For example, to summarize CPU usage from the output of the top command, one can use the following method:

```
top -b -n1 | awk '/Cpu/ { print "CPU Usage: " $2+$4 "%"}'
```

Here, the top command runs in batch mode (-b) for a single iteration (-n1). AWK processes the line containing Cpu and prints a summary of CPU usage by combining user time ($2) and system time ($4).

By leveraging AWK in system administration, administrators can automate routine tasks, thus saving time and reducing the likelihood of errors. AWK's flexibility and efficiency make it a valuable tool for managing and analyzing system data.

10.3 Log File Analysis with AWK

In this section, we will explore how AWK can be effectively employed for log file analysis. Logs are invaluable for monitoring systems, diagnosing issues, and understanding system behavior over time. AWK's capabilities to process and extract meaningful information from log files make it an indispensable tool for system administrators and developers.

Consider a standard Apache access log file, where each log entry consists of several fields such as IP address, date, request method, URL, HTTP status code, and user agent. AWK can parse and analyze these logs to extract insights such as usage patterns, error occurrences, and frequent users.

```
# Sample Apache access log entry:
```

```
192.168.1.1 - - [12/Dec/2022:12:34:56 +0000] "GET /index.html HTTP/1.1" 200 1024 "
    -" "Mozilla/5.0"
```

Firstly, understanding the structure of the log entries is crucial. Each field in the log entry is separated by a space, with specific fields enclosed by square brackets ‘[]‘ or double quotes “""‘. We will use AWK to delimit these fields and perform various analyses.

```
awk '{ print $1, $4, $5, $6, $7, $9 }' access.log
```

The command above extracts and prints the IP address ($1), timestamp ($4), request method ($6), URL ($7), and HTTP status code ($9). The ${4} field includes both the opening square bracket and the timestamp, and the ${5} field includes the closing square bracket. Here, we will focus on more specific use cases.

Counting Requests by IP Address

To identify the IP addresses that access the server most frequently, we can count the occurrences of each IP address in the access log. AWK can tally the requests and sort the results.

```
awk '{ ip[$1]++ } END { for (i in ip) print ip[i], i }' access.log | sort -nr | head -10
```

This script initializes an associative array ip[] where the keys are IP addresses and the values are their corresponding request counts. After processing all log entries, it prints the request count and IP address, which are then sorted in reverse numerical order to display the top 10 IP addresses.

Detecting Error Status Codes

HTTP status codes indicate the result of a client's request. Identifying requests that result in error status codes (e.g., 404, 500) can highlight issues in the web server or application.

```
awk '$9 ~ /^[45]/ { print $1, $4, $7, $9 }' access.log
```

This command filters log entries where the status code ($9) begins with '4' or '5', indicating client or server errors. It outputs the IP address, timestamp, requested URL, and status code for each error entry.

Summarizing Traffic Volume

To summarize traffic on an hourly basis, we can extract the timestamp field and aggregate the number of requests for each hour.

```
awk '{ hour=substr($4, 14, 2); traffic[hour]++ } END { for (h in traffic) print h, traffic
    [h] }' access.log | sort -n
```

This script extracts the hour from the timestamp (substr($4, 14, 2)), increments the count for the corresponding hour in the traffic[] array, and then prints the hourly request count. The results are sorted numerically by hour.

Browser and Operating System Analysis

User agents provide information about the client's browser and operating system. Analyzing user agents can reveal usage patterns and help in making decisions related to browser support and compatibility.

```
awk -F'"' '{ split($6, ua, " "); print ua[1], ua[2] }' access.log | sort | uniq -c | sort -nr |
    head -10
```

Here, the field separator is changed to double quotes (awk -F'"') to isolate the user agent field ($6). The split() function divides the user agent string into components, capturing the browser name and version. The results are sorted, deduplicated, and the top 10 user agent strings by frequency are displayed.

These examples demonstrate the versatility of AWK in processing and analyzing log files. Access logs provide a wealth of information critical for maintaining and optimizing system performance, and AWK serves as a powerful utility for extracting and interpreting this data. Learning to harness AWK's full potential for log file analysis enhances one's capability to manage and troubleshoot systems effectively.

10.4 AWK for Data Extraction and Reporting

AWK, a powerful pattern scanning and processing language, excels in data extraction and reporting tasks. This section delves into the specifics of using AWK for these purposes, providing a comprehensive guide on how to apply AWK scripts to extract meaningful information from various data sources and generate structured reports efficiently.

Consider a scenario where we have a large text file containing employee records with fields such as employee ID, name, department, and salary. The records are delimited by commas:

```
1,John Smith,Engineering,5000
2,Jane Doe,Human Resources,4500
3,Bob Johnson,Marketing,4000
4,Alice Williams,Engineering,5500
```

To extract and report data using AWK, one must grasp its field handling and pattern matching capabilities. Fields in AWK are denoted as $1, $2, etc., with $0 representing the entire record.

First, we will write an AWK script to extract employee names and salaries for those in the Engineering department.

```
awk -F, '$3 == "Engineering" { print $2, $4 }' employee_records.txt
```

In this AWK script:

- -F, specifies the field separator as a comma.
- $3 == "Engineering" is the pattern that matches records where the third field (department) equals 'Engineering'.
- print $2, $4 outputs the second field (name) and the fourth field (salary).

The output of the script will be:

```
John Smith 5000
Alice Williams 5500
```

AWK also allows aggregate operations, such as calculating the total and average salary of employees in a specific department. Below is an AWK script to determine these metrics for the Engineering department:

```
awk -F, '$3 == "Engineering" { total += $4; count++ }
    END { if (count > 0) print "Total: " total, "Average: " total/count }'
        employee_records.txt
```

This script includes:

- total += $4; which accumulates the salary values.
- count++ which keeps a tally of records that match the pattern.
- The END block, executed after all records are processed, prints the total and average salaries.

Output:

```
Total: 10500 Average: 5250
```

In many scenarios, the extracted data needs to be formatted into structured reports. AWK facilitates the generation of tabular reports by specifying custom output formats. Here is an example that creates a report summarizing salaries by departments:

```
awk -F, '
{ dept[$3] += $4; count[$3]++ }
END {
  printf "%-20s %-10s %-10s\n", "Department", "Total", "Average"
  for (d in dept)
    printf "%-20s %-10d %-10.2f\n", d, dept[d], dept[d]/count[d]
}' employee_records.txt
```

Key aspects of this script include:

- dept[$3] += $4; which stores total salaries by department in the associative array dept.
- count[$3]++; counts the number of employees per department.
- The END block utilizes printf for formatted output, where:
  - %-20s reserves 20 characters for the department name.
  - %-10d and %-10.2f format the total salary and average salary, respectively.

Output:

```
Department          Total      Average
Engineering         10500      5250.00
Human Resources     4500       4500.00
Marketing           4000       4000.00
```

AWK's versatility also covers filtering and preprocessing data. For instance, imagine a file employee_records_mixed.txt that may contain some malformed lines. We can use AWK to cleanse the data before reporting to ensure only valid records are processed.

```
awk -F, 'NF == 4 { dept[$3] += $4; count[$3]++ }
END {
  printf "%-20s %-10s %-10s\n", "Department", "Total", "Average"
  for (d in dept)
    printf "%-20s %-10d %-10.2f\n", d, dept[d], dept[d]/count[d]
}' employee_records_mixed.txt
```

Here, NF == 4 filters out lines that do not have exactly four fields, preventing malformed records from influencing our report.

These examples illustrate that AWK is a potent tool for data extraction and reporting. Proper understanding and application of its pattern matching, field handling, aggregation, and formatting capabilities enable effective manipulation and presentation of data, rendering AWK an indispensable asset for tasks requiring concise and powerful data processing.

10.5 AWK in Software Development

AWK, a powerful text processing tool, possesses versatile features that make it highly useful in software development. Its ability to manipulate and analyze text streams is invaluable in a developer's toolkit. This section delves into several practical applications of AWK that developers frequently encounter, enhancing their workflow and productivity.

Developers often deal with configuration files that are primarily text-based. AWK can be used to read, modify, and validate these files efficiently. Consider a configuration file where each line follows the format key=value. To extract all keys and values, one can use the following AWK script:

```
awk -F '=' '{ print "Key: " $1 ", Value: " $2 }' config.txt
```

This script uses the -F option to define the field separator as the equals sign (=) and prints each key-value pair in a structured format. The flexibility of AWK allows developers to easily adapt this script for more complex configurations where nested or hierarchical formats might be present.

Unit testing is an integral part of software development. AWK can be employed to parse test output logs, summarizing results and highlighting failures. Assume the output from a unit test suite is stored in test_results.log and contains lines like:

```
PASS test1
FAIL test2
PASS test3
FAIL test4
```

To count the total number of passed and failed tests, the following AWK script can be utilized:

```
awk '/PASS/ { pass_count++ } /FAIL/ { fail_count++ }
END { print "Passed tests: " pass_count; print "Failed tests: " fail_count }'
    test_results.log
```

This script increments the counters pass_count and fail_count based on whether a line contains the string PASS or FAIL. After reading the file, it prints the summary of the test results.

Code metrics, such as line counts and comment density, are vital for maintaining code quality. AWK can assist in calculating these metrics. For example, to count the number of lines of code (LOC), the number of comment lines, and compute the comment density in a source code file:

```
awk '{
  total_lines++
  if ($0 ~ /^\/\// || $0 ~ /^\/\*/) comment_lines++
}
END {
  print "Total Lines: " total_lines
  print "Comment Lines: " comment_lines
  print "Comment Density: " (comment_lines / total_lines * 100) "%"
}' source_code.cpp
```

This script increments total_lines for each line in the file, while checking for comment lines that start with // or /* and incrementing comment_lines accordingly. The END block subsequently calculates and prints the comment density.

Developers frequently need to transform code or documentation, such as converting between different markup formats. AWK scripts can facilitate these conversions. Consider converting Markdown headers into HTML headers in a documentation file:

```
awk '{
  if ($1 ~ /^#$/) {
    print "<h1>" substr($0, 3) "</h1>"
  } else if ($1 ~ /^##$/) {
    print "<h2>" substr($0, 4) "</h2>"
  } else {
    print
  }
}' README.md
```

This script checks for Markdown headers starting with one or two hash (#) symbols and replaces them with corresponding HTML tags, while preserving the rest of the document structure.

For software localization, developers often work with gettext PO files. AWK can extract untranslated strings and count their occurrences. Given a PO file with the format:

```
msgid "Hello"
msgstr ""

msgid "World"
msgstr "World"
```

To identify and count untranslated strings, the following script is useful:

```
awk '/^msgid/ { id = $0 } /^msgstr/ && $0 == "msgstr \"\""{ untranslated[id]++ }
END {
  for (id in untranslated) {
    print id
  }
  print "Untranslated Strings: " length(untranslated)
}' messages.po
```

This script captures lines starting with msgid and checks if the following msgstr is empty. If so, it tracks this untranslated entry in an associative array untranslated. Finally, it prints all untranslated strings and their count.

Furthermore, AWK proves useful for extracting and generating project metadata, such as version numbers, from source files. Consider a source file version.h where the version number is defined:

```
#define VERSION "1.2.3"
```

To extract this version number, the following script can be used:

```
awk '/#define VERSION/ { print $3 }' version.h
```

This script identifies the line defining the version and prints the version number.

AWK's applicability extends beyond these examples, supporting a myriad of operations essential to software development tasks. From parsing and generating project documentation to automating conversion tasks and aggregating log data, AWK remains a irreplaceable tool in a developer's toolkit for efficient and effective text processing.

10.6 Text Data Transformation

Text data transformation is a crucial operation in numerous domains such as data science, software development, and systems administration. AWK provides powerful text transformation capabilities that allow for efficient data manipulation and extraction. This section delves into various techniques for transforming text data using AWK, from basic substitutions to more advanced text restructuring.

AWK's text processing capabilities primarily reside in its pattern-matching and action specifications. For example, to replace a text pattern within a file, we can use AWK's substitution command. Consider the following example, which demonstrates substituting all occurrences of the word "foo" with "bar" in a file:

```
awk '{gsub(/foo/, "bar"); print}' input.txt > output.txt
```

In this command:

- gsub(/foo/, "bar") is used to perform a global substitution within each line.

- print outputs the modified line.
- input.txt is the source file, and output.txt is the destination file.

More complex text transformations often require conditions to determine when a substitution should occur. The following example shows how to apply a substitution only to lines containing a specific pattern:

```
awk '/pattern/ {gsub(/foo/, "bar"); print}' input.txt > output.txt
```

Here, the substitution gsub(/foo/, "bar") is applied only if the line matches the pattern pattern.

In addition to straight substitutions, AWK can rearrange and format data. Consider a scenario where the input file contains data in the following format:

```
John Doe,1980-04-15,5000
Jane Smith,1979-08-30,6000
```

We want to transform this data to display the name in the format "Last, First", the birth date in "MM/DD/YYYY" format, and enclose the salary in parentheses. Using AWK, we can achieve this as follows:

```
awk -F, '{
  split($2, date, "-");
  formatted_date = date[2] "/" date[3] "/" date[1];
  print $2, $1, formatted_date "(" $3 ")";
}' input.txt > transformed.txt
```

Explanation:

- -F, sets the input field separator to a comma.
- split($2, date, "-") splits the birth date field into year, month, and day.
- formatted_date constructs the new date format.
- print $2, $1, formatted_date "(" $3 ")" rearranges and formats the output.

For more advanced text restructuring, consider a task where we need to transpose the rows and columns of a CSV file. AWK's associative arrays are practical for this type of transformation.

```
awk -F, '{
  for (i=1; i<=NF; i++) {
```

```
    a[NR,i] = $i
  }
  max_col = (NF > max_col) ? NF : max_col
  max_row = NR
} END {
  for (i=1; i<=max_col; i++) {
    for (j=1; j<=max_row; j++) {
      printf("%s%s", a[j,i], (j == max_row ? "\n" : ","))
    }
  }
}' input.csv > transposed.csv
```

Explanation:

- -F, sets the field separator to a comma.
- The for loop assigns each field to the array a with the row and column indices.
- max_col and max_row track the maximum number of columns and rows.
- The END block prints out the transposed array, ensuring each field is separated by a comma and each line ends with a newline character.

Text data transformation with AWK extends to altering the case of text. To convert all text to uppercase, use the following AWK script:

```
awk '{print toupper($0)}' input.txt > uppercase.txt
```

To convert text to lowercase, use:

```
awk '{print tolower($0)}' input.txt > lowercase.txt
```

These examples demonstrate the diverse capabilities of AWK in text data transformation, providing efficient and effective methods to manipulate and restructure text data according to specific requirements.

10.7 Processing CSV and TSV Files

Comma-Separated Values (CSV) and Tab-Separated Values (TSV) files are widely-used formats for storing tabular data. Their popularity stems from the simplicity and ease of manipulation using text processing tools. AWK is particularly effective for processing CSV and TSV files, given its powerful pattern matching and field manipulation capabilities.

When dealing with CSV and TSV files, one of the primary tasks is to correctly specify the field separator. In AWK, this is accomplished using the -F option or by setting the FS (Field Separator) variable. For CSV files, the field separator is a comma (','), while for TSV files, it is typically a tab character ('\̂').

```
# Example command to process a CSV file
awk -F, '{print $1, $2}' data.csv

# Example command to process a TSV file
awk -F'\t' '{print $1, $2}' data.tsv
```

In the case of the CSV file data.csv and TSV file data.tsv, the above commands print the first and second fields of each row. Let's delve deeper into some common operations and techniques for processing these file formats with AWK.

Reading and Writing Columns: One common operation is extracting specific columns from a CSV or TSV file. For this, AWK's ability to reference fields using $n (where n is the column number) is particularly useful.

```
# Extract the third and fifth columns from a CSV file
awk -F, '{print $3, $5}' data.csv

# Extract the first and third columns from a TSV file
awk -F'\t' '{print $1, $3}' data.tsv
```

Filtering Rows Based on Column Values: Another common task is filtering rows based on conditions applied to specific columns. This can be easily accomplished using AWK's conditional expressions.

```
# Filter rows where the value in the second column is greater than 50 in a CSV file
awk -F, '$2 > 50 {print $0}' data.csv

# Filter rows where the value in the first column matches a specific string in a TSV file
awk -F'\t' '$1 == "specific_value" {print $0}' data.tsv
```

Performing Calculations: AWK excels at performing calculations on numeric columns. For instance, we can calculate the sum or average of a column across all rows.

```
# Calculate the sum of the third column in a CSV file
awk -F, '{sum += $3} END {print sum}' data.csv

# Calculate the average of the second column in a TSV file
awk -F'\t' '{sum += $2; count++} END {print sum/count}' data.tsv
```

Handling Quoted Fields in CSV: One complication with CSV files is that fields may be enclosed in quotes, especially if they contain commas. This requires additional processing to handle correctly. The following AWK script provides an approach to deal with quoted fields.

```
# Handle quoted fields and extract properly
awk -v FPAT='([^,]+)|(\"[^\"]+\")' '{print $1, $2}' data.csv
```

Here, the FPAT variable is set to a regular expression that matches either non-comma sequences or quoted strings, allowing AWK to correctly interpret fields even when they contain commas.

Modifying and Writing Files: Often, it is necessary to modify CSV or TSV files and write the results to a new file. This can be done using AWK in combination with redirection.

```
# Modify the value in the second column of a CSV file and write to a new file
awk -F, '{OFS=","; if($2 > 50) $2 = $2 * 2; print $0}' data.csv > new_data.csv

# Lowercase the values in the first column of a TSV file and write to a new file
awk -F'\t' '{OFS="\t"; $1 = tolower($1); print $0}' data.tsv > new_data.tsv
```

Joining CSV or TSV Files: Joining data from multiple CSV or TSV files based on a common column is another frequent requirement.

```
# Join two CSV files on the first column
awk -F, 'NR==FNR{a[$1]=$2; next} $1 in a{print $0, a[$1]}' file1.csv file2.csv

# Join two TSV files on the first column
awk -F'\t' 'NR==FNR{a[$1]=$2; next} $1 in a{print $0, a[$1]}' file1.tsv file2.tsv
```

In the above commands, the first file is read and an associative array a is created with keys from the first column. The second file is then read, and rows with matching keys are printed along with the corresponding value from the array.

Dealing with Missing Data: Handling missing data is essential in data processing. Missing data in fields can be managed using conditional statements.

```
# Replace missing values in the third column of a CSV file with a default value
awk -F, 'BEGIN{OFS=","} {if($3 == "") $3 = "N/A"; print $0}' data.csv

# Fill empty fields in the second column of a TSV file with a zero
awk -F'\t' 'BEGIN{OFS="\t"} {if($2 == "") $2 = 0; print $0}' data.tsv
```

Sorting Data: Sorting data by a specific column is often required for analysis or reporting.

```
# Sort a CSV file by the third column numerically
awk -F, '{print $0 | "sort -t, -k3,3n"}' data.csv

# Sort a TSV file by the first column alphabetically
awk -F'\t' '{print $0 | "sort -t$'\t' -k1,1"}' data.tsv
```

Utilizing these techniques ensures robust processing of CSV and TSV files, enabling effective handling of various data manipulation tasks.

10.8 AWK in Network Monitoring

Network monitoring is a critical aspect of maintaining the health, security, and performance of computer networks. AWK, with its powerful text processing capabilities, is a valuable tool for network administrators to parse and analyze network traffic data. This section delves into practical approaches to utilize AWK for network monitoring tasks, including analyzing network logs, extracting relevant information, and generating summary reports.

Network devices such as routers, switches, and firewalls often generate log files that record various types of network events. These logs are typically structured text files, making them suitable for parsing with AWK. Consider a sample log file generated by a firewall.

An example entry in a firewall log might look like this:

```
Mar 10 21:15:32 firewall1 kernel: iptables: IN=eth0 OUT= MAC=02:42:c0:a8:00:02
:02:42:c0:a8:00:01:08:00 SRC=192.168.0.2 DST=192.168.0.1 LEN=60 TOS=0x00
PREC=0x00 TTL=64 ID=54321 DF PROTO=TCP SPT=443 DPT=80 WINDOW=
65535 RES=0x00 SYN URGP=0
```

To extract specific information such as source IP address (SRC) and destination IP address (DST) using AWK, the following command can be employed:

```
awk '{for(i=1;i<=NF;i++) if ($i ~ /SRC=/) src=$i} {for(i=1;i<=NF,i++) if ($i ~ /
    DST=/) dst=$i} {print substr(src,5) " -> " substr(dst,5)}' firewall.log
```

In this command:

- The for(i=1;i<=NF;i++) loop iterates through each field in the log entry.
- The condition if ($i ~ /SRC=/) checks if the current field matches the pattern SRC=.
- When a match is found, src=$i stores the source IP address field in the src variable.
- The substr(src,5) function removes the SRC= prefix from the source IP address field, extracting the actual IP address.

- The same process is applied to the destination IP address with DST=.
- The final print statement outputs the extracted source and destination IP addresses in a readable format.

Firewalls and other network devices often produce large amounts of log data. Summarizing this data helps in detecting patterns and anomalies. For example, to count the number of connections per source IP address, the following AWK command can be utilized:

```
awk '{for(i=1;i<=NF;i++) if ($i ~ /SRC=/) src=$i} {src_ip[substr(src,5)]++} END {
    for (ip in src_ip) print ip, src_ip[ip]}' firewall.log
```

This command does the following:

- Extracts the source IP address from each log entry.
- Increments the count in the src_ip associative array using the source IP address as the key.
- In the END block, iterates over the array to print each source IP address along with the number of occurrences.

AWK can also be employed for monitoring specific types of network traffic. Suppose you wish to identify and analyze HTTP traffic specifically. Analyzing such traffic involves filtering log entries based on the destination port (DPT) commonly used by HTTP (port 80):

```
awk '{for(i=1;i<=NF;i++) if ($i ~ /DPT=80/) print $0}' firewall.log
```

In this command, only the log entries matching the destination port DPT=80 are printed, effectively filtering out HTTP traffic.

To demonstrate the flexibility of AWK in more complex scenarios, consider analyzing the frequency of network traffic over an hourly period. Assume the log entries include timestamps. The goal is to count the number of log entries per hour:

```
awk '{split($3, time, ":"); hour=time[1]; count[hour]++} END {for (h in count) print h,
    count[h]}' firewall.log
```

In this command:

- The split($3, time, ":") function splits the timestamp field (assumed to be the third field) into an array time using the colon (:) as the delimiter.

- The hour component of the timestamp is extracted into the hour variable.
- The count associative array is incremented for each hour.
- The END block prints the number of log entries for each hour.

For network performance monitoring, calculating metrics such as the average packet size can be insightful. If the log entries contain the packet length (LEN) field, the average packet size can be computed as follows:

```
awk '{for(i=1;i<=NF;i++) if ($i ~ /LEN=/) len=$i} {total+=substr(len,5); count++}
    END {print "Average packet size:", total/count}' firewall.log
```

In this script:

- The packet length is extracted and summed in the total variable.
- The count variable keeps track of the number of log entries.
- In the END block, the average packet size is calculated and printed.

Network monitoring often requires real-time analysis. Although AWK is not inherently a real-time tool, combining it with other utilities like tail can approximate real-time processing:

```
tail -f firewall.log | awk '{for(i=1;i<=NF;i++) if ($i ~ /SRC=/) src=$i} {print "New
    connection from", substr(src,5)}'
```

By using tail -f to follow the log file and piping the output to AWK, this command prints a message for each new connection detected, offering a simple form of real-time monitoring.

Through these practical examples, the versatility of AWK in network monitoring is demonstrated. Whether parsing log files, summarizing traffic data, filtering specific types of traffic, or integrating with real-time log streams, AWK proves to be an indispensable tool for network administrators.

10.9 Automating Tasks with AWK

Automating repetitive tasks is an essential aspect of efficient system administration and data processing. AWK, with its textual data manipulation capabilities, excels in automating tasks that involve pattern matching, data extraction, and text transformation. This section delves into various aspects of automating tasks with AWK, providing detailed examples and explanations to ensure comprehensive understanding.

Consider a scenario where you are required to rename multiple files based on a pattern. AWK can be employed to simplify this process by generating the required shell commands. Assume you have a directory with multiple text files named as file_001.txt, file_002.txt, etc., and you want to rename them to document_001.txt, document_002.txt, etc. An AWK script can be written to achieve this:

```
ls *.txt | awk '{ printf("mv %s %s\n", $1, substr($1,1,5)"document_"substr($1,6)) }'
```

The command above performs the following steps:

- ls *.txt: Lists all text files in the current directory.
- Pipe (|) is used to pass the list of files to AWK.
- In the AWK script, $1 refers to the file name from the list.
- substr($1, 1, 5) extracts the first five characters (used here as a fixed part for demonstration).
- substr($1, 6) extracts the characters starting from the sixth position.
- printf("mv %s %s
  n", $1, substr($1,1,5)"document_"substr($1,6)): Constructs the mv command to rename the file and prints it.

```
mv file_001.txt document_001.txt
mv file_002.txt document_002.txt
...
```

Executing the above AWK-generated commands will rename the files as desired.

Another common task is processing and summarizing log files to identify specific patterns or anomalies. Consider an example where you need to count the number of login attempts by different users from a log file named auth.log. Each line in the log file might look like:

```
Jan 10 10:00:01 server1 sshd[12345]: Accepted password for user1 from 192.168.1.1 port 22 ssh2
```

To count the number of login attempts for each user, the following AWK script can be used:

```
awk '/Accepted password/ { user[$10]++ } END { for (u in user) print u, user[u] }'
    auth.log
```

Explanation of the script:

- /Accepted password/: Pattern to match lines containing "Accepted password".
- user[$10]++: Increments the counter for the username found in the tenth field.
- END { for (u in user) print u, user[u] }: After processing all lines, iterates through the user array and prints each username and the corresponding count.

Sample output might look like:

```
user1 5
user2 3
user3 2
```

This script automates the task of summarizing login attempts, providing useful insight into user activity.

In scenarios where data needs to be extracted and reformatted from CSV or TSV files, AWK simplifies the process significantly. Suppose you have a CSV file named sales.csv with the following content:

```
Date,Item,Quantity,Price
2023-01-01,Apple,10,1.50
2023-01-01,Banana,5,0.75
2023-01-02,Apple,8,1.50
2023-01-02,Banana,7,0.75
```

To calculate the total sales for each item and generate a summary, the AWK script can be written as follows:

```
awk -F, 'NR>1 { sales[$2] += $3 * $4 } END { for (item in sales) printf "%s: $%.2f\n
    ", item, sales[item] }' sales.csv
```

Explanation:

- -F,: Sets the field separator to a comma.
- NR>1: Skips the header line.
- sales[$2] += $3 * $4: Sums the sales value for each item.

- END { for (item in sales) printf "%s: $%.2f
n", item, sales[item] }: Iterates through the sales array and prints each item with the total sales value.

Sample output:

```
Apple: $27.00
Banana: $9.00
```

In advanced scenarios, AWK can interface with other utilities to achieve higher levels of automation. Suppose you are managing a server and need to monitor disk usage and notify the administrator if usage exceeds a certain threshold. A shell script combined with AWK can achieve this:

```
#!/bin/bash
threshold=80
df -h | awk -v threshold=$threshold '
NR>1 {
  gsub("%","",$5)
  if ($5 >= threshold) {
    printf "Warning: Disk usage on %s is %d%%\n", $6, $5
  }
}
'
```

The script executes the following steps:

- threshold=80: Sets the threshold for disk usage.
- df -h: Retrieves human-readable disk usage statistics.
- NR>1: Skips the header line.
- gsub("%","",$5): Removes the percentage symbol from the disk usage value.
- if ($5 >= threshold): Compares the disk usage with the threshold.
- printf "Warning: Disk usage on %s is %d%%
n", $6, $5: Prints a warning message if the threshold is exceeded.

If any disk partition exceeds the specified usage threshold, the script outputs a warning:

```
Warning: Disk usage on / is 85%
```

This demonstrates how AWK can be integrated into bash scripts for system monitoring and automation tasks. This ability to handle text processing and generate commands makes AWK an indispensable tool for automating various tasks in system administration, data processing, and beyond.

10.10 AWK for Bioinformatics

Bioinformatics involves the development of methods and software tools for understanding biological data, primarily where the data is large and complex. AWK, with its powerful text processing capabilities, is well-suited for handling various bioinformatics tasks. This section discusses how AWK can be leveraged in bioinformatics settings, from sequence data analysis to statistical computations.

One of the primary uses of AWK in bioinformatics is the processing of sequence data files, such as FASTA or FASTQ files, which are ubiquitous in genetic research. The following example demonstrates how to extract sequence identifiers from a FASTA file.

```
awk '/^>/{print}' sequences.fasta
```

This command reads the input FASTA file sequences.fasta and prints any line beginning with the > character, which denotes sequence identifiers in FASTA format.

To count the number of sequences in a FASTA file, one can execute:

```
awk '/^>/{count++} END{print count}' sequences.fasta
```

This script increments a counter each time a sequence identifier is encountered and prints the total count at the end of the file.

In some applications, researchers might need to filter sequences based on specific criteria. The following AWK script demonstrates how to extract sequences longer than a specified length, for example, sequences longer than 100 nucleotides:

```
awk 'BEGIN{RS=">"; ORS=""} length($2) > 100 {print ">"$0}' sequences.fasta
```

Here, the script sets the record separator (RS) to >, enabling it to treat each sequence as a single record. The output record separator (ORS) is set to an empty string to ensure proper formatting. The length($2) > 100 condition filters sequences, printing only those longer than 100 nucleotides.

Next, consider the analysis of SAM (Sequence Alignment/Map) files, which store large amounts of sequence alignment data. Researchers often need to parse these large files to extract useful information, such as alignment scores or specific sequence matches. A common task is calculating the average mapping quality score:

```
awk '{sum += $5; count++} END {if (count > 0) print sum/count}' alignments.sam
```

This command extracts the mapping quality score from the fifth field of each line (represented by $5), accumulates the scores, and computes their average. The average is only printed if there is at least one record in the file.

Furthermore, AWK can be used to process Variant Call Format (VCF) files, which contain information about variants found in sequencing data. To filter SNPs (Single Nucleotide Polymorphisms) with a minimum quality score of 30:

```
awk '$1 ~ /^#/ || $6 >= 30' variants.vcf
```

In this command, lines beginning with # (the header) are printed unconditionally. For other lines, only those with a quality score field ($6) greater than or equal to 30 are printed.

Performing statistical analysis on biological data often requires the calculation of various summary statistics. AWK's built-in arithmetic functions can be utilized to calculate mean, median, mode, and standard deviation directly from data sets. For instance, finding the mean and standard deviation of column values in a text file:

```
awk '{sum += $1; sumsq += $1*$1; count++}
    END {mean = sum/count;
        stddev = sqrt((sumsq - sum*sum/count)/count);
        print "Mean:", mean, "\nStandard Deviation:", stddev}' data.txt
```

This AWK script accumulates the sum and sum of squares of the values from the first column. It calculates the mean by dividing the total sum by the count of values. Standard deviation is computed using the formula sqrt((sumsq - sum*sum/count)/count).

Combining AWK with other command-line tools like grep and sed can further enhance its power in bioinformatics workflows. For example, you can preprocess data with grep or sed before passing it to AWK for analysis. Here is a pipeline to filter sequences containing a specific motif and then calculate their length:

```
grep -B 1 'TGCA' sequences.fasta | grep -v '^--$' | \
awk 'BEGIN{RS=">"; ORS=""} {if ($0 ~ /TGCA/) print ">"$1"\n" length($2) "\n"}
'
```

This pipeline first uses grep to select sequences containing the motif TGCA, then removes the separator lines added by grep using grep -v, and finally pipes the result to AWK. AWK processes the remaining sequences, outputting each sequence identifier and its length.

In bioinformatics applications, efficient data processing is crucial due to the large volumes of data. AWK scripts can be optimized for performance by minimizing string operations and avoiding unnecessary computations. For example, instead of calculating certain values within the main processing loop, intermediate results can be stored and processed in the END block.

AWK proves to be an invaluable tool in bioinformatics for its text processing capabilities, ease of use, and efficiency. Its ability to handle diverse data formats and perform complex data manipulations makes it an essential component in the bioinformatician's toolkit.

10.11 Case Studies of Successful AWK Projects

1. Monitoring System Performance

A well-known high-frequency trading firm implemented AWK to monitor and analyze the performance of their trading systems. Given the high volumes of data generated, an efficient system was crucial. Specialists employed AWK scripts to parse system logs, extract relevant performance metrics, and report anomalies. Below is an example AWK script used to identify occurrences where CPU utilization exceeds 85%:

```
#!/usr/bin/awk -f
$3 > 85 { print "High CPU Usage Detected:", $0 }
```

Sample log file content:

```
timestamp: 2023-04-01 08:00        CPU: 83%
timestamp: 2023-04-01 08:05        CPU: 87%
timestamp: 2023-04-01 08:10        CPU: 90%
```

Running the script on the sample log file would produce:

```
High CPU Usage Detected: timestamp: 2023-04-01 08:05        CPU: 87%
High CPU Usage Detected: timestamp: 2023-04-01 08:10        CPU: 90%
```

2. Streamlining Customer Feedback Analysis

A multinational retail corporation utilized AWK to streamline the analysis of customer feedback data stored in CSV format. Employee-created scripts automate the extraction of specific sentiments and product-related issues, providing valuable insights to improve customer satisfaction. Below is an example AWK script that extracts entries with a rating of 2 or lower:

```
#!/usr/bin/awk -F, '{
    if ($3 <= 2)
        print "Low Rating Feedback ID:", $1, "Rating:", $3, "Comment:", $4
}'
```

Sample feedback file content:

```
1,2023-04-01,5,Excellent product!
2,2023-04-02,2,Not satisfied with the quality.
3,2023-04-03,1,Poor performance.
```

Executing the script on the provided feedback data yields:

```
Low Rating Feedback ID: 2 Rating: 2 Comment: Not satisfied with the quality.
Low Rating Feedback ID: 3 Rating: 1 Comment: Poor performance.
```

3. Genomic Data Filtering in Bioinformatics

In bioinformatics research, AWK is frequently used to filter and manipulate large genomic data sets. A research team working on human genome variation data employed AWK for initial data filtering as part of their pipeline, which significantly reduced preprocessing time and errors. The following script isolates variations on a specific chromosome with a frequency greater than 0.05:

```
#!/usr/bin/awk -F'\t' '{
    if ($1 == "chr17" && $5 > 0.05)
        print $0
}'
```

Sample genomic variation file:

```
chr17    1539240    .    A    T    0.03
chr17    2102311    .    C    T    0.12
chr18    5623412    .    G    A    0.07
```

Output after running the AWK script:

```
chr17    2102311    .    C    T    0.12
```

4. Automating Network Usage Reports

Organizations managing large IT infrastructures often need to monitor network traffic efficiently. A leading telecom company implemented AWK scripts to automate the generation of network usage reports from log files. These reports help in identifying bottlenecks and planning network upgrades. The script below extracts data transfer events greater than 100MB:

```
#!/usr/bin/awk -F' '{
    if ($4 == "MB" && $3 > 100)
        print "High Data Transfer Event:", $0
}'
```

Sample network log:

```
2023-04-01 08:00    user1   50     MB
2023-04-01 08:05    user2   120    MB
2023-04-01 08:10    user3   200    MB
```

Executing the above script provides:

```
High Data Transfer Event: 2023-04-01 08:05    user2   120    MB
High Data Transfer Event: 2023-04-01 08:10    user3   200    MB
```

Each case study illustrates the applicability of AWK in diverse domains. The ability to quickly extract, analyze, and report data using concise and efficient scripts makes it an invaluable tool across industries.

Made in the USA
Monee, IL
07 November 2026

67911525R10164